# MADAME DE POMPADOUR

## NANCY MITFORD

High rouged, unfortunate female of whom
it is not proper to speak without necessity.

THOMAS CARLYLE

Sincère et tendre Pompadour.

VOLTAIRE

PENGUIN BOOKS

# PENGUIN BOOKS

Published by the Penguin Group
Penguin Books Ltd, 80 Strand, London WC2R 0RL, England
Penguin Putnam Inc., 375 Hudson Street, New York, New York 10014, USA
Penguin Books Australia Ltd, 250 Camberwell Road, Camberwell, Victoria 3124, Australia
Penguin Books Canada Ltd, 10 Alcorn Avenue, Toronto, Ontario, Canada M4V 3B2
Penguin Books India (P) Ltd, 11 Community Centre, Panchsheel Park, New Delhi – 110 017, India
Penguin Books (NZ) Ltd, Cnr Rosedale and Airborne Roads, Albany, Auckland, New Zealand
Penguin Books (South Africa) (Pty) Ltd, 24 Sturdee Avenue, Rosebank 2196, South Africa

Penguin Books Ltd, Registered Offices: 80 Strand, London WC2R 0RL, England

www.penguin.com

First published by
Hamish Hamilton 1954
First published in this edition by Hamish Hamilton 1988
Published in Penguin Books 1995

7

Copyright 1954 by Nancy Mitford

Printed in England by Clays Ltd, St Ives plc

TO
DOLLY
PRINCESS RADZIWILL

# CONTENTS

# ACKNOWLEDGMENTS

I should like to thank, for kindness, interest and help, Dr. Alfred Cobban, Mr. Frank McDermot, Mr. Roger Machell, M. van der Kemp, Conservateur du Musée de Versailles, Mademoiselle Langlois and M. Pierre Lemoyne, of the Musée de Versailles, Mademoiselle Joly, of the Bibliothèque de Versailles, Mr. Francis Watson, of the Wallace Collection, and Mrs. Watson, le Marquis de Lasteyrie, M. Gaston Palewski, Vice-Président de l'Assemblée Nationale, M. Georges Benda, M. Richard Pénard y Fernandez, Mr. Stuart Preston, Mr. Heywood Hill, Mr. Cecil Beaton and Mr. Roger Senhouse.

N.M.

*Chapter One*

# VERSAILLES AND LOUIS XV

AFTER the death of the great King, beautiful Versailles, fatal for France, lay empty seven years while fresh air blew through its golden rooms, blowing away the sorcery and bigotry which hung about the walls like a miasma, blowing away the old century and blowing in the new. Louis XIV died in 1715. He had outlived his son, his grandson, and his eldest great-grandson, had reigned seventy-two years, too long for the good of his country. Even then he was so strong that he could not die until half eaten away with gangrene, for which Dr. Fagon, killer of Princes, prescribed asses' milk. At last the Duc de Bouillon, wearing a black feather, went out on to the balcony and announced to a waiting crowd, curious but not sad, 'Le Roi est mort.' He retired into the palace, put on a white feather, came back and announced 'Vive le Roi'.

The reign of Louis XV had begun; like his great-grandfather he was five years old when he succeeded to the throne of France. He had neither father, mother, brothers nor sisters; all had been killed by the wretched Fagon. He himself would no doubt have followed them to the grave had not his nurse, the Duchesse de Ventadour, hidden him away during that terrible fortnight when the rest of his family was dying of measles, bleedings, purges and emetics. His father's brother was still alive, but useless as an uncle for a little boy; he was the King of Spain, imprisoned in the etiquette of his own palaces and by now far more Spanish than French. They never saw each other. Louis XV was brought up without the natural family love which should surround a child, without hugs and kisses and without slaps. 'First of all he must live', Madame de Ventadour used to say and she never allowed him to be crossed. At the age of seven he was taken, crying dreadfully, away from her and handed over to a governor. He then retired into a world of his own, concealing all his thoughts and feelings from those around him, and nobody ever knew much about them for the rest of his life. He was an intensely secret man.

The Regent of France, Philippe, Duc d'Orléans, was the next heir to the throne, because the Duc d'Anjou had formally re-nounced his rights to it on becoming King of Spain. People were not wanting who said that the Duc d'Orléans had poisoned the heirs of Louis XIV; if so his conduct towards the one that survived was very notable. As soon as his uncle had breathed his last he took the little boy, who stood between him and the throne, away from Versailles and established him in the Tuileries Palace, across the road from his own Palais Royal. For the rest of his life he faithfully served this child. France was at peace; the religious quarrels of the last century had lost their venom, her frontiers were established and no enemy was attempting to cross them; the claim of her King to his throne was unquestionable; the air was full of new ideas. An even greater century than the *Grand Siècle* might now have been inaugurated, if the Regent had only had the energy to enforce certain changes in the constitution.

As a young man the Duc d'Orléans had been intelligent and ambitious; it was one of Louis XIV's grave mistakes that he had allowed him to take so little part in public life. Determined as he was to make the nobles politically impotent, he kept the Princes of the Blood even more strictly in their place. He was too much blinded by his theories to see what a loyal and honourable man his nephew was and how useful he could have been to France. So the Duc d'Orléans turned his attention to the pleasures of this life, and a more perfect rake has seldom existed. When, at the age of forty-one, he found himself ruler of France, he was still intelligent, but energy and ambition had been sapped by years of wenching and the cruder forms of dissipation. He did envisage fundamental constitutional changes; he tried to bring back the great nobles into the government of France and to rule by councils instead of bureaucratic secretaries of state. But these lords had lost the habit of being useful; Louis XIV had trained them so well that they had even lost the habit of being a nuisance. The councils fell into the hands of officials and the last serious attempt to bring back aristocratic government in France collapsed. The Regent then settled down to govern as the old King had governed and to bring up the new King to be as much like his ancestor as possible. It was noticed that he even had the same manner towards him, the same deep respect, tinged, however, with love and humour instead of with hatred and fear. He loved the child far more than his own dreary son. He explained every political step to him, saying, 'you are the master, I am only here to tell you what is happening, to make suggestions, to carry out your orders'. The little boy was charmed; he attended the Council meetings, clasping in his arms a pet cat which the Ministers called his colleague; he was too proud and too shy ever to say a word. This pride and this shyness were to remain with him throughout his life. His only attempt at a protest was when the Regent announced his betrothal to a little Spanish first cousin, a baby Infanta of two. The King cried throughout the whole Council, but without making any observations.

When Louis XIV decided, after the civil war known as the Fronde, to keep the great nobles under his eye and to rob them of power, he had cunningly played upon the French love of fashion and fun; all fashion and all fun were gathered together at Versailles. Parisian society, though very middle-class, hummed with life and could be enjoyed from time to time as a change from the Court; the provinces were unthinkable. The heaviest blow that could befall a man was banishment to his estates; this not only meant loss of place and influence; the exile, condemned to live in the country, became ridiculous in the eyes of his friends. Let him embellish his house and garden, let him give expensive parties and make a social and intellectual centre for the whole neighbourhood, the poor man was a dowdy provincial; he counted for nothing any more. The memoirs of the time dramatize to the full these banishments, *disgraces*, as they were called. 'On hearing of his disgrace the Duke, who is religious, behaved with Christian submission; when they went to tell the Duchess she thought, from their faces, that her son must have died.' Living in their beautiful houses in the beautiful French countryside, with the administration of huge estates to interest them, these exiled nobles were considered, and considered themselves, as dead. In fact, they generally became either very fat or very thin, and departed life rather quickly.

This policy, by which the greater nobles had become a *noblesse de cour* and were cooped up in a perpetual house party at Versailles, divorced from public opinion in their native provinces, as well as from the sources of their wealth, was disastrous to French economy. While the Ile de France was like an enormous park or garden, containing thousands of glorious houses, rural France was a desert.[1] The road between Paris and Versailles was a perpetual double file of carriages being driven at full speed—English visitors then, as now, remarking that French noblemen like to drive very fast—that between Paris and Orléans was empty but for an occasional post chaise. Agriculture was fearfully neglected, even those landlords who did sometimes visit their estates, in the intervals of duty at Court, took no interest in it whatsoever; their

[1] Many thousands of noble families did live in the provinces, on their estates, because they had not the *entrée* at Court, but they were nearly all wretchedly poor and all without any sort of political influence. They can in no way be compared to our landed gentry.

only outdoor pursuits were hunting and gardening. Game was carefully preserved, poaching was still punishable by death, and as a result the land was overrun with stags, wild boars, wolves and the hunt itself. Louis XV, when out hunting, was always most careful not to ride over the crops and was furious with anybody who did so, but many sportsmen of the day were quite unscrupulous in this matter. It would never have occurred to a landlord to invite one of his farmers to hunt with him, and indeed it would have been against the law—none but the nobles were allowed to hunt or fish. Most of the great nobles were total absentees from their estates; they revolved round the Court, with a town house in Paris, a country villa within easy reach of Versailles, and, if they were lucky, a flat in the palace itself. About a thousand nobles lived, or had a *pied à terre* there, at the time of Louis XV. One result of this curious system is that it is hardly possible to study eighteenth-century French domestic architecture except in, and around, Paris. Nearly all the country houses in the provinces are old fortified castles, with perhaps a few re-decorated rooms, or were built in the nineteenth century. Some rich provincial towns have fine public buildings and bourgeois houses, but there is extraordinarily little of the first importance further from Versailles than a comfortable day's drive.

Versailles was the heart of France, and here the King lived, like a man in a glass house, visible to, and within reach of, his subjects. In those days the palace was even more open to the public than it is now; people wandered in and out at all hours and were allowed into the state rooms as well as into the gardens. When, at the beginning of the Revolution, a furious mob was known to be approaching, the guards tried to shut the gates in vain, a hundred years of rust having soldered them to their hinges. Louis XIV had practically lived in public, but Louis XV, more highly strung than his great-grandfather, arranged a suite of rooms for himself where he could be away from the crowd. This suite, though it consisted of fifty rooms and seven bathrooms, and was in itself like a country house, was known as the *petits appartements*; even the courtiers could only go there if they had the privilege of the *grandes entrées* or by invitation. As time went on, the King arranged other, more private apartments, where he could be entirely undisturbed; and at last the north wing of the palace became a perfect net-work of secret passages, hidden staircases, and tiny rooms looking on to interior courtyards. 'Rats' nests,' said the son of Robert de Cotte, thinking with regret of the noble monuments built by his father and Mansard. Louis XV was fond of little things, exquisite in quality, and these rats' nests were embellished with some of the finest decoration ever seen, much of which still exists to-day. But although Louis XV hated public appearances, he never shirked what he believed to be his duty. He got up, dined, prayed, had his hunting boots pulled off, and went to bed in public. The *lever* and the *coucher* were formal ceremonies; he never slept in his state bedroom. Everybody knew quite well that he had often been up and working for hours before the *lever*—lighting his own fire sometimes so as not to wake the servants—and often went to amuse himself in Paris, or the town of Versailles, after his *coucher*. If he omitted to say his prayers, it was a sign that he was not going to bed in order to sleep. The fire-place in the state bedroom always smoked, so that in cold weather the *lever* and the *coucher* were very uncomfortable affairs.

As for the courtiers, they lived and prayed and hunted and danced and ate to iron rules, and a timetable which made the days slip by and gave them the illusion of being always busy. The functions which they were obliged to attend were so near to-gether in time, and so far distant in space, that they spent much of their lives running from one end of the palace to the other. They were like a huge family whose head was the King. They could do nothing, not even go to Paris for the day, or be inoculated against smallpox, certainly not arrange marriages for their children, without his express permission. Their privileges were enormous, and their power non-existent.

French historians have always been inclined to explain the trend of events in the eighteenth century by dwelling on the characters of their Princes. Much ink is expended on the various heirs to the throne killed off by Fagon and his successors. The father and the son of Louis XV are regretted. Perhaps if the Duc de Bourgogne, eldest son of the Dauphin of Louis XV, had lived to reign instead of Louis XVI, things would have been different; he seems to have been superior to the three sad kings, his brothers. But he died at the age of ten. To an English reader all this is rather surprising since we are inclined to think that unless a monarch has genius, or is mad or wicked, his personality is of small account. In those days any dull German could make as good a King of England as the bonniest of native princes. But in France the situation was quite different. There the King was Lord High everything; all was directed by him and he alone could provide the inspiration which made the wheels of government go round. The French loved their Kings as the English never have, with an unreasoning love which was later to turn to an unreasoning hatred. The personality of the King of France was therefore of great importance.

Now Louis XV was by very far the most considerable of Louis XIV's descendants. As a child he was full of promise, religious, pretty, clever, brave and shy, with a shyness that had nothing gauche about it and on the contrary engendered a regal formality of manner, thought quite perfect by all who saw him. He grew up to be a charming man and an intelligent ruler with a high sense of duty, loving and, for many years, loved by his people. But the machinery by which he was expected to govern was long since worn out, and neither he nor his counsellors had the genius to devise anything better. He knew that something

was wrong somewhere, but he was for ever caught in the terrible
web spun by his terrible ancestor.

Perhaps the fate of the French monarchy was sealed when, in
1722, the Regent took the Court back to Versailles. Kings always
live in a cage, but if the cage is in the capital city some echo of
public opinion may penetrate its bars. No King has ever been
more cut off from his people than Louis XV. Cardinal Dubois,
the Regent's adviser, insisted on the step, hoping thereby to prolong the life of his master, and thinking that he might be induced
to live more temperately away from the Palais Royal. The move
seems to have been effected with no trouble or fuss, everybody fell
back into the little miseries of etiquette as if they had never been
away. A few months later Cardinal Dubois died. The King came
of age officially the following year—he was thirteen—and the
Regent continued to govern. But the excesses of that strange man
had undermined his health. One day, in a mood of black depres-
sion, he sent for the little Duchesse de Falaris to gossip with him,
before he went upstairs to work with the King. Sitting in front of
the fire, he asked her whether she believed in a future life; she
replied that she did, and he said in that case he found her conduct
on this earth incomprehensible. 'Well now,' he said, after a silence,
'tell the news.' As she opened her pretty little mouth to recount
the latest piece of scandal, Philippe d'Orléans rolled to the floor
and died.

The King, stunned, shaken and intensely sad, raised no objection
when the Duc de Bourbon came to him and proposed taking over
the government of France. He nodded his head without a word.
'M. le Duc', an appellation reserved at Court for the head of the
Bourbon Condé family, was not very brilliant, no match for
Cardinal Fleury, the King's tutor; Fleury was determined himself
to rule the country and immediately set on foot a series of intrigues to that end. In three years' time he stepped into the shoes

of M. le Duc, who found himself exiled to his estates at Chantilly. Nobody regretted this most unattractive individual, though his mistress, Madame de Prie, had been rather nice and pretty. She, poor woman, killed herself when she realized the full horror of life in the country. Their rule had not been without results. Before he went, M. le Duc had taught the King to love hunting—the Condés were men of the forest, enormous hunters—and was responsible for his marriage.

At fifteen the King was a big strong boy, forward for his age. His fiancée, who lived in the palace, was still only five; a golden-haired darling, she appeared with him at all the State functions, trotted round after him like a little pet, and was considered absolutely sweet. But boys of fifteen loathe sweet little girls and he felt humiliated at having such a small fiancée. He sulked whenever he saw her. The marriage was to be consummated in ten years' time, and meanwhile what? The King was obviously quite ready to consummate something at once; the sooner this last descendant of a royal line, this 'conjugation of the blood of Henri IV', five of whose children were his ancestors, was given a chance to breed, the better. M. le Duc was very much of this opinion because the next heir to the throne was the Duc d'Orléans, and the Orléans and Condé branches of the Bourbon family were at daggers drawn. (The feud between them was fanned by the Dowager Duchesses who were sisters, daughters of Louis XIV and Madame de Montespan.) Furthermore, if the King were not married soon, one of two things could be expected to happen. Either he would take a mistress, who, at his age, would certainly acquire a dangerous influence over him, or he would turn to the boys. Pederasty was by no means unknown in the Bourbon family; Louis XIII had certainly preferred men to women, while many of the courtiers could remember the egregious Monsieur, with his bracelets, and high-heeled shoes, and high-pitched squabbles. He was a direct ancestor of Louis XV. There had recently been a homosexual scandal among young dukes, attached to the King and very little older than him. The Regent had taken measures at once, and they had received the heavy punishment of exile to their estates, accompanied by wives who had quickly been found for them. When the King asked what they had done he was told that they had torn up railings in the park; he made no comment, but he must have known that they would not have been sent away for that. Thereafter they were always called 'les arracheurs de palissades'. The First Gentleman of the Bedchamber, the Duc de la Trémoïlle, agreeable, polite and amusing, was seen to have the tastes of a young lady; he spent his time eating sweets and doing embroidery. He too was married off and sent home, so furious that for seven years he turned his back on his unlucky wife. After a great deal of hesitation, pushed to it finally by a serious illness of the King, M. le Duc made up his mind that the Infanta must return to Spain and the King be married to somebody of an age to have children; the risk of offending the Spaniards was less grave than that of waiting any longer.

In fact, Philippe V was exceedingly angry. 'Ah! the traitor!' he cried, and the courtiers in his ante-room were filled with a terrified curiosity to know who the traitor might be. However the Queen, Elizabeth Farnese, who ruled the King, remained calm and merely said: 'We must send at once to meet the Infanta.'[1]

The hurdle of the Infanta's return having been cleared without mishap, M. le Duc began to study lists of princesses to take her place. There were nearly forty in all, but they boiled down to very few suitable ones. French and Lorrainer princesses were ruled out at once because they all had Orléans or Bourbon Condé blood and neither family would consent to such an elevation of the other. Princess Anne of England was a Lutheran and the English would not allow her to change her religion; the daughter of Peter the Great, the future Tzarina Elizabeth, was too parvenue

[1] This Infanta eventually became Queen of Portugal.

and was also said to show signs of incipient madness, as did the King of Portugal, who had an otherwise eligible daughter. The Princess of Hesse Rhinevelt would have done very well if her mother had not been in the habit of giving birth alternately to daughters and hares; M. le Duc, thinking, perhaps, that there was room for any amount of hares at Chantilly, finally married her himself.

Enormous bets were placed on these various ladies, odds lengthening and shortening according to the day's rumours; the Court seemed to be living on the eve of some important race. At last the choice fell upon a very dark horse indeed, Marie Leczinska, daughter of the penniless, exiled Stanislas Leczinski, King of Poland. A Princess who knew no cosmetics but water and snow and who spent her time embroidering altar cloths was not at first sight a very suitable person to reign at Versailles. No doubt M. le Duc and Madame de Prie thought that, since she would owe everything to them, she would help them to keep their position. In fact, the marriage, regarded as a final proof of their incompetence, greatly facilitated Fleury's efforts to get rid of them. It was a poor marriage for the King of France, this lady, '*dont le nom est en ski*', being endowed with neither worldly goods, nor powerful family connexions, nor beauty, nor even youth, since she was seven years older than the King. But she had a sweet nature and regal manner, as even the most disagreeable of her subjects were obliged to admit, when they knew her; above all she was very healthy.

When Stanislas received a letter asking for her hand he could not believe his luck. He rushed to his daughter's room crying: 'Kneel, kneel and give thanks to God Almighty!'

'What has happened—are you going back, as King, to Poland?'

'Far better than that, you are going, as Queen, to France.'

As soon as she arrived at Versailles the King fell in love with her and fell into bed with her; on their wedding night he gave her proof of his love seven times. The courtiers were delighted, and Maréchal de Villars said that none of his cadets at St. Cyr could have done better. Nine months later she produced twin daughters, Madame Première and Madame Henriette; by the time the King was twenty-seven they had ten children, of whom six daughters and a son reached maturity. He thought, and continually said, that his wife was the most beautiful woman at Versailles, and for years this marriage went very well. They might have been happy ever after, that is to say, Marie Leczinska might have played the part of mistress as well as that of wife, if she had had more character. Louis XV was a man of habit, a faithful man at heart, so shy, too, that he found it very difficult to make advances to any woman; he disliked new faces, and beautiful faces intimidated him. His little love affairs with girls of easy virtue, found for him by his valets, meant nothing at all to him, and his family meant a great deal. Unfortunately the Queen, though an exceedingly nice woman, was dowdy and a bore; she was incapable of forming a society that would attract a gay young husband, and she surrounded herself with the dullest, stuffiest element at the Court. After the birth of her children she settled comfortably, and rather selfishly, into middle age; she made no effort to remain attractive to her young husband, to share his interests or to entertain his friends; fashion and fun meant nothing to her. She had no temperament at all, complaining that she was for ever 'in bed, or pregnant, or brought to bed' and any excuse was good enough to keep the King out of her bed. As she was extremely pious, he had never been allowed there on the days of the major saints. By degrees the saints for whom he was excluded became more numerous and less important; finally, he was kept out by one so utterly unknown that he flew into a temper. He told Lebel, the palace *concierge*, to bring him a woman. Lebel went off and found a pretty housemaid, and the result was 'Dorigny le Dauphin', who became an art dealer of some distinction.

Nobody quite knows when the liaison between Louis XV and the Comtesse de Mailly began, but the King himself cannot have thought it very serious until 1739. That year he refused to go to his Easter duties. Asked by the Bishop whether he would touch for the King's Evil as usual on Easter Day, he said no, since this ceremony could only take place after communion and he did not intend to communicate. His Jesuit confessor, Père de Lignières, wishing to avoid a scandal, suggested that Cardinal de Rohan might say a low mass in the King's cabinet, after which nobody would know for certain whether he had or had not confessed. The King absolutely refused to lend himself to such a fraud. He was living in adultery and had no intention, for the present, of mending his ways; but at the same time he was not going to make a mockery of his religion.

Madame de Mailly was a daughter of the Marquis de Nesle. Their family name was Mailly; she had married her first cousin. Madame de Nesle, her mother, was a lady-in-waiting to the Queen, and the King had always known the Mailly sisters. She was not a beauty, or in any way very romantic, but a jolly, downright, sporting woman with whom he felt at ease. She never asked for anything, neither for power nor for money; she loved him. But in 1740 he fell in love with her sister, whom she had unwisely invited to all her suppers and parties; the Marquise de Vintimille was even less of a beauty and much less nice than Madame de Mailly, and behaved with the greatest unkindness to her. The affair did not last very long; Madame de Vintimille died giving birth to the King's baby, the Comte du Luc. The King was heartbroken; he went back to Madame de Mailly and she adopted the baby, who was exactly like him to look at, and always known as *le demi-Louis*. But this lady's troubles were not yet over. Very soon the King fell desperately in love, much more than he had been with Madame de Vintimille, with yet another sister, the Duchesse de Châteauroux.

Madame de Châteauroux was a beauty, even nastier than
Madame de Vintimille, rapacious, implacable, and very ambitious.
She made the King work harder with his ministers than he had
ever done before. Seeing that he was still rather fond of her sister
she made him exile her from the Court; poor Madame de Mailly
went off in floods of tears and was thereafter known as The
Widow. The King missed her, and corresponded with her surrep-
titiously; but Madame de Châteauroux soon found out and put a
stop to that. 'Madame, you are killing me,' he would say as she
insisted that he should give his attention more and more to the
dull details of public affairs. 'So much the better, Sire, a King
should continually die and be resuscitated.' She was odious to the
poor Queen and made a breach between her and the King which
was never repaired; husband and wife never felt easy in each
other's company again.

Madame de Châteauroux was the central figure in the famous
'Metz incident' which made a deep impression on the King; to
the end of his days he could not speak of the scenes of Metz without horror. Fond of campaigning, as he was fond of hunting, he
went, in 1744, to join his army on the Eastern frontier and took
with him an enormous train, including Madame de Châteauroux
and yet another Mailly sister, the Duchesse de Lauraguais. At
Metz he fell seriously ill, with pains in the head and a high fever;
the usual bleedings and purges had no effect and the doctor
announced that his life was in danger. Immediately there was talk
of the Last Sacrament which would, of course, entail confession
and the departure of the mistress. She, meanwhile, mounted
guard over him, with her great friend the Duc de Richelieu,
First Gentleman of the Bedchamber. Nobody else was allowed to
see him alone and they pretended to him that his illness was
nothing at all. It could not be kept up. He knew that he was very
ill indeed, and getting worse all the time; at last he kissed her and
said: 'Princess' (his pet name for her), 'I think we shall have to

part.' He gave orders that she and Madame de Lauraguais should go at once, and that the Queen should be sent for; then he confessed.

The Bishops of Metz and Soissons, about to bring the Holy Sacrament from the cathedral to the King's bedside, heard that Madame de Châteauroux and her sister were still in Richelieu's house in the town; they sent a message to the effect that Our Lord was awaiting the departure of the Duchesses, who then had no choice but to leave for Paris. Before communicating, the King was induced by the Bishops to make a public statement of repentance; all those who were in his ante-room, that is to say the officers of state and the high *bourgeoisie* of Metz, were brought in to his bedside to hear him do so. He was very weak and hardly spoke as if he wanted to recover; he said that perhaps it was God's will to give his people a better King. When the Queen arrived, he received her affectionately and begged her pardon. He was very civil to the Dauphin, never a pleasant apparition to a possibly dying young King, and seemed in fact to be in a repentant state of mind and to have every intention, should he live, of changing his ways.

But the French clergy, who had taken the affair in hand, made blunder after blunder. To an intensely shy, reserved and proud man, the thought of his public confession was humiliating enough as he came back to his normal state of health; now it was printed and distributed to every parish in France so that each priest could make a sermon on it, embellished with his own views on the sin of adultery. This proceeding shocked many sensible and God-fearing citizens, who felt that the King should have been allowed to repent in private, and that all the women of the Court should have been sent away together, so that the affair with Madame de Châteauroux could have ended without publicity. As soon as the King was better, a lady-in-waiting, prompted by his confessor, put a second pillow into the Queen's bed. Rumour had it that the Queen had taken to rouge again. At the most frivolous Court in the world, where everything was treated as a joke, all this provoked gales of laughter, and M. de Richelieu, who held a watching brief for Madame de Châteauroux, certainly did not shelter the King from these gales. The country, however, felt very differently about the whole matter. The handsome young King was enormously popular and the French had worked themselves up to a state of despair when they believed him to be dying. The reaction to better news caused a mafficking such as has rarely been seen in Paris—people embracing each other in the streets and embracing the horses which had brought the messengers. It was at this time that Louis XV received the name of Well Beloved. But in their transports of joy his subjects did not omit to underline their detestation of his mistress; and, whenever she appeared in public, she was booed, hissed, pelted with eggs and almost lynched. She retired to bed with a complete breakdown.

With his courtiers giggling in his ante-room and his clergy and people moralizing to his face, the King forgot all his good resolutions. He had but one idea, to show that he was not going to be bullied into a new life, to show who was the master; besides he longed very much for Madame de Châteauroux. As soon as he got home to Versailles he sent for her. She was in her house in the rue du Bac, feverish and furious. When the King's message came, not wishing to delay their reunion, she got up, had a bath, and prepared to leave. The effort was too much for her; she collapsed and died of pneumonia.

The King was now thirty-four years old.

*Chapter Two*

# PARIS AND MADAME D'ETIOLES

VERY little of Paris as we know it to-day existed in the 1720's; no Place de la Concorde, Madeleine, or rue de Rivoli, the Louvre half its present size, no Ecole Militaire or Panthéon, no bridge between the Pont Royal and the Pont de Sèvres, no big thoroughfares or *boulevards*. The lay-out was that of an overgrown village; narrow streets surrounded the houses of rich merchants and of the ennobled lawyers known as the *noblesse de robe*, very much despised by the *noblesse d'epée*, the old feudal families. The streets were noisier, with even more terrible traffic blocks, than to-day. They were filthy dirty and it was impossible to walk in them when there had been rain without getting mud up to the knees. On the outskirts of this town, rich nobles and merchants were building a garden city, the *faubourgs*, whose wide streets led out to the country. Each house, of a pale honey colour, weather and soot not yet having done their horrid work, stood in its own big garden, full, in summer, of orange trees and olean-ders. Every house of any size had an orangery. The quays did not exist; gardens went down to the river where the boats and barges of their owners were moored. Many of these houses are still in existence, but, too often, squashed between nineteenth- or twen-tieth-century blocks of flats, they would be unrecognizable to their former owners. A few *Hôtels*, Matignon, Biron, and the Elysée, for instance, have kept their gardens, and from them we can judge how the others must have looked. The forest was at their door; La Muette, in the Bois de Boulogne, was still one of the King's hunts.

Jeanne-Antoinette Poisson, the future Marquise de Pompadour, was not born in one of these splendid new mansions, but in the rue de Cléry, then, as now, situated in the heart of the town. Her mother was a beauty, so she has been accorded various fathers by various biographers, but it is probable that her mother's husband, M. Poisson, was the real one. He certainly thought so. Poisson was a jolly *bourgeois*, steward to the Pâris brothers, who ran the economy of France. The Pâris were nearly as important in the life of Mlle Poisson as her own family—indeed Pâris-Duverney is one of the possible fathers—and they were deeply attached to her. Pâris-Monmartel, the little girl's godfather, was Court banker; Pâris-Duverney supplied the army; their power was almost un-limited. They could support or starve out the generals at the front, make or ruin politicians; the King himself was dependent on them when he wanted to realize large sums of money for any reason and he used them in all his financial transactions. They were responsible to no government department and always refused the various ministries which were offered them. Their own riches were said to be fabulous, but when Pâris-Duverney died he left so little money that, in the nineteenth century, his coffin was opened to see if he had not, by any chance, been buried in gold. Of course they have been called rogues and worse, but on the whole the verdict of their contemporaries was favourable. Maréchal de Saxe thought the world of them, and said that they were entirely public spirited; they always supported him up to the hilt, partly, no doubt, because they saw he was worth supporting. But whether these mysterious brothers—there were four of them, but only two come into this story—were good or bad, or like most people, a mixture of both, it was clearly a wrong principle for the country's finances to be in the hands of one family con-cern. In private life they were patrons of art, great collectors, and frequented the cultivated society of other rich *bourgeois*; their clever, reassuring, genial faces, above a broad expanse of embroidered waistcoat, look out from several canvases of the day; they must have been delightful fellow-guests.

François Poisson was doing well. He had moved from the rue de Cléry to a big house in the rue de Richelieu, with *boiseries* and modern comfort, sumptuous, up to date. But in 1725, when his little girl was four years old, there broke some sort of black market scandal to do with corn supplied to the population by the Pâris brothers. Owing to a succession of cold, wet summers, there was a famine in the capital, tempers were running high, and Poisson seems to have been made a scapegoat. He got over the German frontier only just in time to avoid arrest, leaving Madame Poisson to cope with his affairs, and saying, rather sadly perhaps, that as she was so very pretty she would surely fall on her feet. He was quite right, she did; but not before she had suffered trials and humiliations, the house in the rue de Richelieu, with all its contents, being seized and sold over her head. She was rescued from her misfortunes by M. Le Normant de Tournehem, one-time ambassador to Sweden, now a director of the *Compagnie des Indes*, and a *fermier général*, or collector of indirect taxes. The *fermiers généraux* were always respected *bourgeois* of the financial world; and he was a great friend of the Pâris. (Tournehem is often credited with the paternity of Mlle Poisson, but this does not seem very likely. Had he already been Madame Poisson's lover, he would hardly have left her for months in horrid embarrassment after the flight of her husband.)

This very nice, rich fellow cherished Madame Poisson and took charge of the whole family. He saw to the education of the children, Jeanne-Antoinette and her younger brother Abel; he finally made it possible for François Poisson to come back to Paris, after an exile of eight years. He was completely cleared of the charges against him and was given an important job to do with army supplies. From now on, Tournehem and the Poissons all lived cheerfully together.

Little is known of Jeanne-Antoinette's childhood; the lives of children were not carefully documented in those days. At the age of nine she went to a fortune-teller who told her that she would reign over the heart of a king—in her accounts twenty years later, there is an item of six hundred livres to this woman, 'for having predicted, when I was nine, that I would be the King's mistress'—after this she was called Reinette by her family. By the wish of her father, she spent a year in a convent at Poissy, where his two sisters were nuns. They wrote to him, in Germany, saying that when he sent money he had better let them have it direct, and not through Madame Poisson. Reinette was very delicate and spent much of her time there in bed, with whooping cough and sore throats. Whatever else the good nuns may have taught the little girl, they certainly failed to give her any understanding of the Roman Catholic religion. After leaving the convent she was educated at home, under the eye of Tournehem and of her mother, and this worldly education left nothing to be desired; a more accomplished woman has seldom lived.

She could act and dance and sing, having been taught by Jéliotte of the Comédie Française; she could recite whole plays by heart, her master of elocution was Crébillon, the dramatist; she played the clavichord to perfection, a valuable gift in those days, when tunes could not be summoned by turning a knob. She was an enthusiastic gardener and botanist, and knew all about the wonderful shrubs which were pouring into France from every quarter of the globe; she loved natural history, and collected rare and exotic birds. Her handwriting, curiously modern, was both beautiful and legible. She painted, drew and engraved precious stones. Last, but not least, she was a superlative housekeeper. Abel, too, was taught everything considered necessary to a rich young man of the day. What was even more important than lessons, the Poisson children were brought up among people of excellent taste, who had knowledge of and a respect for art in all its forms; honest *bourgeois* who, when they patronized an artist, paid for what they ordered. Both the children profited in later life from this example which was not always followed by the highest in the land.

From the earliest days Reinette was a charmer. She charmed her 'stepfather' Tournehem; she charmed the nuns at the convent who loved her tenderly, and took an interest in her long after she had left them; her father, mother and brother worshipped the ground she trod on. She grew up endowed with every gift a woman could desire but one, her health was never good. Without being a regular beauty, she was the very acme of prettiness, though her looks, which depended on dazzle and expression rather than on the bony structure, were never successfully recorded by painters. Her brother always said that not one of her many portraits was really like her; they are certainly not very much like each other. We recognize the pose, the elegance, but hardly the face. More informative are the descriptions by various contemporaries, written in private journals and memoirs, which did not see the light for many years after her death.

Dufort de Cheverny, himself of *bourgeois* origin, always deeply jealous of her brother, says:

'Not a man alive but would have had her for his mistress if he could. Tall, though not too tall; beautiful figure; round face with regular features; wonderful complexion, hands and arms; eyes not so very big, but the brightest, wittiest and most sparkling I ever saw. Everything about her was rounded, including all her gestures.

'She absolutely extinguished all the other women at the Court, although some were very beautiful.'

The Duc de Luynes, a dry old member of the Queen's set, rather fond of dwelling on the physical appearance of Court ladies in the most denigrating terms—their cheeks too flat, their noses too fat, their figures almost deformed and so on—is obliged to admit that she is *fort jolie*.

The Prince de Croÿ, who disapproved of her, says over and over again that it would not be possible to be prettier.

Président Hénault, the Queen's greatest friend, writes: 'One of the prettiest women I ever saw.'

An honest, rather unimaginative soldier, the Marquis de Valfons writes: 'With her grace, the lightness of her figure, and the beauty of her hair, she resembled a nymph.'

Le Roy, a gamekeeper at Versailles, after praising all her features, her figure and her beautiful light brown hair, goes on: 'Her eyes had a particular attraction, perhaps owing to the fact that it was difficult to say exactly what colour they were; they had neither the hard sparkle of black eyes, nor the dreamy tenderness of blue, nor the special delicacy of grey; their indeterminate colour seemed to lend them to all forms of seduction and shades of expression. Indeed her expression was always changing, though there was never any discordance between her various features; they all unfolded the same thought, which presupposes a good deal of self control, and this applied to her every movement. Her whole person was half way between the last degree of elegance and the first of nobility.'

Finally, the Marquis d'Argenson, who hated her so terribly that his whole diary is really written with the aim of destroying her in the eyes of posterity, finds nothing worse—at the beginning—to say than: 'She is snow white, without features, but graceful and talented. Tall, rather badly made.'

By the time she was of marriageable age, she was already spoken of in Paris society as fit for a King; and she herself had lived in a dream of love for the King ever since her visit to the fortune-teller, a dream which was most unlikely to come true, since it was impossible for a *bourgeoise* to be presented to him, and he had a mistress already. Meanwhile her parents were not finding it easy to marry her; the reputations of both left too much to be desired. Poisson was an amusing rough diamond, but he had been mixed up in shady business, some said hanged in effigy by the public hangman after his flight, and his origins were lower rather than middle class; he had never tried to seem other than he was, or bothered the least bit about appearances, and many people would not have cared to have him in the family. As for lovely Madame Poisson, she was clever and cultivated but not, alas, virtuous; alas too, this jolly but doubtful couple was not even very rich. However, M. de Tournehem, who was, now took the affair in hand. He suggested to his nephew, M. Le Normant d'Etioles, that he should marry Reinette. D'Etioles did not like the idea, but Tournehem offered such excellent terms—an enormous dowry, a guarantee that the young couple should live with him for the rest of his life, all expenses, even the wages of their personal servants, paid, and should inherit his fortune when he died—that d'Etioles gave way. They were married in March, 1741.

The young couple and M. and Madame Poisson lived with M. de Tournehem in the Hôtel de Gesvres, rue Croix des Petits Champs, and at the Château d'Etioles in the forest of Sénart. One of the most delicious of the many houses lived in and arranged by Reinette, Etioles did not escape the bad luck with which they have nearly all been cursed. Its owner pulled it down early in this century to avoid paying rates on it. Le Normant d'Etioles was no sooner married than he fell passionately in love with his wife and she, for her part, often said that she would never leave him— except, of course, for the King. This seems to have been a family joke, but it was more than a joke to Madame d'Etioles.

Her daughter, Alexandrine, was born when the King was ill at Metz; somebody told her that his life was said to be in danger, whereupon she had a relapse and nearly died. (Alexandrine was her second child; a little boy had already died in infancy.) Yet if, like many women, she had dreams of a different life, her real life was most agreeable. She was young, beautiful and rich, surrounded by relations whom she loved, and who regarded her as the pivot of their world. She did not have to express a wish before it was granted. At Etioles a big theatre was built, with proper stage machinery, for her to act in; soon she was recognized as one of the very best amateur actresses in France. Her horses and carriages were the envy of the countryside and so were her jewels and dresses; she was of an extreme elegance, a more difficult achievement then than it is to-day, as the great dressmakers did not exist, and each woman invented her own clothes.

Madame d'Etioles was a person of decided character who knew what she wanted in life, and generally got it. Now that she was married and 'out' in society she thought that she would like to have a *salon* and entertain the intellectuals of her day. This was a career for which her talents and fortune obviously fitted her. The intellectual life of Paris centred round those writers, known as the *philosophes*, who were presently to compile a great encyclopædia of human knowledge; a spectacular occupation and one that continually got them into trouble with the Church and the Court. They lived in a blaze of publicity, with the eyes of the world upon them, partly because of this encyclopædia and partly because Voltaire belonged to their group. He was one of those people with a talent for attracting the attention of their fellow men. Their ideas produced the moral climate in which the French Revolution finally took place; but had they lived to witness the Revolution, it would have horrified them one and all. Though they were not Christians, they were, for the most part, neither atheists nor anarchists; Voltaire believed in God and loved Kings. But they did want to prevent the dead hand of the Church from producing, in France, the intellectual paralysis which we see to-day in Spain. Where government was concerned they wanted more justice and less secrecy, a few mild reforms. Unfortunately the system left by Louis XIV was impervious to mild reforms, it had to be blown up by a bomb.

These *philosophes* lived and worked in Paris, Voltaire not having, as yet, cast its dust from his feet; and they frequented the houses of certain hostesses, where they were able to exchange ideas in an atmosphere whose component parts, of exalted mutual admiration and miserable little jealousies, proved intensely stimulating. The talk, always good in France, has probably never reached such heights, before or since, as the conversations between Voltaire, Vauvenargues, Montesquieu, Marivaux, Fontenelle, and Helvétius. The stars, of course, would be Voltaire, with his enormous stock of interesting information, his brilliant flashes of fun, and his tender regard for the other star, Vauvenargues, who, in his turn, had a deep respect for Voltaire's genius. The lesser lights, but not to be despised, were Marivaux, waiting impatiently for the ball to come his way; Montesquieu waiting too, but rather more calmly; Fontenelle who, though over ninety, was always ready when it did come with some appropriate story or remark that never took more than a minute; and Helvétius, fonder of listening than of talking, storing it all up in his memory. This miraculous entertainment went on round the supper tables of a few women, Mesdames Geoffrin, du Deffand, de Tencin, Madame Denis, the niece of Voltaire, and one or two others. Madame d'Etioles, with her gifts and her fortune and the liking she always had for clever men, seemed ideally suited to be such a hostess and this very soon became her object in life. She probably thought she would beat the old ladies at their own game: better educated than Madame Geoffrin, more cheerful than Madame du Deffand, less bossy than Madame de Tencin, richer than Madame Denis and prettier than any of them. Already the potential guests were very well-disposed towards her; Crébillon, Montesquieu and Fontenelle went to her house, she had been painted by Nattier and Boucher, and Madame du Deffand had written to the Président Hénault saying, 'don't be unfaithful to all of us with Madame d'Etioles.' Voltaire took an almost proprietary interest in her; 'well brought up, amiable, good, charming and talented,' he said. 'She was born sensible and kind hearted.'

But Madame d'Etioles had enough worldly wisdom to realize that it is never enough for a young woman to receive; she must also be received. She knew, too, that writers like meeting society people; a *salon* only frequented by the intellectual *bourgeoisie* lacks elegance. The Marquise de la Ferté d'Imbault, daughter of Madame Geoffrin, says that two difficulties stood in the way of Madame d'Etioles' ambition at this time. One was pretty Madame Poisson, who was received by certain hostesses, Madame de Tencin, for instance, but was considered rather too disreputable by others, including Madame Geoffrin. The Geoffrins lived only four doors from the Hôtel de Gesvres and one day, rather to their horror, Madame Poisson and her daughter paid them a call.

'The mother,' says Madame de la Ferté d'Imbault, 'had such a bad reputation that we could not possibly have made friends with her; the daughter, however, was quite another story. I had no wish to seem rude, and it was difficult to see one without the other, but in the end I managed to return Madame d'Etioles' call and not Madame Poisson's. Madame d'Etioles asked my mother if she could often go and see her, to improve her knowledge of the world. . . . One New Year's Day, she and her husband called on me at my *toilette*, so polite to me that I scolded her in a laughing way; next New Year's Day, at her own *toilette*, she had the whole Court, and the Princes of the Blood, bowing to the earth. I still laugh when I think of it.'

The other difficulty was that his business as *fermier général* compelled M. de Tournehem to receive a great many bores at the Hôtel de Gesvres, where his niece acted as hostess. Amusing people like the Abbé de Bernis and the Duc de Nivernais, whom she often met, and would have liked to entertain, would not fit in at all with Tournehem's financial friends.

The first of these obstacles was soon removed in a very sad way;

Madame Poisson was laid low with a cancer. She was forced to give up society and prepare to face an agonizing and lingering death. Madame d'Etioles, on her own, was a highly desirable guest, with her looks and elegance, and possessing as she did that intense love of life, and interest in human beings, which is perhaps the base of what we variously call charm, sex appeal or fascination. She was not only clever and amusing, but modern in her outlook, quite prepared to 'think philosophically' and never likely to be shocked even by the most outrageous sallies of the *philosophes*.

She was soon asked everywhere; her name began to be known at Versailles, where the love of gossip extended to tales about people who would never be seen at Court. Curiously enough it seems to have been the Widow Mailly who first spoke of her there, having met her at a party, and been so carried away by her singing, and playing of the clavichord, that she gave her an enthusiastic hug. The King soon knew her by name; he also knew her by sight; she was a country neighbour. His favourite hunt was in the forest of Sénart where he had a hunting lodge called Choisy, his own little house, altered for him by Gabriel, and which he loved more than any of his palaces, some said more than any of his mistresses. He came here for privacy and fun, bringing with him six ladies and various men friends, but no spoil-sport husbands; life was so free and easy that the women were allowed to float about without panniers, an unheard-of licence in a gentleman's house. A mechanical table came up from the kitchen with the food already on it so that there need be no servants in the dining-room; after dinner the King made the coffee himself. Let nobody think, however, that orgies took place; they were not at all to the taste of Louis XV.

Although the *bourgeoisie* was never allowed to ride with the King's hunt, only families noble since 1400 having that privilege, the rule was relaxed in favour of near neighbours, who had permission to follow it in carriages. Madame d'Etioles took full advantage of this opportunity. She drove her own phaeton, knew the forest like the palm of her hand, and was always popping up in the path of the King. Dressed in pink, driving a blue phaeton, or in blue driving a pink one, a vision of prettiness, a skilful, dashing driver, she could hardly have failed to attract his attention. He was too shy to speak to a stranger, but he did sometimes send a present of game to her house. Meanwhile somebody else had noticed her, and with no friendly eye. The Duchesse de Chevreuse, who had known Madame d'Etioles from a child, happened to mention her name in front of the King, whereupon Madame de Châteauroux stepped so hard on her foot that she nearly fainted from the pain. Next day Madame de Châteauroux called on her to apologize, saying: 'You know they talk of giving that little d'Etioles to the King.' After this, Madame d'Etioles was warned to keep away from the hunt, and had no choice but to do so; it would have been madness to provoke the enmity of Madame de Châteauroux.

Fate now took a curious turn. Madame de Châteauroux died; the second of the Mailly sisters to be removed from the King by death. As in the case of Madame de Vintimille he was heartbroken if not inconsolable; this time, however, he did not return to Madame de Mailly. Naturally there was now but one topic of conversation in society, both at Versailles and in Paris; who would be the next mistress? At first it was taken more or less for granted that it would be the fourth Mailly sister, Madame de Lauraguais. The King, sad and out of spirits, supped with her every night, but this was really from habit; she had been the inseparable companion of Madame de Châteauroux. The Duc de Richelieu was known to support her candidature; he also had one or two other duchesses up his sleeve, and his influence with the King in these matters was great.

Meanwhile every pretty woman in the Ile de France nurtured

a secret conviction that she would carry off the prize. Such was the prestige of a monarch in those days, so nearly was he considered as a god, that very little shame attached to the position of his mistress, while the material advantages to her family were enormous. The monstrous fortunes of the Gramont, Mortemart, la Vallière and d'Estrées families were founded upon such relationships with various Kings. The Queen having settled into a dreary little life with her unfashionable friends, gaiety and amusement centred on the King's set and was led by his mistress. Besides all this, Louis XV was extremely attractive. He was tall and handsome, he had a most caressing look, a curious husky voice which nobody ever forgot who had once heard it, and a sexy moodiness of manner irresistible to women; the haughty air, which came in reality from shyness, in no way detracted from his charm. The wives of his subjects had no difficulty in falling in love with him, and Madame d'Etioles was not the only one who had done so. It was put about in Paris that he was tired of aristocratic mistresses, with their political ambitions and their grasping families; the *bourgeoises* were one and all agog.

But how to meet him? This was indeed a problem. True he often went, masked, to the public balls, both in Paris and in the town of Versailles. It was a pastime of which he was uncommonly fond, but the moment his identity was known, as it always was because of the way he carried his head and the unmistakable timbre of his voice, he would be mobbed; nobody could have a private word with him after that. A possible way would be an introduction through one of his body servants. These men, whose functions were handed down from father to son, whose families always ended by being ennobled, and who themselves employed between ten and twenty servants, were very important in the palace hierarchy. In some respects they had more influence with the King than any of his courtiers; he confided many things to them and was very fond of them. Madame d'Etioles had a distant cousin, one Binet, who was body servant to the Dauphin and who often, in the course of his duties, saw the King alone; no doubt she was in touch with him, but for the moment she did not make use of him.

At this juncture there were signs that the King would have liked to reform, and go back to the Queen. He was a religious man, a family man at heart. The Metz affair had not failed to make an impression on him; he was devoted to his daughters, growing up apace, and had no wish to offer a bad example to them, or to the Dauphin, who was nearly sixteen and just about to be married. Mesdames de Vintimille and Châteauroux had been extremely grasping, and had made themselves obnoxious to the Queen who, though most long-suffering as a rule, had once turned on Madame de Vintimille, when she asked for some favour, with 'You are the mistress here, Madame.' The King hated this sort of incident; it embarrassed him and he hated being embarrassed. But he also hated being bored, and if he had ever seriously considered a return to conjugal life, one look at the Queen's existence must have made him realize that it would be more than he could bear.

Marie Leczinska was said by her intimates to be not only very good but also very amusing. They said that she had a noble mouth but a malicious eye, and hinted that, when her devotions were finished, she kept her friends in a perpetual roar of laughter. This we must beg leave to doubt. People lucky enough to belong to the circle of royal personages are fond of letting it be understood that they are less dull than they look; the friends of Marie Leczinska were no exception, but they cannot persuade us that she was anything but a very nice old bore. Her jovial father, Stanislas, always said the dullest queens in Europe were his wife and daughter: 'When I'm with her I yawn like at Mass.' The amusing element at Court had always avoided her; now, in the midst of the liveliest society France has ever seen, she was living

like a nun. Most of her day was spent in prayer, her only outings
being to charitable entertainments or the convent where her unfashionable dresses were embroidered.

In the morning, between Mass and her state visit to the King,
she read some moral tale, or did a little painting, for which her
talent was pathetically meagre, as we can see by the example of
her work which still remains at Versailles. She dined at 1 p.m.,
in public, eating enormously. After dinner she sewed for the poor
until it was time for cards. Gambling was a great feature of the
life at Versailles, enormous sums were won and lost, and everybody spent hours at the tables, even the young Princesses. The
Queen's game was Cavagnole, played with dice; it had long
been out of fashion; Comète and Piquet were now all the rage.
Nothing is so frumpish as last year's gambling game and the
courtiers complained terribly when they were made to play *la
triste Cavagnole* with the Queen. Two or three times a week her
tables were put in the state rooms where the public was admitted,
but nobody ever bothered to go and watch. After supper, her
evening was given over to social life. Her ladies, who were
chosen by the King, because they amused and attracted him,
scampered off to the *petits appartements* and she was left with her
elderly friends the Duc and Duchesse de Luynes.

The Duc de Luynes kept a journal in which almost every hour
of life in the palace is accounted for. He is not a great writer like
Saint-Simon, and three-quarters of his journal, devoted to questions of etiquette and usage, is almost unreadable; but he inspires
confidence, he never writes anything of which he is not quite certain, and from time to time, in some anecdote or physical descrip-
tion, his pages come to life. Enormously rich, he and his wife were
also close-fisted and dowdy, as is evident from the fact that they
did not pull down Dampierre and build a modern château in its
place, as almost anybody else would have. Beautiful Dampierre, a
jewel of Louis XIII architecture, stands unchanged in its park, and

still belongs to the Duc de Luynes. The Queen supped at least every other day with these friends; the Duke noting each year how many times. It was very expensive for them, and she once said to his brother that she really must make it up to them in some way; they waited, hopefully, but in the end only received gracious compliments.

The other guests at these suppers were always the same: Luynes' son and daughter-in-law, the Duc and Duchesse de Chevreuse; his brother, the Cardinal de Luynes; Président Hénault, and Moncrif; all, except the Chevreuses, were over sixty. François de Moncrif, whose origins, certainly Scotch, are rather mysterious, was one of those hangers-on who, in all societies and in all ages, manage to create and maintain a position for themselves, for no very evident reason. He must have been extremely cosy. He was the 'historian of cats' and it was said that he got on in life by never scratching, having velvet paws and never putting up his back, even when startled. The Queen thought he was so good as to be almost saintly; she little knew that in the passages of the Opéra hung a notice: 'If one of the young ladies would care to sup with a nice little old man, she would find ninety-two steps to climb, quite a good supper and could earn ten *louis*.' The nice little old man was Moncrif; the ninety-two steps led to his lodging in the Louvre, given to him by his friend the Queen.

The Duc de Chevreuse, who truly was all piety and goodness, was in love with the Queen and horribly jealous of Président Hénault; the King, the Dauphin and even the Queen herself used to make jokes about it. This little company sat sleepily round the fire, evening after evening; one or more of them would generally nod off, lulled by the snoring of Madame de Luynes' old dog, Tintamarre. The Cardinal once woke up with a jump and called for an immediate meeting of the chapter.

Such evenings were not likely to attract the presence of Louis XV.

## Chapter Three

# THE BALL OF THE CLIPPED YEW TREES

IN February, 1745, the Dauphin was married to the Infanta Marie-Thérèse-Raphaele, sister of the King's little rejected fiancée. He was the second of Louis XV's children to marry. The eldest daughter was now wife of the King of Spain's second son, the Infant Philippe; she was always known as Madame Infante.

A great round of festivities celebrated the Dauphin's wedding. Though he and his sisters disliked balls, their father did not; he declared that at their age it was good for them to dance, and during the whole month of February they were given the opportunity of doing so nearly every night. There were balls in the apartments of Mesdames (the Princesses), in the town of Versailles, and in the palace riding school; the King danced continually and always with the same person. She was masked, but rumour had it that she was the lovely Madame d'Etioles. These fêtes culminated in a great ball at Versailles, and another at the Hôtel de Ville in Paris.

A few days before the palace ball was to take place, when nobody was talking of anything else, Président Hénault met Madame d'Etioles. He asked if she was going to it? Yes, she was. He said, with the fatherly solicitude of an old Lothario, that he hoped she had made suitable arrangements for accommodation; he had heard that every room in the whole town of Versailles was taken. She replied demurely that her cousin, the Sieur Binet, was kindly seeing to it for her.

The ball for the Dauphin's marriage was perhaps the most

splendid ever known in all the history of Versailles. The palace was illuminated inside and out; it glowed like a great bonfire at the end of the Avenue de Paris, which in its turn was a river of light, from the double line of coaches, all laden with guests, coming from the capital. Candles, torches, brands and flares, cast a warm and variable radiance, very much more beautiful than electric headlights and flood lighting. The guests drove across the great courtyard, and got out of their carriages at the foot of the marble staircase in the south wing. Never had there been such a crowd at any previous ball, every pretty woman in Paris was there to try her chances with the King. When balls were given in the state apartments they were entirely open to the public; it sufficed to be properly dressed to be admitted. The men were obliged to carry swords, but even this regulation was arbitrary; everybody knew that the palace *concierge* did a brisk trade hiring out swords to would-be guests. At the top of the staircase one member of each party was required to unmask and give his name; otherwise there were no rules and no invitations were issued. On this occasion, the man who was supposed to take the names very soon gave up the unequal struggle; the crowd surged past him into the great reception rooms, through the Queen's rooms, including her bedroom, into the Galerie des Glaces. These rooms each had a buffet and a band; it was hoped that too great a crush in the gallery would thus be relieved. But the guests, who behaved in a very free and easy way the whole night, shocking the courtiers with their lack of manners, merely paused to help themselves to food—fish, as Lent was in progress, fresh salmon, and soles, and *pâté* of trout—and then pushed on, clutching plates and glasses. The prophecy of Nostradamus, that the floor would give way and only the King and the thirty people near him would be saved, was gallantly disregarded.

For a long time the King, and other royalties, were sought in vain; none had yet appeared. At last, one of the looking-glass doors was thrown open, and in came the Queen; she was unmasked, her dress was covered with bunches of pearls and the two famous diamonds, the Régent and the Sancy, sparkled on her head. She was followed by the Dauphin and his new wife, dressed as a gardener and flower-seller, and the Duc and Duchesse de Chartres. All the other royalties present were masked; they included Prince Charles Edward of England, so soon to embark on his disappointing adventure. Time went on, and still no sign of the King. The Chartres vanished from the party; they were so fond of making love that they could hardly bear to take any time off, when they dined out they generally asked for the use of their hostess's bed during the course of the meal; at Versailles they had their own to go to. The Princesse de Conti, mother of the Duchesse de Chartres, removed her mask in the supper room imagining that somebody would spring up to give her a chair; nobody recognized her, nobody budged; she stumped away furiously muttering that she had never, in a long life, seen such impossible people.

The Dauphine danced with a Spanish grandee who knew all the gossip of Madrid and was clearly of great importance; he refused to reveal his identity although she begged him to do so. Presently the Marquis de Tessé, himself a grandee of Spain, had a long talk with him, found him absolutely delightful and invited him to dinner; the Spaniard never unmasked, and presently he vanished. Next day M. de Tessé's Spanish cook confessed to him that the mysterious hidalgo had been none other than himself. This story went all round Versailles and was thought particularly enjoyable because of the Dauphine's character. Like all the Spanish royal family she was extremely stiff, penetrated with the sense of her own importance. The French never liked her. She made it quite clear that she thought many of their customs too common for words, the use of rouge, for instance, and their passion for jokes. She was never seen to laugh at a joke, either with friends or at the play, and made it quite clear that she would not tolerate them from her ladies-in-waiting. The King put himself out for her to a touching extent, trying, in a hundred little ways, to make her feel at home; she was always most dis-agreeable to him, possibly from shyness but more likely, it was thought, because she disapproved of him. M. de Luynes, to whom anybody royal appeared in rather a rosy light, says that she would have been pretty had it not been for her red hair, white eyelashes, and an enormous nose which seemed to grow straight out of her forehead without any roots. She was, however, elegant and a beautiful dancer; the Dauphin, extremely uxorious like all his family, had fallen in love with her at once.

At last, the door leading to the *Oeil de Bœuf*, ante-chamber to the King's apartment, was opened; everybody pressed forward. A very curious procession lurched blindly into the ballroom; eight yew trees, clipped like those in the garden outside, in the shape of pillars with vases on them. The King had made up his mind that, for once, he would be unrecognizable. In the print by Cochin of the scene in the great gallery, lit by eight thousand candles, many fancy dresses can clearly be made out and the yew trees are mingling with the crowd. Presently one of them went off with pretty Présidente Portail to a dark and solitary corner of the palace. She thought he was the King, and nestled happily among the twigs; but when she returned to the ballroom what was her fury to see that the real King, who had taken off his head-dress, was engaged in a laughing conversation with Madame d'Etioles, dressed as Diana and also unmasked. 'The handkerchief is thrown,' said the courtiers. It was now quite clear to them that a love affair was beginning. Before they parted the King had arranged to meet her the following Sunday at the ball in Paris.

Next morning at eight o'clock the last carriage still had not left Versailles.

The Paris municipality now put its best foot forward. The

Spanish marriage was very popular; it was supposed to have eliminated the Pyrenees and turned them into a *temple d'amour*—such rubbish, said the courtiers—thus lessening the chances of war with Spain. The Dauphin was known to be in love and this was considered very nice and romantic; and then the King, the adored, the idol, was in such an interesting situation. The mood of the capital was one of benevolent jollity. The festivities on this Sunday evening must have been very much like those of a modern fourteenth of July, only far more elaborate, with free food and wine galore. As it was winter and therefore impossible to dance in the streets, seven ballrooms were built—at the Hôtel de Ville, which had its courtyard roofed in, at the Place Dauphine, two in the Place Louis le Grand (Vendôme), at the Place du Carrousel, in the rue de Sèvres and the Place de la Bastille. These ballrooms were designed with an attention to detail which has hardly been bestowed, since the eighteenth century, on something only intended to last one evening. They were like large summer houses, Chinese in feeling, their walls were of pink marble and trellis work filled with vine leaves, bunches of grapes and flowers. Real palm trees, whose stems were garlanded with roses, and draperies of pink velvet fringed with gold, outlined the buffets which groaned with turkeys, boars' heads and other delicacies. The chandeliers hung from garlands of flowers, and, outside, the walls and roofs were covered with candles. Everywhere there were pictures and statues of the Royal Family; marble fountains flowed with wine. Except for the Hôtel de Ville all these ballrooms were open to the public; the poorest of the poor came with their wives, their families and even their dogs to eat, and drink, and dance, and amuse themselves all night. There was also a subscription ball at the Opéra.

The Dauphin was to attend the masked ball at the Hôtel de Ville without his father, and there to thank the Parisians for their good wishes. It was expected that the King would look in later, in disguise. This ball was by invitation, but there had been considerable mismanagement, twice too many cards had been sent out and the crowd was so immense as to be almost dangerous. In spite of a second ballroom in the courtyard the guests could hardly move, it took hours to get up or down the stairs, and the women's dresses were torn to pieces by the crush. The whole thing was a scandal, said the Parisians, who grumbled about it for weeks afterwards; the food had given out by three in the morning, and it was alleged that several people had died, of heat, or cold, or fatigue or asphyxiation.

The King and the Duc d'Ayen, his boon companion, left Versailles immediately after the King's *coucher*, at about midnight; they were in black dominoes. First they went to while away an hour or two at a public ball in the town; then they started off for Paris, a drive which, with the King's special horses, known as *les enragés*, took about an hour and a quarter. At Sèvres they met the Dauphin going home to his darling new wife; he had thanked the Parisians very charmingly for their kind enthusiasm, after which it had been almost impossible for him to get through the crowd at the Hôtel de Ville, even with a guard clearing the way. The two carriages stopped, and the Dauphin crossed the road to tell his father what it had been like at the ball; he very much advised him not to go on. Himself lazy, religious and home-loving, he always disapproved of his father's passion for gay society; no doubt he thought him far too old to go dancing all night. The King, however, had a tryst which he fully intended to keep.

When he arrived in Paris he went to the Opéra; here he trod a measure or two and then, sending away his own carriage, he took a cab to the Hôtel de Ville. He soon found Madame d'Etioles, very much dishevelled, as were all the women by then, but none the less pretty for that. They got somehow into a private room and had a little supper, after which even the King decided that the crowd was too much for enjoyment; he asked if he could take her home. D'Ayen went for a cab and the three of them got into it. The streets were almost as crowded as the ball, and at one moment the cab was held up by the city police. The King, rather nervous by now, said, 'Give them a *louis*.'[1] 'No, no, Sire,' said d'Ayen, 'if we do that we shall be recognized at once and your escapade will be in the police reports to-morrow.' The King, who greatly enjoyed reading about other people's escapades in the police reports, but had no wish for his own to be all round the town, sat as far back as he could while d'Ayen handed the cab driver an *écu*; the man whipped up his horses, they galloped through the cordon and Madame d'Etioles was duly deposited at the Hôtel de Gesvres. The King got back to Versailles at 9 a.m.; he changed his coat and went to Mass, 'no good sinning in every direction', after which he slept until five o'clock. According to Court language 'day broke in the King's room at five.'

By now, tongues were wagging. Those who had seen the King and Madame d'Etioles leaving the Hôtel de Ville together supposed that she had gone back with him to Versailles; at Versailles itself the courtiers were wondering how long it would be before she appeared there again, and whether this was a passing attraction or a serious affair. People who knew the King well bet on the former. Never, they said, would he bring a *bourgeoise* to Versailles as mistress; in the annals of the Kings of France such a thing was unknown, and it would create an impossible situation. The King's mistress, after all, had an enormous position at the Court which somebody not born and bred there would never be able to carry off. Indeed, at this point the King himself seems to have hung back, probably because he was not sure of his

[1] A *louis*, in those days, was exactly a guinea. The Duc de Luynes says, 'they give in London a guinea for a *louis* and in Lille a *louis* for a guinea.' An *écu* was half a crown. The *livre* varied in value according to the monetary policy of the government. During the reign of Louis XV it was about twenty-four to the *louis*.

own feelings. Madame d'Etioles was not the sort of person with whom one could play fast and loose, or treat as the little mistress of a few days, taking her from husband and family, and then casting her off again; it had to be all or nothing. She was rather middle-class in her behaviour; she spoke, and even thought, quite differently from the courtiers, and while this amused the King when they were alone together, he may have feared that it would embarrass him in front of such as the Duc de Richelieu. He was certainly anxious to establish a permanent mistress; he told the Sieur Binet that he was tired of going from one woman to another. In that case, said Binet, he could hardly do better than Madame d'Etioles, who was so madly in love that she could neither eat nor sleep. It seems that Binet had taken the affair in hand. The Bishop of Mirepoix, also attached to the Dauphin's household, and leader of the extreme Catholic party at the Court, now threatened him with dismissal. Binet ran to the King, who was infuriated by this tactless step. There was no question, he said, of any dismissal at all.

Madame d'Etioles was soon to be observed flitting in and out of the palace. Nobody knew whether she slept there and if so in which room, but the King often supped alone at this time and her carriage was constantly on the road to Paris. When Binet was questioned, as he was night and day by curious courtiers, he said that she was soliciting a place as *fermier général* for her husband. The husband, however, was quite unaware of these goings-on. M. de Tournehem, whom Reinette could twist round her little finger, had sent him on a business journey to Provence. By the time the poor man, quite unsuspecting, came back to Paris, the affair with the King was sufficiently advanced for Tournehem to break the news to him that he had lost his wife for ever. D'Etioles fainted away, was stricken with terrible grief and wrote a pathetic letter, imploring her to come back to him. Madame d'Etioles, who had an extremely frank and open nature and never could keep anything to herself—out it all came, with her, it was part of her charm—immediately showed this letter to the King, at first sight not a very clever move. Ever since the Marquis de Montespan had driven up to Versailles in a coach draped in black, with a pair of stag's antlers wobbling about on its roof, the Kings had had a healthy respect for husbands and their possible reprisals. Louis XV would never have got over such an incident. He thought it very indelicate of Madame d'Etioles to show the letter, bad form, exactly what one would expect of somebody with her upbringing, and handed it to her saying, coldly, 'Your husband seems to be a very decent sort of man, Madame.'

However, the letter, indicating that d'Etioles was back in Paris and knew all, gave the King food for thought. The moment had clearly come when he must decide whether he was going to install the lady as his titular mistress, or allow her to go back to a husband who was still ready to receive her, but would not be so indefinitely. The King was in love; he had seen enough of her by now to feel certain that she would never bore him, and she could soon be taught not to embarrass him. 'It will amuse me,' he said, 'to undertake her education.' Besides, she worshipped the ground he trod on, a fact to which no man can ever be quite indifferent. The upshot was that Madame d'Etioles remained at Versailles, lodging in a little flat which had once belonged to Madame de Mailly, and which was connected with the King's room by a secret staircase. The first time she was publicly seen at Court was on the 3rd April, when she appeared at the Italian comedy in the palace theatre.

The King and Queen were there in two boxes, one above the other; Madame d'Etioles was in a box on the opposite side of the stage, clearly visible to both. Naturally all eyes were upon her, and the Duc de Luynes, in attendance on the Queen, was obliged to admit that she was wonderfully pretty and well-dressed. After the play the King supped with his two great friends, the Duc d'Ayen and the Comte de Coigny, Madame d'Etioles making a fourth. She began to appear at small supper parties given by the King to his intimates; surprisingly little adverse comment seems to have been made on her at this time—all agreed that they were passionately in love with each other.

An adulatory letter arrived from Voltaire who obviously hoped great things of his friend in her new position. Her parents were in the seventh heaven and so was Uncle Tournehem; only the husband was distracted with grief, but nobody seems to have given him another thought. Louis XV was quite right when he said that Le Normant d'Etioles was a very decent fellow; he sought no advantage from his wife's position and answered any communications she chose to make him with perfect dignity. The rest of his family remained on excellent terms with her; his sister, Madame de Baschi, was always one of her greatest friends. She took her husband's cousin, Madame d'Estrades, with her to Versailles as a sort of unofficial lady-in-waiting; nothing was ever too much for her to do for any member of the Le Normant family. When Le Normant d'Etioles' father died, she went into mourning for him as a daughter-in-law, and cancelled a party to which she had invited the whole Court. D'Etioles and Abel Poisson remained lifelong friends and were constantly to be seen about Paris together. But he never spoke to his wife again.

## Chapter Four

## FONTENOY

THE War of the Austrian Succession was now in its fifth year. The Emperor had died in 1740 leaving an only daughter, Maria Theresa; during his lifetime the Princes of the Empire and the sovereigns of Europe had agreed to respect her rights, but as soon as he was dead the temptation to fish in troubled waters became too strong for them. The electors of Bavaria and Saxony, the Kings of Spain and Sardinia put forward claims to the Imperial Crown, in the name either of their wives or of female Hapsburg ancestors. The King of Prussia did not bother to put forward a claim at all; he acted. In December 1740 he invaded Silesia. A general war broke out in which France ought never to have joined; it was neither praiseworthy nor politic of her to have done so; many sacrifices and few advantages accrued, and the expense led to a fatal neglect of her navy. Louis XV who, much as he personally enjoyed battles, was an extremely pacific man, had always been against it, and so had Cardinal Fleury; but when it broke out the Cardinal was dying and the King was overruled by the military clique. Hatred of the Empire was the strongest common denominator of French political thought in those days, as the King was to find out later, to his cost.

Cardinal Fleury died in 1743, aged ninety. He had been to Louis XV what Cardinal Richelieu was to Louis XIII. An exceedingly clever man and able ruler, in whom the King had perfect confidence, he had directed the policy of France without fear of being dislodged by the intrigues either of Court or of Church.

This situation was never repeated in the life of Louis XV; he never found another Fleury.

In 1745 the French army, led by Maurice de Saxe, was enjoying a period of victories. The King had recently created him Marshal of France, and had promised his new Marshal that he and the Dauphin would go campaigning with him in the Spring; the time had nearly come for them to be off. The Dauphin must be dragged from the arms of his bride, and he himself from those of his lovely mistress. He had no intention of taking her with him to risk the scenes of Metz all over again. Besides, he had a plan for her. She was to retire to Etioles in the company of two courtiers, chosen by himself, who would teach her the customs, manners and usage of Versailles. Some such education was quite necessary, if she was not to make a series of appalling solecisms, and to become the laughing stock of a society on the look out for any excuse to mock and be disagreeable.

The Court was always referred to, by those who belonged to it, as *ce pays-ci*, this country, and indeed it had a climate, a language, a moral code and customs all its own. It was not unlike a public school and just as, at Eton, a boy cannot feel comfortable, and is, indeed, liable to sanctions, until he knows the names of the cricket eleven; various house colours; who may, or may not, carry an umbrella; or on which side of a street he may or may not walk, so, at Versailles, there were hundreds of facts and apparently meaningless rules which it would be most unwise to ignore. People sometimes broke them on purpose, hoping thereby to gain a little more privilege for their families; a Princess of the Blood would arrive in the Chapel followed by a lady-in-waiting with her purse on a cushion, or a Duchess be carried to the royal rooms in an armchair—thin end of the wedge for a sedan chair—but somebody always reported it, and a sharp message from the Monarch would bring the culprit to heel. To break the rules out of sheer ignorance would be thought barbarous.

Madame d'Etioles would have to learn the relationships of all the various families, who was born what, married to whom and ennobled when. The two different sorts of nobility, the *noblesse de robe* and the old feudal aristocracy, must be clearly distinguished and their connexions known. This was becoming complicated because the old nobility, unable to resist the enormous fortunes of the new, had swallowed its pride and married wholesale into plebeian families. Very important it was to know who had done so. There were not a few in the same case as M. de Maurepas, who, with a mother born la Rochefoucauld and a *bourgeois* father, was, like the mule, more ready to remember his mother the mare than his father the ass. So others had to remember for him. There was a special salute for every woman at the Court, according to her own and her husband's birth; the excellence of her housekeeping, the quality of her suppers, also entered into the matter. Variations of esteem were expressed in the curtsey. A movement of the shoulder practically amounting to an insult was a suitable greeting for the woman of moderate birth, badly married and with a bad cook, while the well-born Duchess with a good cook received a deeply respectful obeisance. Few women, even when brought up to it, managed this low curtsey with any degree of grace. The most ordinary movements, the very look and expression, were studied as though on a stage; there was a particular way of sitting down and getting up, of holding knife, fork and glass, and above all of walking. Everybody could tell a Court lady from a Parisienne by her walk, a sort of gliding run, with very fast, tiny steps so that she looked like a mechanical doll, wheels instead of feet under her panniers.

The look and general demeanour must be happy. Cheerfulness was not only a virtue, but a politeness, to be cultivated if it did not come naturally. If people felt sad or ill or anxious they kept it to themselves and showed a smiling face in public; nor did they dwell on the grief of others after the first expression of sympathy.

It was estimated that each human being has about two hundred friends; out of this number at least two must be in some sort of trouble every day, but it would be wrong to keep worrying about them because the others also had to be considered.

As in all closed societies certain words and phrases were thought impossible. *Cadeau*, which should be *présent*; *je vous salue*; *aller au français* instead of *à la comédie française*; *champagne* instead of *vin de champagne*; *louis d'or* for *louis en or*. *Sac* was pronounced *sa*, *tabac*, *taba* (as it still is), *chez moi*, *cheu moi*, *avant hier*, *avant-z-hier*, and so on. It was all quite meaningless, and so was much of the Court etiquette which had come down through various dynasties and whose origins were long since forgotten. An usher opening a door stood inside it when certain people passed through, and outside for others. When the Court was campaigning the *Maréchal des Logis* allotted rooms. On certain doors he would write: *pour le Duc de X* whereas others would merely get: *le Duc de X*; people would do anything to have the *pour*. The occupant of a sedan chair must stop and get out when meeting a member of the royal family. The occupant of a carriage, however, must stop the horses and not get out; people who got out of their carriages showed ignorance of Court customs. The Dukes were allowed to take a *carré*—the word *coussin* was tabu—to sit or kneel on in the chapel, but they must put it down crooked; only Princes of the Blood might have it straight. The Dukes would edge it round more and more nearly straight until a royal reprimand got it back to the proper angle. There was a running feud between the French Dukes and the princely families of the Empire, who, their estates having at one time or another, by conquest or marriage, passed to France, were now French subjects. (Prince, unless of royal blood, is no more a French title than it is an English one.) The most pretentious of these princely families were the Rohans and the La Tour d'Auvergnes, but they were all considered by the native French as rather too big for their boots; while they themselves were never happy until they received French dukedoms.

Another feud was that between the Ambassadors and Princes of the Blood. The former, regarding themselves as representatives of the person of their sovereigns, claimed equal rights with the Princes who, of course, resisted the claim and would not give way one inch. The Comte de Charolais, brother of M. le Duc, and a man of violent rages, seized a whip and himself chased the Spanish ambassador's coachman out of the *cul de sac*, a parking place near the Louvre, to which the Princes considered that they had the sole rights. Then there was the burning question of the *cadenas*. At State banquets the Princes were each given a silver gilt casket, with lock and key, containing their knives, forks and goblets; the Ambassadors were not, and considered this omission extremely insulting to their sovereigns. They appealed to the Master of the Household, the Prince de Condé, who was only eight. A Prince of the Blood himself, he was entirely against giving *cadenas* to the Ambassadors. Further to complicate everything, etiquette was different in the different palaces. Somebody who was only supposed to sit on a folding stool at Versailles might easily get a proper stool at Marly, and a chair with a back to it at Compiègne.

The four months of the King's absence would not be too long for Madame d'Etioles to learn the hundreds of details of which these are a very few examples. Her teachers, and she could not have had better, were the Abbé de Bernis and the Marquis de Gontaut. Bernis was one of those men whom every pretty woman ought to have in her life; a perfect dear, smiling, dimpling, clever, cultivated, with nothing whatever to do all day but sit about and be nice. Presently he was just enough in love with his beautiful pupil to add a flavour to their relationship. At the age of twenty-nine he was already a member of the Académie française, to which, however, he had been elected more for his agreeable company than for his literary talent; his verses were excessively flowery. Voltaire always called him Babet la Bouquetière. Like everybody who knew the little Abbé he could not but be fond of him but he was furiously jealous over the Académie; he longed to be of it as much as he affected to despise it.

Bernis was a real Abbé de Cour, that is to say a courtier first and a priest second; cadet of a good old country family, he was so poor that his greatest ambition was to be given a small attic in the Tuileries palace. As he was a friend of Pâris-Duverney, he had already met the Poisson mother and daughter, but had decided not to frequent them. He rather liked Madame Poisson; he said that as well as being perfectly lovely she had wit, ambition and a great deal of courage; but he could see at once that she was not and never would be in society, and accordingly she did not interest him. But Madame d'Etioles in her new situation was nothing if not interesting and when somebody approached him, on the King's behalf, and asked whether he would consent to see a good deal of her during the next few weeks, he really could not resist. He did go through the motions of hesitating and asking advice; his friends strongly urged him to accept, he had so much more to gain than to lose, they said, thinking perhaps of the longed-for attic in the Tuileries. When he spoke of his cloth, they pointed out that the affair between Madame d'Etioles and the King had been none of his making, and nobody, not even the Almighty himself, could pretend that it was in any way his fault. It was now an accomplished fact, and the plain duty of one and all was to make the best of it.

The Marquis de Gontaut was quite a different sort of person. He belonged to the Biron family, the very highest aristocracy, and was a member of the King's intimate circle. Nobody ever had a word to say against this charming man; he was a faithful friend to Madame d'Etioles until the day of her death.

Reinette spent a very happy last summer at Etioles. She was

savouring the joys of anticipation without the possible disappoint-
ments and weariness of fulfilment. The rest was good for her
after all her recent emotions; she only ever felt really well in the
country, where she could keep reasonable hours and live on a
milk diet. To one so devoted to her family the company was
perfect; she had her parents with her as well as Abel and M. de
Tournehem. Madame Poisson was ill, getting worse every day;
but extremely courageous and sustained by the joy she felt at her
daughter's new position. The baby, Alexandrine, was out at
nurse in a nearby village where her mother often went to see her.
Another relation staying in the house was a widowed cousin of Le
Normant d'Etioles, the Comtesse d'Estrades; this young woman
belonged to a rather better society than the Poissons and was
inclined to show off about it. She was already great friends with
Babet la Bouquetière. Madame d'Etioles looked up to her,
admired her and thought her in every way perfect; they were
each other's confidants and bosom darlings.

Voltaire wrote and suggested himself. 'I have your happiness at
heart, more perhaps than you imagine, more than anybody else in
Paris. I'm not speaking now as an ancient old lady-killer, but
as a good citizen when I ask you if I may come to Etioles and say
a word in your ear, this month of May.' He stayed, off and on,
most of the summer, in one of those good-tempered moods the
charm of which comes to us down the ages, making it impossible
not to love him. He wrote to Président Hénault, from Etioles:
'At her age she has read more than any old lady of that country
where she is going to reign and where it is so desirable that she
should reign.' The *philosophes* were naturally enchanted that their
young friend and admirer should queen it at Versailles; they
counted perhaps on a little more protection than they got from
her. When she first arrived there she was not powerful enough
to stand up to the Jesuits and later on she rather changed her views
about the *philosophes* and their revolutionary ideas. All the same,

without her, they would have fared much worse than they did.

This charming house party was not without various excitements as the long summer days went by. Collin, a young lawyer, said to have a dazzling career in front of him, came from Paris with a deed of separation between Le Normant d'Etioles and his wife. It had been effected, by decree of the Parlement, at six o'clock one morning; there was no publicity. D'Etioles was away, as usual, on some interminable journey to do with M. de Tournehem's business. A few months later Reinette asked Collin if he would give up his practice and devote himself to looking after her affairs; she told him to think it over well, as, should the King get tired of her, he would find himself out of a job. He took the risk, and never regretted having done so.

Every day a courier arrived from the Grande Armée with one or two letters from the King: *à Madame d'Etioles à Etioles*, sealed with the motto *discret et fidèle*. One night a powder magazine blew up at the nearby town of Corbeil; there was a tremendous bang and the drawing-room door was blown in. Was it an omen? The very next letter, *discret et fidèle*, was addressed *à Madame la Marquise de Pompadour, à Etioles*. It enclosed title deeds to an estate of this name and an extinct Marquisate revived in favour of Reinette. Her new coat of arms, also enclosed in the same thrilling packet, was three castles on an azure ground. Voltaire and Bernis wrote poems for the occasion in which Etioles and Etoiles were synonymous and Pompadour rhymed with Amour; everything was as merry as a marriage bell.

The King too was enjoying himself. He slept on straw, sang ditties with his soldiers in his curious loud cracked voice, all out of tune, and wrote his letters to Etioles on a drum. The campaign went very well; Ghent was taken and Fontenoy was a resounding victory. This battle is supposed to be the classic illustration of French and English military virtues; English doggedness and

endurance, against French flexibility and powers of recuperation.
It was a very close-run thing. The King and the Dauphin, covered
with gold lace, their great diamond St. Esprits glittering on their
breasts, took up a position, at daybreak, on a little mound overlooking the village of Fontenoy. They were guarded by *la
Maison du Roi*, the Household cavalry. Fontenoy was held by the
French, as was a nearby coppice, the Bois de Berri, and another
village, Anthoin. The King was in high good humour; he
remarked that never since Poitiers had a French monarch gone
into battle with his Dauphin and that not since the days of St.
Louis had one carried off in person a victory against the English.
When a cannon ball rolled towards his horse he cried, 'Pick it up,
M. le Dauphin, and throw it back to them.'

At 6 a.m. the big guns on both sides opened fire; the English,
led by the Duke of Cumberland, attacked Fontenoy three times
and were driven off with heavy losses. Their allies the Dutch,
meanwhile, launched an attack on Anthoin, were driven off and
never seen again that day. Cumberland decided to force a passage
between the Bois de Berri and Fontenoy. A solid formation of
about fourteen thousand English and Hanoverian troops advanced, at the slow regular pace of the parade ground; they were
shot at from both sides and suffered many casualties but came
steadily on until they found themselves face to face with the
French guards regiments. The Englishmen halted, their officers
took off their hats, the French officers acknowledged the saluta-
tion.

Then cunning, or chivalrous—according to whether a French
or English historian tells the tale—Lord Charles Hay cried,
'Gentlemen of the French guards, fire!' To which the chivalrous,
or cunning, Comte d'Auteroches replied, 'No, no, my lord, we
never fire first.' Everybody knew that whichever side opened fire
would be left at a disadvantage, virtually unarmed, for several
minutes, while the soldiers were recharging their muskets. After a

pause the English opened the steady, deadly and murderous fire for which, since the days of bows and arrows, they have been renowned; the results for their enemy were fearful. Every single French guards officer was killed or wounded, and the ranks were decimated; with no officer to rally them they wavered and broke. The redcoats resumed their advance. Maréchal de Saxe's whole plan of battle was thrown out by this defection of his infantry; the French guards, like the English, were supposed to stand and die, and it was many years before they lived down the disgrace of this day. The Duc de Biron, with the *Régiment du Roi*, slowed up the advance for a while—suffering fearful casualties, 460 of his men falling at a single volley—but it seemed that nothing could stop it. Useless to throw cavalry against that dogged mass; and on it came. Saxe now sent a message to the King that his position was becoming dangerous and that it would be better for him to retire. The King said he was perfectly certain that the Comte de Saxe (as he always called him) had the matter well in hand, and he would stay where he was.

Maurice de Saxe, too ill with dropsy either to stand or ride, had a little wicker carriage drawn by four horses; in this he galloped up and down the lines. The Maréchal de Noailles, though senior to him and very jealous of him, forgot these considerations and was acting as his A.D.C. More and more units engaged the Englishmen, but in vain; certain, now, of victory they came on shouting and cheering. The English general of German blood roared that he would get to Paris or eat his boots; the French general of German blood was told this and said, 'He must let us cook them first.' But he thought the day was lost, and sent another message to the King, imploring him to go. The battle was now so near the royal party that King and Dauphin were separated by riderless horses and had lost sight of each other in the general confusion.

Then up to the King galloped Richelieu, adorer of battles,

who 'despised death as a gambler despises ruin'; he had been all over the front and was so covered with dust as to be unrecognizable. 'What news?' The reply was most unexpected: 'The battle is won. We must use our cannon and then the King's Household will charge.' There were only four guns left, they opened fire on the English column with some effect, after which Richelieu, Biron and d'Estrées took the King's bodyguard into action, leaving the King and the Dauphin with nobody to defend them. It was a bold stroke and it succeeded perfectly. The English, on the face of it still as unshakable as ever, had really had about enough; under the impact of Richelieu's charge they positively melted away. 'It was like fighting against magic regiments which could be visible or invisible at will.' Cumberland and his officers were the last to leave the field.

No doubt the presence of the King had greatly contributed to this victory; his soldiers could hardly allow their monarch and his only heir to be taken prisoner before their very eyes, and the fresh troops of his bodyguard had formed an invaluable reserve. When he had warmly thanked Saxe, the other general officers, Biron and the *Régiment du Roi* which had played such a glorious part earlier in the engagement, with a special word to Richelieu, he took the Dauphin round the battlefield. The slaughter had been terrible, and the King, always a pacifist at heart, wanted his son to realize at what a cost such victories are won. The wounded, French and English alike, were carted into Lille where hospital arrangements were better than they had ever been after a battle; the rich merchants' wives gave up all frivolity, turned themselves into nurses and looked after the soldiers very well indeed.

There was no singing with his men that night; the King retired to bed early and slept very little. He was heard to sigh, often and deeply.

The battle of Fontenoy marked the apogee of Louis XV's

popularity, never again was the mystical link between him and his people, of all classes, to be so strong. Voltaire pounced upon the occasion to write a laudatory poem, *La Bataille de Fontenoy*, dedicated to *Notre Adorable Monarque*, for which he dug out a good many epithets and mythological allusions formerly applied by Boileau to Louis XIV. Richelieu, a great friend of Voltaire's, got even more praise in it than he deserved; and the cunning old poet mentioned a lot of other people who might be useful to him. Soon he was besieged by women begging a line or two for sons and lovers. This poem sold ten thousand copies in ten days, mostly to the army; subsequent editions brought in so many sons and lovers that the thing became a farce.

The population of Paris arranged fêtes and ceremonies, lasting three days, to welcome the King on his return from the front, and received him with delirium. The Queen, the Princesses and all the Court came up from Versailles and stayed at the Tuileries with him. He had not one moment to himself, but sent various friends to call on Madame de Pompadour at her uncle's house. During the great banquet at the Hôtel de Ville she and her family dined upstairs in a private room; the proud Dukes of Richelieu, Bouillon and Gesvres left the King's table in turns with messages for the newly-made Marquise.

On the 10th September the Court returned to Versailles; and that same evening one of the royal carriages drove up to a side door. Madame de Pompadour got out of it, accompanied by her cousin Madame d'Estrades, and went quickly upstairs to an apartment which had been prepared for her. Next day the King supped there with her alone; her reign of nearly twenty years had begun.

## Chapter Five

# PRESENTATION AT COURT

'AND which of our trollops is going to present this adventuress to the Queen?' An Abbé de Cour threw the question at the tittering, twittering company in general. 'Shut up, Abbé, for it's me.' It was indeed the disreputable old Princesse de Conti, who would at any time perform any service for her cousin the King so long as he would go on paying her gambling debts. She had covered herself by going to see the Queen and explaining that it was hardly her fault if she was obliged to be a party to something utterly repugnant, so much against both her wishes and her principles. Alas, she had received the royal command; no more to be said. Fontenoy, as a topic, had now entirely lost interest and nothing was spoken of but the presentation; everybody was busily making plans for the great event. The Duchesse de Luynes, who had been going to Dampierre for a little holiday, thought that the least she could do would be to stay and support the Queen, while the Queen's father, Stanislas, who was on his way to visit her, thought it would be more seemly for him to wait in Paris until all was over. In the end he compromised and went to Trianon. Everybody else flocked to Versailles to see the fun; there had seldom been such an enormous crowd in the state apartments.

At 6 p.m. the Princesse de Conti left her room accompanied by her own lady-in-waiting, as well as by the new Marquise, the Comtesse de Lachau-Montaubon and the Comtesse d'Estrades, whose presentation had taken place the day before. They all wore thickly embroidered satin skirts over enormous panniers; short muslin sleeves; small white feathers, held in place on their lightly powdered hair with diamonds; and narrow trains. Their little sliding footsteps took them through lanes of sight-seers in the state rooms, through the *Œil de Bœuf* packed with courtiers, to the King's council chamber. His Majesty stood by the chimney piece, deeply embarrassed, scarlet in the face, and looking very sulky indeed. When the Marquise de Pompadour was named he muttered something which nobody heard and dismissed her with a freezing nod. She, too, was seen to be very nervous; but her three curtseys were impeccable, and masterly was the kick with which she got her train out of the way so that she could walk backwards, the most difficult part of the whole proceeding.

The intimidating journey now continued, back across the *Œil de Bœuf*, to the Queen's room. This was even more packed with people than the King's, as everybody was curious to know what the Queen would say to her new rival; no doubt she would compliment her on her dress in one sentence, or at the most two, before dismissing her. It was the usual way, at Versailles, of saying nothing at all. But the Queen was quite well aware that the interview had been settled for her, and preferred to take a line of her own. She spoke to Madame de Pompadour of Madame de Saissac, asking if she had seen her lately, and said that she herself had been so delighted to have a visit from her the other day in Paris. Now the Marquise de Saissac was one of the few aristocrats whom the Poisson family had always known; by speaking thus, in such a natural and friendly way, of a mutual acquaintance the Queen gave the onlookers to understand that, in her view, Madame de Pompadour was perfectly admissible at Court. She must have known that this would annoy the courtiers and was perhaps not averse to doing so; she had many a little score to pay back herself.

As for the Marquise, she was quite thrown off her balance by the unexpected kindliness of this opening; she seems to have become almost hysterical, and burst out, not at all as a noblewoman would have done, with assurances of love and respect for the Queen, and her determination to do all that she could to please her. The Queen seems to have been gratified rather than annoyed by this vehemence and the two women then exchanged no fewer than twelve sentences (eagerly counted up, and reported that very night to Paris). The bystanders were, of course, longing for Madame de Pompadour to make some fearful slip but the only small incident that occurred was when she removed her glove to take the Queen's skirt and kiss it; she tugged too nervously and pulled off a bracelet which fell on to the floor. The Princesse de Conti picked it up for her. She was then conducted downstairs to the Dauphin's apartment where she was coldly received; he spoke of her dress in one sentence only, dismissed her, and—some say—put his tongue out at her as she went.

Her ordeal was over. She had come out of it pretty well, her grace, her beauty and her extreme elegance could not be denied, even by those who could hardly bear to think of a *bourgeoise* in the sacred purlieus. As for the Queen, she was much relieved that this new mistress was at least respectful, perhaps really rather nice; she had suffered from the Maillys who had subjected her to every sort of petty humiliation and had done all they could, only too successfully, to estrange her from the King. Any change from such hateful, if well-born women, was for the better as far as she was concerned.

Louis XV, after so many months away from his beloved, now very naturally wanted to be able to enjoy her company in peace and quiet for a while. He carried her off to Choisy with a small house party, Mesdames de Lauraguais, St. Germain, Bellefonds, Messieurs de Richelieu, Duras and d'Ayen; people in whose company she was going to live from now on. The Marquise was allowed to invite a few of her own friends, Voltaire, Duclos and

the Abbé Prévost; an experiment which seems not to have been
a success, as we never hear of them coming in this way again.
The writers dined by themselves, in a special room, not at all the
same as dining in the dining-room. The King, so fond of artists,
gardeners and architects, to whom he would allow every sort of
familiarity, never felt at his ease with writers, and Madame de
Pompadour, who would have liked to live in their company,
suffered from this. She once pointed out to him that Frederick the
Great always asked the intellectuals to his own table; the King
replied, with some truth, that it was all very well for the King of
Prussia, a country devoid of intellectuals, but that if the King of
France introduced this custom, he would have to begin by getting
an enormous table. He then counted up on his fingers: Mauper-
tuis, Fontenelle, La Mothe, Voltaire, Piron, Destouches, Montesquieu, the Cardinal de Polignac. 'Your Majesty has forgotten
d'Alembert and Clairaut.' 'Yes,' he said, 'and Crébillon and
Lachaussée.' 'Then there's Crébillon's son and the Abbé Prévost
and the Abbé d'Olivet.' 'There you are!' said the King, 'for twenty-
five years I should have had all this dining and supping with me.'

At Choisy Madame de Pompadour commissioned Voltaire to
write an opera, in celebration of Fontenoy: *Le Temple de la Gloire*,
in which Louis XV is represented as Trajan. *Chez lui les autels de
Vénus sont dans le Temple de la Gloire*. When this opera was finally
given at Versailles, Voltaire, always at his insufferable worst with
the King, went too far as usual. Bold as brass, he advanced to
where the King was chatting with Richelieu, and said, loudly, 'Is
Trajan pleased?' He then took the King by the sleeve to tell him
something. He had already been invited to supper after the performance, but it was noticed that the King never once spoke to
him. Such manners simply did not do at Versailles, and Madame
de Pompadour must have suffered to see her friend behaving so
stupidly. For let it not be thought that Voltaire was indifferent to
royal personages. He was one of the great snobs of history and it

was only when he saw that there was no place for him at the Court
of his own King—entirely, it must be said, owing to his incon-
ceivable tactlessness—that he went off, first to that of King
Stanislas at Lunéville, and then to that of King Frederick at
Potsdam. Meanwhile he had been given, and kept through all his
vicissitudes, a post and pension at Versailles, as well as that most
coveted of favours, a room in the palace. (This he did not keep;
there was a chronic housing shortage there and empty rooms were
snatched up at once). As soon as he was in it he began to demand
every kind of improvement and repairs to the room itself, adding
that in his view the public privies at the bottom of his staircase
ought to have a door to them. The King having personally inter-
vened with the Jesuit members, Voltaire was at long last elected to
the Académie française.

All this he owed entirely to Madame de Pompadour, whose
attitude towards him, then and thereafter, was beyond praise. She
had the rare capacity of understanding a creative artist; she saw
that underneath the grimaces, the pushfulness, the frantic giggles,
the pretensions and follies of a man like Voltaire lay an inferno of
uncertainty and sensibility. She was aware too, and this was perhaps more remarkable, not only of his genius but of his essential
goodness, and for that she forgave him everything, even the cruel
verses he wrote about her in *La Pucelle*. In his heart of hearts he
was grateful to her, and loved her. When the final accounts were
made up he had done her more good than harm: *Sincère et tendre
Pompadour* might well serve as her epitaph.

While Louis XV was away at the war, Choisy had been exten-
sively altered and re-decorated under the supervision of Gabriel;
possibly in order to eliminate too many souvenirs of the Maillys
who had each reigned there in turn. The King certainly appeared
to be haunted by no sad memories now; he proceeded to eat,
drink and make love with such excessive enthusiasm that he was
soon taken violently ill. The doctor put him to bed, purged him

and bled him and gave him emetics, probably in this case the most sensible treatment. He had a high temperature, so it was thought necessary to inform the Queen; a messenger was sent to Versailles and came back with a letter asking if she might visit her husband. He answered that he would be enchanted to see her and that, if she gave herself the trouble to come, she would find excellent food and plenty of religious services in the neighbourhood. He had not been so friendly for many years; she hurried over to Choisy at once, to find him still in bed, though mending fast.

She was taken round and shown all the improvements, a new, long terrace on the river, the re-decoration of the house, the pictures of battles by Parrocel, and bigger and better quarters for the servants; altogether she was given a very nice welcome. But—and there was a but—Madame de Pompadour, unlike the writers, dined in the dining-room. The Queen was obviously put out by this; she turned grumpy and only spoke in order to praise the food, having lived long enough in France to be unable to pass over good food in silence. After dinner she suddenly rounded on the Duc d'Ayen, saying he made far too many jokes about his fellow courtiers and that he must be more careful or soon he would not have a friend left in the world. Great was the relief when she ordered her carriage and went back to Versailles.

A few days later King Stanislas very tactlessly arrived to in-quire after his son-in-law, who was not fond of him, although in many ways they were so much alike.[1] The King was up, not dressed, playing cards in his bedroom with a few friends; Madame de Pompadour, in her riding habit, was there. Poor old King Stanislas was clearly given to understand that he was not wanted. He took himself off again with hurt feelings.

As soon as the voyage to Choisy was over, it was time for the

[1] Stanislas was now Duke of Lorraine, a compensation provided for him by the Polish treaty. He led a happy, carefree, *opéra bouffe* existence in his palace at Lunéville.

annual voyage to Fontainebleau. This word, voyage, simply meant that the King went from one of his houses to another. He was for ever on the move, though long journeys through beautiful France were almost unknown; he gyrated in the same little circle, Choisy, Marly, la Muette, Trianon, and later Bellevue, Crécy, St. Hubert and Petit Trianon. The parties which went with him to the small houses were limited to a few close friends; he went for a night or two, to one or another, almost every week. Marly and Trianon were more of a business and more people had the right to be asked. Marly itself only held 15, but the outside pavilions held 153 and were always full. Madame de Pompadour never liked Marly where the drawing-rooms were too small to hold such a crowd.

Twice a year, in July and October, the whole Court moved off, for six weeks at a time, to Compiègne, for army manœuvres, and Fontainebleau for hunting; and that was indeed an upheaval in *ce pays-ci*. The royal family, courtiers, Princes of the Blood and ministers got on to the road; followed by the state papers, archives and a great deal of furniture, silver and linen. The whole thing entailed enormous trouble and expense. The dates for these journeys were fixed by the King at Christmas and nothing but death could alter them.

At Fontainebleau, as at Versailles and Marly, Madame de Pompadour was given Madame de Châteauroux's old rooms, very large and beautiful ones on the ground floor, communicating with those of the King by a small staircase. She was, indeed, rather haunted by her predecessor; when, with the curiosity of a true Parisian, she asked the Court hairdresser how he had become so fashionable, he replied, laconically, 'I used to do the other one's hair.' The other had only been dead such a very little time; the Queen still thought of her and was terrified one night by seeing her ghost. 'As if poor Madame de Châteauroux would be looking for the Queen,' said the wags.

Madame de Pompadour settled down to her new existence. She had to make acquaintance with those who were to be friends and enemies, as well as with those who would form the backcloth of faces against which all the scenes of her life would be played from now on—hundreds of courtiers who hung about the King without ever getting to know him. Very sensibly she had brought M. Benoît, her excellent cook; less sensibly, perhaps, she had also brought Madame d'Estrades, from whom she was inseparable. No doubt she felt the need for one familiar face in the new strange land; also she was of an age when everybody must have a best friend, and Madame d'Estrades filled this role. It was to prove an unfortunate choice in the long run, but at the beginning it worked very well. The two of them supped every night with the King and a few men friends, or he with them in Madame de Pompadour's rooms; he took a fancy to Madame d'Estrades, who was gay and amusing and a wonderful gossip; she would have been quite pretty, says M. de Luynes, had it not been for her pendulous cheeks. For years the King sat between her and Madame de Pompadour at all the suppers; she was of all the voyages and she became a fixture of Court life.

Another fixture was the Duc de Richelieu, charming, handsome, brave, wicked and corrupt, a traitor in his soul, one of those to whom all is permitted and all forgiven. Madame, the Regent's mother, said of him: 'If I believed in sorcery I should think that the Duke must possess some supernatural secret, for I have never known a woman to oppose the very least resistance to him.' Nor did men oppose much resistance; not nearly enough. When he was a young colonel, in the garrison at Bayonne, he had offered to sell the town to the Spaniards; the Regent came into possession of four letters from him to the Spanish commander and said: 'If M. de Richelieu had four heads I have in my pocket enough to cut off each one of them.' For some unexplained reason he was merely sent to the Bastille where he was allowed his books, his servant, a viola and a backgammon board. After a few days, out he came, back to the Court and more army commands. He went to the Bastille on two other occasions; once at the request of his stepfather who could do nothing with him; and once for killing a cousin of his wife's in a duel on active service, but he always reappeared at Versailles as if nothing whatever had happened. He had a great hold over Louis XV, and over the Regent: he made them laugh. He never could endure Madame de Pompadour and was soon her declared enemy. He was perfectly odious to her, teased her in every possible way, never laughed at her jokes, praised her suppers or admired her clothes. One night at la Muette, when he knew she was sleeping badly, he banged about overhead, danced and jumped with hardly a pause. He told his friends that Mistress though she might be, of King and Court, he would torment little Pompadour and wear her down. At last he made her life such a misery that she begged the King to leave him out of their supper parties and voyages. But the King only laughed, 'You don't know Son Excellence, put him out of the door and he'll come back by the chimney.' The King had special names for many people and Son Excellence had stuck to Richelieu since he was once, for a short time, ambassador at Vienna.[1]

The King's two other cronies, the Duc d'Ayen and M. de Coigny, both loved the Marquise and became her true friends. They were much younger than Richelieu, about the King's age, and their fathers, Maréchaux de Noailles and de Coigny, were still alive. Both were married, but their wives lived in Paris and hardly ever appeared at Court. The King very rarely invited husbands and wives together; it did not make for sparkle. The Abbé de Bernis was of this voyage to Fontainebleau, though not

---

[1] It was the custom for the King to address people by their names and titles; he would not, like everybody else, say Monsieur, when speaking to a man, or Monsieur de X when speaking of him, but always Comte de X.

at the suppers, because there was a strict rule that priests never
ate with the Monarch. He brought Moncrif to see Madame de
Pompadour, who made his conquest, a triumph for her as he was
such a faithful member of the Queen's set.

Madame de Pompadour did not forget, or in any way modify
her behaviour to old friends and relations now that she was so
grand. She begged Madame de la Ferté d'Imbault to come and
settle at the Court, she said she knew that the King would like her.
But Madame de la Ferté d'Imbault declined for reasons of health.
Perhaps she did not care for the idea of being sponsored by her
hitherto so humble little friend. Certainly she flew into a rage
when somebody suggested that Jeanne Poisson would soon be
playing a part in the destinies of France—never heard such rubbish in her life, she said. Like most people at this time she regarded the liaison as a fancy of the King's which was unlikely to
last very long.

Madame de Pompadour had her father to stay at Fontainebleau and, in spite of the fact that he was a real fish out of water
there, she was perfectly natural with him; the idea that she might
be ashamed of him never crossed her mind. The King gave him a
property called Vandières, and though Poisson himself said that
nothing would induce him to change his name, at his age, Abel
was henceforward known as M. de Vandières (*avant hier*, said the
wags). In 1750 the King gave Poisson another estate, Marigny.
Again the old boy refused to change his name, but Abel became
M. de Marigny and in 1754 was made a Marquis. To save confusion I will call him Marigny from now on.

Madame de Pompadour's Uncle Tournehem received the important post of Intendant Général des Bâtiments du Roi, the equivalent of our Ministry of Works, with the understanding that it
would go to Marigny at his death. The young man already
thought of nothing but art and architecture and his sister encouraged this bent by every means in her power. He was her

constant companion and came to all her little suppers, where he was given a high place at her table—quite wrongly from every point of view, since in France relations of the host always go to the bottom of the table. A certain nobleman, furious at sitting below this proletarian hobbledehoy aged twenty, complained to the King. He got no satisfaction whatever, the King merely observing that when he condescended to sup with his subjects they were equal in his eyes.

Madame de Baschi, Le Normant d'Etioles' sister, did not live at the Court with Madame de Pompadour, but constantly paid her visits. On one occasion, when the King was inviting no women but the wives of ministers to Marly, Madame de Pompadour said that she counted as a minister of state and would bring Madame de Baschi as her wife. The King laughed very much and allowed her to come.

The courtiers, always on the look out for any sign that the King might be cooling off his new mistress, began to say that she would bore him to death with her family; she never seemed to talk of anything else. But he was not bored, quite the contrary, and he shrieked with laughter when she called her brother Frèrot in front of him. It was against Court etiquette to use any diminutive, or the second person singular, in the King's presence, even brothers being obliged to say *vous* to each other. He had certainly never heard such a word as Frèrot in all his life. He himself called Abel *petit frère* and soon became extremely fond of him. The fact is that the King liked family life, and could hardly have enough of it. This the courtiers, who saw him so regal and terrifyingly aloof, could never understand. As for the *bourgeois* idiom of his mistress, he thought it quite delightfully funny, and very soon he was heard calling his daughters by the most outrageous nicknames: Loque for Madame Adélaïde, Coche for Madame Victoire, Chiffe for Madame Louise. Madame de Pompadour had nicknames for everybody all her life; her friends, her pet animals, even her houses were continually called by new names when she spoke or wrote of them.

She was indeed a change from the women of the Court, who, with certain notable exceptions, were self-conscious, artificial, preoccupied with their rank and privileges, and very dull. The French aristocrats, since they were also courtiers, had nearly all adopted the muted tones and careful behaviour of that profession. Breezy, eccentric noblemen, so common in England, where they led an independent life on their own estates, were almost unknown in France. Certain members of the royal family were an exception. The Comte de Charolais was a rip-snorting oddity; he dressed like a gamekeeper and ordered his coachman to run over any monks he might see on the road, but he could afford such vagaries as he was a cousin of the King's.

Madame de Pompadour never became a courtier in her manners. There was no nonsense about her. She gave herself no airs; on the contrary she hardly bothered to change her *bourgeois* ways at all. Her loud forthright voice, using a language which would seem much more familiar to us than the almost Racinian idiom of the Court, never altered its tone or lessened its emphasis. Her laugh, an enchantment, says Croÿ, rang out freely, very different from the discreet and smothered giggles to be heard in the galleries and ante-chambers when the King was about. Her maiden name, thought so despicable by the courtiers, the subject of so many bad jokes, seemed quite all right to her; in fact both she and her brother were proud of it. On one occasion Marigny was seen paying respectful attentions to a certain lady; when asked who she was, he replied: 'She bears a name to eclipse all but the greatest; born Poisson, married to a Poisson, she will end a Poisson.' The courtiers were furious and told each other that 'Marinière' was really too embarrassing. Whenever a fine piece of celadon or porcelain in the shape of a fish came the King's way, he would buy it and have it mounted in ormolu for

Madame de Pompadour; she signed her own engravings with a huge baroque fish, and Marigny took fishes as his coat-of-arms. But all these piscine decorations must have seemed rather natural to the French, accustomed as they were to the Dauphin's dolphins splashing about the palaces.

As soon as the King was dressed in the morning he went down to Madame de Pompadour's rooms where he stayed until it was time for Mass; on non-hunting days he would have a bite of something, a cutlet or a wing of chicken at dinner (our luncheon time), and stay the whole afternoon, chatting, until at six he went off to work with his ministers. The Court was at Fontainebleau on purpose to hunt, and Madame de Pompadour, who rode, as she did everything else, very well, sometimes went out with Mesdames, the Princesses. The royal family was quite civil to her, except the Dauphin, and he sulked for many a long year.

Members of the Queen's little set, even the Duc and Duchesse de Luynes, were soon forced to admit that, given the painful though not surprising circumstances, Madame de Pompadour's behaviour was perfect. She was exceedingly polite, never said horrid things about people or allowed them to be said in her presence, at the same time she had high spirits and was excellent company, gay and amusing. Whenever she could do a good turn to anybody she did it and she put herself out to any extent to please the Queen. The Queen was fond of flowers, so was she. They were one of her passions in life, and very soon the hot-houses of all the Royal Gardens were re-organized under her supervision. As soon as flowers in profusion filled her rooms they filled the Queen's rooms too. The poor lady had never received so much as a bunch of daisies before. The Duc de Luynes says it was a pity Madame de Pompadour made it so obvious that they came from her, and that this rather took away from the Queen's pleasure. Unfortunately both women were but human. The Queen had no desire whatever to be a real wife to her husband, but she was jealous of Madame de Pompadour, who, on her side, though infinitely good natured, was not always very delicate; she was too open and straightforward to include tact among her virtues.

While she was at Fontainebleau she found out that the Queen was tormented by her gambling debts which were enormous; she was not very good, it seemed, at Cavagnole. If she did have a little win she spent it all on charity. Madame de Pompadour made the King pay up, a thing he had never yet done for his wife. He really could afford to. He had been winning such enormous sums at piquet, that the men who had lost to him had to be given until January to pay. The Marquise seemed to take a genuine interest in the Queen's affairs, listening with breathless attention when a lady-in-waiting expounded upon some detail of the royal health. When she was herself not well and unable to go to a tedious charity bazaar organized by Her Majesty, she sent her deepest apologies, with a *louis* for the cause, saying over and over again how dreadfully disappointed she had been. Nobody else ever bothered about the Queen's feelings in this way; she had no influence whatever with her husband and therefore the courtiers neglected her entirely.

When the time came to leave Fontainebleau the Queen was asked to choose a day that would suit her, and she was invited to break her journey at Choisy. The King always did this but the Queen had never done so before. As a result there was such a large party, with her followers as well as his, that card tables overflowed even into the bathroom. The King and Madame de Pompadour were most attentive to her and played Cavagnole at her table for a while. She talked a great deal to Madame de Pompadour, whose manner was perfect, neither too familiar nor too respectful. The Queen, in a very good temper, kept saying she would not go away until she was chased, and it was past midnight when she got back to Versailles. Here she found, to her delight, that her room had been done up during her absence, the panelling re-gilded and her bed, which had become very shabby, covered with a new tapestry of a religious design. As time went on, and the King felt less guilty about her, he became much nicer to her and altogether she had cause to bless Madame de Pompadour. 'If there has to be a mistress,' she would say over and over again, 'better this one than any other.'

But in spite of her charm, good nature and desire to please, Madame de Pompadour had and always would have enemies. To the aristocrats she was the incarnation of Parisian *bourgeoisie*. While the nobles, living in a delightful insouciance at Versailles, neglecting their estates, gambling all of every night for enormous sums, spending far more than they could afford on horses, carriages and clothes in order to impress each other, were getting steadily poorer and more obscure, the *bourgeoisie* was getting richer and more powerful. They hated it, and hated her for belonging to it. Those who knew her well seem to have loved her, except Richelieu, some of them quite against their will; but the ordinary courtiers would have done anything to bring about her downfall. However, if they wanted to wage war Madame de Pompadour had big guns on her side, not counting the biggest gun of all. The Pâris brothers and their colleagues were her firm supporters, and after five years of expensive warfare, with the country in a state of near-bankruptcy, financiers counted for very much. There was trouble at this time between the Pâris and Orry, who as Controller General was in charge of the nation's finances as well as of most of the internal administration: for some months there had been talk of replacing him and in December 1745 he was dismissed. Rightly or wrongly this dismissal was put down to the Marquise; it was the first hint, at Court, that her influence was extending beyond the domain of party-giving, and many felt it as a chill wind.

*Chapter Six*

# MOURNING

SOON after her arrival at Versailles, one of the two great sorrows of her life fell upon Madame de Pompadour; she was in the Chapel on Christmas Eve, 1745, when they came and told her that her mother was dying. She hurried out of church and left immediately for Paris. It was said that Madame Poisson, clever as four devils, occupied her last hours advising Madame de Pompadour how to behave in her new, her glorious and her undoubtedly difficult position. Of course her position must really have been made much easier by the removal of this masterful beauty, in her early forties, but Madame de Pompadour did not think so; she was thrown into fearful grief, and so were the two widowers, Poisson and Tournehem. They sobbed in each other's arms, and for the rest of their lives were inseparable. The King, who generally shunned the grief of other people in an agony of embarrassment, was extremely kind to Madame de Pompadour on this occasion; he supped night after night alone with her and Frèrot and presently took her off to Choisy, where he invited a small party, to try and cheer her up. Thinking that a projected voyage to Marly might be too much for her, he suggested putting it off; but this she wisely would not allow. The women had already bought their dresses, she said. Meanwhile the Queen had been made very happy; for the first time since many a day the King gave her a New Year's present, a beautiful gold snuff box with a jewelled watch set in the lid. Everybody at Court knew perfectly well that it had been ordered, originally, for Madame Poisson.

In the Spring of 1746 Louis XV once more went off to his army, but only for a few weeks. The Dauphine was expecting a baby and he intended to be back in time for this great event; the Dauphin remained with his wife whom he loved more than ever. While the King was away Madame de Pompadour stayed at Choisy. She seems to have been pregnant, or perhaps simply over-tired, not very well. She was to rest and live quietly, only going to Versailles to pay her court to the Queen twice a week. She was occupied just now with the first of her many houses, Crécy, near Dreux. By an arrangement with the brothers Pâris she appeared to have bought it herself, but it was really a present from the King. The house, which already existed, was altered and greatly enlarged by the architect Lassurance; Falconnet, Coustou and Pigalle worked on the decorations and the gardens were laid out by d'Isle, under the close supervision of the Marquise herself. M. de Tournehem and Marigny also helped her with it.

The Dauphine seemed very well, and in July her baby was born. The lady-in-waiting who carried it off to be dressed made a face which plainly told the crowd in the ante-room that it was only a girl. Nobody was very much put out by this; next year there would surely be a Duc de Bourgogne. But four days later the Dauphine suddenly died, to the utter despair of her husband; the King had to drag him forcibly from her bedside. Versailles was now plunged into all the ceremonial gloom with which a royal death was attended in those days: the black hangings over everything, even the furniture, and the courtyard outside; the professional weepers, the chanting of monks and nuns, the open-ing of the body (obligatory in the case of a royal person; the doc-tors said they found a great deal of milk in her brain) and the removal of its heart, handed on a salver to a lady-in-waiting; the lying in state, the struggling crowds and fainting courtiers, ceremonial visits to the baby, who had been given the title of Madame, the endless, torchlit journey by night to the royal mausoleum of St. Denis. Worst of all, what the French call *figures de circonstance*, suitable but fictitious expressions of grief on every face. On every face but the Dauphin's. The little girl, so shy that some people thought her half-witted, had made no impression whatever on those around her, and this must have aggravated his misery, poor fellow; he had nobody with whom he could talk about her. By way of consolation people pointed out her defects, both physical and mental, to him, and began talking of his second wife; the first was not even buried before rooms were being allocated to *Madame la future Dauphine*. He knew quite well that his father's friends were waiting impatiently for the period of mourning to be over so that they could start amusing themselves again.

According to custom, the royal family prepared to leave Versailles while the Dauphine still lay there in state. But where could they all go at such short notice? Choisy was full of workmen, Meudon had no furniture, the big palaces, Fontainebleau and Compiègne, could not be got ready in a hurry, Trianon was too near. Marly was out of the question, since it was to Marly that the Court had repaired after the death of the King's mother, and there that his father and elder brother had died, less than a week later. So Choisy it had to be. It was very uncomfortable and Madame de Pompadour was obliged to give up her room to one of the Queen's ladies.

The boredom which assailed them all during this visit was remembered long afterwards. No hunting, no gambling, and the King, as always when thoroughly out of humour, turned a bad colour—'That yellow colour which isn't good for him,' Madame de Pompadour used to call it—which meant that he was bored and liverish. The party was only kept going at all by the affair of the holy water. The Princely families of Rohan and La Tour d'Auvergne, whose *prétensions chimériques* had never for one moment been allowed by Louis XIV, claimed the right to throw holy water over the Dauphine before the Dukes. The King having gone away without leaving any very precise orders on the subject, a violent dispute broke out at Versailles. Messengers hurried to and from Choisy, and the King tried to regulate the affair as tactfully as possible by laying it down that no men were to throw holy water, only women. He had forgotten the various Duchesses who had the privilege of going into the death chamber in attendance on Princesses of the Blood. A horrible scene over the Dauphine's dead body, between these ladies and the Princesse de Turenne (La Tour d'Auvergne), was only avoided by the decency of Mesdames de Brissac and Beauvilliers who voluntarily gave up their rights. The King thanked them, afterwards. The pros and cons of this affair, hotly disputed, occupied many an idle hour at Choisy. The conclusion was that the Rohans and La Tour d'Auvergnes had won this time, by taking everybody unawares, but must never be allowed to do so again.

The King was getting yellower every day and began to talk of going back to the army. But Madame de Pompadour, who had foreseen this, and dreaded losing him again so soon, had been in touch with the Maréchal de Saxe. Saxe, very intimate with the Pâris brothers, was an old acquaintance of Madame de Pompadour. He was to become one of her greatest friends. As may be imagined, the presence of the King, while flattering in the extreme, was a continual worry and responsibility to the Marshal and he was only too glad to combine with her to keep him at home. He wrote saying that no engagement of importance was likely for the rest of that summer and that it would hardly be worth the King's while to move again.

So the King invited himself to stay at Crécy. This was exactly what the Marquise had been hoping for; enchanted to have him as her guest for the first time, she went ahead with the women of the party, the Princesse de Conti, Mesdames du Roure and d'Estrades, to make all the necessary arrangements. The next day the King followed with two large berlines full of dukes, including d'Aumont, d'Ayen, la Vallière, Villeroy and, of course, the inevitable Richelieu. Two Princes of the Blood, Conti and Chartres, arrived under their own steam; Lassurance and Marigny were there already, supervising the work in hand. The King, interested as he always was by any sort of building or planning, soon turned a better colour. There were two new wings to the house itself, not to speak of a mountain which was rising in the park—but which, considered rather too bare, was transformed into a grassy amphitheatre—the windmill, the dairies, and the distant views leading to cascades. Plans were also under consideration for stables to hold two hundred horses, a cottage hospital for the village, the removal of some cottages which spoilt the view, and improvements in the parish church. The King sat down there and then and designed a green and gold uniform for Crécy—each of the royal houses had its own, worn by all the male guests. Benoît excelled himself at every meal and the King said he had never seen a better kept house; in short the visit was a radiant success and augured well for the future. Madame de Pompadour saw that this was an excellent way of getting her lover to herself and planned to acquire other houses, nearer Versailles.

The only fly in the ointment, as usual, was Richelieu. Under a mask of grave politeness, Son Excellence continued his guerrilla warfare against the Marquise. Every woman knows how dangerous the great friend of the beloved can be, and every clever woman uses all her powers of seduction to get him on her side. Madame de Pompadour did her very best, she was always charming to him and even supported his ambitions, most unfortunately as it was to turn out. But nothing was of any avail. In his eyes she incarnated the abominable bourgeoisie, the wrong people, with their deplorable ton, who were gradually accumulating money and power at the expense of the right people.

Until Cardinal Richelieu had put it on the map, the du Plessis family was noble, but of the very minor nobility. The Duke could hardly bear the fact that he should owe his position to the merits of his great-uncle rather than to his own birth; it irked him all his life. He was not quite sure enough of himself, in fact; and whereas d'Ayen and Gontaut, serene in the knowledge of their unassailable ancestry, could make friends with anybody they liked, Son Excellence could not. Also he was jealous of the Marquise. Hitherto he had been entertainer in chief to the King and, in his capacity of First Gentleman of the Bedchamber, had had all the palace amusements under his control; now he smelt a rival. So he ragged and bullied her unmercifully and no doubt had disloyal jokes about her with the King as soon as her back was turned. At last, enormously to her relief, he went off to conquer Parma for Madame Infante. This eldest and beloved daughter of Louis XV longed for an establishment of her own so that she could leave Madrid. For some time now, the swaggering form and unsmiling face of Son Excellence were no longer to be seen on Madame de Pompadour's staircase.

## Chapter Seven

# THE STAIRCASE

'IT isn't you he loves,' the Maréchale de Mirepoix used to say. 'It's your staircase.' And very naturally indeed the King loved the staircase at the top of which he found this delicious creature, this lively clever companion, waiting to concentrate on him and his entertainment. The rooms to which the staircase leads are on the second floor of the north wing; the visitor to Versailles, coming into the garden through the usual entrance, should turn left and count the nine top windows from the north-west corner; they were Madame de Pompadour's at this time. We still see what she saw from her little balcony between the statues on the colonnade—the Parterre du Nord, the fountains of mermaids and cupids, the avenue of trees, cut into solid walls of leaves, which leads to the Bassin de Neptune, and, over the tree tops the forest of Marly stretching to far horizons. We still hear the great clock on the parish church, the organ in the palace chapel—so few yards away—the birds in the park, and the frogs in the fountains quacking like ducks. But we do not hear the King's hunt in the forest, the hounds and the horns and the King's curious high husky voice giving the view halloo. The rooms, so empty to-day, so cold with their northern light, were crammed to bursting point when she lived in them; crammed with people, animals and birds, pictures, bibelots, curiosities of all sorts, furniture, stuffs, patterns without number, plans, sketches, maps, books, her embroidery, her letters, her cosmetics: all buried in flowers, smelling like a hot house; it is a mystery how they can have held so much. The walls, which were originally lacquered by Martin in the bright delicate colours she loved, have been painted white, but the panelling is still the same and the structure of the flat unchanged. The little room where her maid, Madame du Hausset, lived is still there, with the funnel through which she listened to the King's conversation—greatly to our advantage, as she used to write it down word for word. We can still see the lift shaft which contained a flying chair; the Marquise was hauled up in this by her servants to save the long, steep drag upstairs. On a lower level, looking out on to a dismal little courtyard, is the flat of Madame de Pompadour's doctor and great friend, Quesnay.

Madame de Pompadour was hardly settled at Versailles before she began to direct and inspire the artists of her day. She had all the gifts of a great amateur, erudition, tireless energy in searching for perfection, and an intuitive understanding of the creative temperament, which enabled her to make an artist do better than his best, and to impose her own ideas on him, without hurting his feelings. Until the outbreak of the Seven Years War she also had unlimited credit, since the King, who had hitherto been regarded as rather close-fisted, never seemed to care how much she spent. Probably this was because she knew how to approach him. 'He doesn't mind signing for a million,' she told her maid, 'but he hates to part with little sums out of his purse.' She was often herself short of cash and used to say that she had been much richer when she lived in Paris. When she died a few *louis* were found in a drawer. She had long since sold her diamonds and Collin had to borrow money for current expenses. But she left enough works of art to fill several museums—the sale of them took eight months— and she had lived in the middle of an intense artistic activity which was meat and drink to her. Unlike her successors, Madame du Barry and Marie Antoinette—and vastly superior to them—she always looked after her artists and never owed them a penny. Altogether, and it was the great complaint against her, she was supposed to have cost the King 36 million *livres* (the Seven Years War cost 1350 millions), but her various houses were built on his land and all but Ménars reverted to him at her death.

These houses, and her objects of art, would have been a good investment for France had not nearly everything she created been destroyed or dispersed during the Revolution. Crécy, Bellevue, Brimborian, the Hermitage at Compiègne, utterly destroyed; the Hermitage and the Reservoirs at Versailles, the Elysée, her rooms at Versailles, Fontainebleau, Trianon and Compiègne, altered beyond recognition; her belongings scattered to the four winds, sometimes to be seen in a museum or a private collection—the little boudoir from Brimborian, the celadon fishes, a morocco binding with castles and griffins, a painted commode, an engraved jewel—'This was the Pompadour's fan.'

Soon the King began to share her love of beautiful objects and nothing could have been more felicitous for him. Up to now his private life had been devoid of serious interests. He did not care for literature nor had he that passion for music shared by all his children. Politics occupied much of his attention, but he never talked about them outside the council chamber because he knew that everything he said would be repeated, and this applied also to gossip. As the only pastime he really cared for was hunting, and as it was a perfectly safe topic, he ended by talking of little else—not enough for an intelligent man. Madame de Pompadour, following her own inclinations, had found him a hobby which he could discuss with perfect safety. Houses were bought, or built, altered, decorated and surrounded with beautiful gardens; at the big palaces the King's private rooms were always being re-decorated; furniture, pictures, statues, vases and bibelots were chosen and ordered; rare materials were brought from all over the world to be mounted in gold or bronze or silver; roof gardens and aviaries were filled with curious plants, birds and beasts. The King ran up her staircase knowing that, in her warm and scented rooms, he would find some fascinating new project on foot, plans and designs waiting for his approval, bibelots and stuffs for him to buy if he liked them.

Then there were the hours of chat, and here Madame de Pompadour had an enormous asset in his eyes; she was very funny. Hitherto the King's mistresses had told few jokes and the Queen even fewer, he had never known that particularly delightful relationship of sex mixed up with laughter; all the laughter in his life had been provided by his men friends, especially by Richelieu and Maurepas. He was a great tease and used to read sermons on chastity aloud to the Maillys, who never thought it at all amusing; with Madame de Pompadour he could laugh away to his heart's content. Chat was the pastime of the age, cheerful, gossipy, joking chat, running on hour after idle hour, all night sometimes; and at this the Marquise excelled. She knew a hundred stories to amuse him; she read the police reports from Paris, the equivalent of our yellow press, and told him all the tit-bits she found in them; she also read quantities of private letters abstracted from the post and no doubt their contents gave rise to many a joke (it must be said that everybody knew quite well that a censorship existed). If he felt inclined for a tune she played and sang better than anybody. She knew whole plays by heart and could recite speeches from them for hours on end. He had never cared much for the theatre but she began to interest him in it. She provided exactly the right company for his supper parties; a few congenial friends, no surprises, and no new faces, and added a gaiety and a lightness all her own.

Sadly enough, the only thing that was not perfect in this relationship was its sexual side. Louis XV was a Bourbon, and had their terrible temperament, while Madame de Pompadour was physically a cold woman. She was not strong enough for continual love-making and it exhausted her. She tried to work herself up to respond to the King's ardours by every means known to quackery, so terrified was she that he would one day find out her secret; but she began to make herself ill. Madame du Hausset, her maid, spoke of this to the Duchesse de Brancas—the tall Duchess as she was always called, to distinguish her from her step-daughter-in-law.

'It can't be good for her, she is living on a diet of vanilla, truffles and celery.' 'Yes, I've noticed that,' said the Duchess, 'and now I'm going to scold her, you'll see.' They went together and attacked Madame de Pompadour, who burst into tears. The maid locked the door, and Madame de Pompadour said to Madame de Brancas: 'The fact is, my dearest, that I'm terrified of not pleasing the King any more, and of losing him. You know, men attach a great deal of importance to certain things, and I, unfortunately for me, am very cold by nature. I thought I might warm myself up, if I went on a diet to heat the blood, and then I'm taking this elixir which does seem to be doing me some good.' Madame de Brancas looked at the drug and threw it straight in the fire saying: 'Fi!' Madame de Pompadour said petulantly that she was not to be treated like a baby, and then began to cry again.

'You don't know what happened last week, the King said it was too hot, an excuse to spend half the night on my sofa. He'll get tired of me, and find somebody else.' 'But your diet won't stop him,' said the Duchess, 'and it will kill you. No, you must make yourself indispensable to the King by always being nice to him. Don't rebuff him, of course, at these other moments, but just let time do its work and in the end he'll be tied to you for ever, by force of habit.' The two women kissed each other, Madame de Pompadour swore her friend to secrecy, and the diet was abandoned.

Shortly afterwards she told Madame du Hausset that things were going better. 'I consulted Dr. Quesnay, though without telling him everything. He advised me to look after my general health, and take more exercise, and I believe he's quite right, I feel

a different woman already. I adore that man [the King] and I long
to please him, but he thinks I'm fearfully cold, I know. I would
give my life for him to love me.'

However, in those pre-Freudian days the act of love was not
yet regarded with an almost mystical awe; it had but a limited
importance. Like eating, drinking, fighting, hunting and praying
it was part of a man's life, but not the very most important part of
all. If Madame de Pompadour were not physically in love with
the King, being constitutionally incapable of passion, it would not
be too much to say that she worshipped him; he was her God.
She had other interests and affections, but she made them all
revolve round him; rarely can a beautiful woman have loved so
single-mindedly. Of course her enemies have declared that what
she loved was power and the life at Court; but she never really
liked the Court and was under no illusions as to the nature of
many of its denizens. She constantly declared, and as she was a
very truthful person she can be believed, that had it not been for
the King and her happiness with him, which made up for everything, she never could have endured 'the wickedness, the plati-
tudes, all the miseries of human nature' with which she was
surrounded. A Parisian born and bred, she could not regard a
man with awed respect, simply because he was *Duc et Pair de
France*, and often turned longing eyes towards Paris and the
intellectual feasts there from which she was now excluded.

With the King she was perfectly happy. Often puzzled by his
strange nature which she never quite understood and which, she
told the Duc de Choiseul, on her death bed, was *indéchiffrable*
(undecipherable), but fascinated and happy. We have only to read
the diaries of the day, in which we see her with the King walking,
talking and alive, to recognize the unmistakable signs of true love.
'Put not your trust in Princes' has never been less to the point than
in her case, she put her trust in him and he did not fail her. This
love affair took its course. After a few years of physical passion on

his side it gradually turned into that ideal friendship which can only exist between a man and a woman when there has been a long physical intimacy. There was always love. As in every satisfactory union it was the man who kept the upper hand; Madame de Pompadour was far too strong a character herself, far too clever and downright, to have been happy for long with a man whom she could not respect. She could say exactly what she liked to him, in some ways he spoilt her, but she never ceased to be a little bit in awe of him. She was always terrified of losing him; she strained every nerve to keep up with him in all his activities, he so strong and she so delicate, and in the end it killed her. She had many miscarriages during the first years, which pulled her down and disappointed her, for she naturally longed to have a child with the King. Certainly she never rested enough after them—two days in bed, smelling delicious, is the most we hear of. The King would sup alone, or with one other friend, in her room on these occasions. Then the exhausting life began once more. Seldom in bed before two or three in the morning, she was obliged to be up at eight, dressed as for a ball, to go to Mass in the unheated chapel. For the rest of the day not one moment to herself. She must pay her court to the Queen, the Dauphin and Mesdames, receive a constant succession of visitors, write sometimes as many as sixty letters and arrange and preside over a supper party. At least once a week there would be a voyage of one or two nights, with a house party to entertain, often in a house full of workmen, where improvements, landscape gardening, etc. were in progress and needed supervision. It was too much for her.

'Of all the mistresses so far she is the most lovable, and he loves her more than any of the others.' The Prince de Croÿ, who saw a great deal of them in these early days of their attachment, was a serious, pious young widower. At first he was shocked by this adultery, but rather cynically paid his court to Madame de

Pompadour because he wanted to get on in the world. He wanted
a great deal, and it is easy to guess, reading between the lines of his
invaluable memoirs, that he must have been the Court bore. He
could not be in a room with anybody at all influential without
buttonholing him and trying to further some *affaire* of his own.
There were the *affaires* of the grandeeship of Spain; of the St.
Esprit (or Cordon Bleu, so called because of its blue riband, the
equivalent of our Garter); of the *passe droit*, the Prince de Beauvau
having been allotted higher precedence, which literally made
poor Croÿ ill with rage and humiliation; of the *entrée* to the King's
private rooms; of various embassies he would have liked; of
military commands and governorships which seemed to be his
due; of the marriages of his children. Last but not least he wanted
to be made a French duke. We can see only too well how dreadfully tedious he must have been when prosecuting these *affaires*,
many of which went on for years, most of which he gained in the
end by wearing everybody down. Madame de Pompadour is
often very cold with him; the King gallops off when he comes
face to face with him out hunting; Choiseul, who when Minister
of State kept open table at Versailles, quickly sits between his
own wife and sister when Croÿ presents himself and they chatter
away so that the Prince cannot get in a word. Croÿ notes all
these facts with ingenuous surprise. He was fond of writing memoranda, and pestered the ministers with screeds on every current
subject. He could not even have a chat with Richard, the Irish
gardener at Trianon, without sending him a memorandum on
evergreens.

All the same, we cannot help loving him for the precious
details with which he acquaints us and for his affectionate nature;
he is truly devoted to the King. This priggish young man was
soon under the spell of King and Marquise, and indeed they must
have been a very attractive pair. Impossible, he says, to be nicer,
prettier or more amusing than she, while the King, when at his

ease with close friends, was an excellent talker, gay, funny and ready to be amused. Sometimes his shyness closed in on him; if one of his friends had been away for only a few weeks he could hardly say a word and had to begin, as it were, from the beginning. 'How old are you? How old is your son?' and so on. Then Madame de Pompadour would come forward and smooth everything over and make it easy for him. They teased each other the whole time, nobody could have had a moment's doubt as to their relationship; but she was always deeply respectful, there was never a word out of place.

The King's supper parties were given for the men who had been out hunting with him that day; anybody who had could apply for an invitation, the King was given the list and chose whom he wanted. The would-be guests must then present themselves at the door of his apartments and an usher read out the names of those who were invited. It was rather a lowering occasion for those who were not. Croÿ applied regularly and was by no means always accepted; once when he was not he says that it was particularly disappointing for him because two friends of his up from the country were standing by as sight-seers, and it would have been so agreeable to have gone in while they were watching. Every time he did go, he describes the evening and gives a list of his fellow guests—between eight and twenty in number and always far more men than women.

'30th January, 1747

'We were eighteen, squashed round the table, beginning at my right: Monsieur de Livry, Madame la Marquise de Pompadour, the King, the Comtesse d'Estrades, the Duc d'Ayen, the tall Madame de Brancas, the Comte de Noailles [governor of Versailles], M. de la Suze, le Comte de Coigny, the Comtesse d'Egmont [the Duc de Richelieu's daughter], M. de Croix, the Marquis de Renel, the Duc de FitzJames, the Duc de Broglie, the Prince de Turenne, M. de Crillon, M. de Voyer d'Argenson. The Maréchal de Saxe was there, but he never has supper so he walked about tasting bits of food, for he is very greedy. The King, who still calls him Comte de Saxe, is very fond of him and he seemed quite at home; Madame de Pompadour is devoted to him.

'We were two hours at supper, free and easy but without any excess. Then the King went into the little *salon*, where he made the coffee and poured it out; there were no servants and we helped ourselves. He made up a table of Comète with Madame de Pompadour, Coigny, Madame de Brancas and the Comte de Noailles, the King rather enjoyed that sort of little game, but Madame de Pompadour seemed to hate gambling and to be trying to put him off it. The rest of the company, also playing a small game, was at two tables. The King told everybody to sit down, even if they were not playing—I stood leaning on a screen and watching his game. Madame de Pompadour was very sleepy and kept begging him to break up the party; finally, at two o'clock, he got up and said, half under his breath to her, I thought, and very gaily—"come on then, let's go to bed." The women curtseyed and went out, he bowed and went into his little rooms. The rest of us left by Madame de Pompadour's staircase and came round through the state rooms to his public *coucher* which took place at once.' Croÿ adds that he had a strong impression that beyond these private rooms and this semi-intimacy there were other, smaller, rooms to which only very great friends indeed were admitted.

*Chapter Eight*

# PLEASURE

VERSAILLES, in the eighteenth century, presented the unedifying but cheerful spectacle of several thousand people living for pleasure and very much enjoying themselves. Pleasure, indeed, had an almost political significance since the nobles, removed from their estates and drugged with useless privilege, had to be kept contented and amused. A state department, *Les Menus Plaisirs*, was devoted to its promotion, drew upon unlimited funds and was sought after as a profession by promising young men. People in those days approved of pleasure. When the Duc de Nivernais left on his very serious and tricky mission to London after the Seven Years War, he was described as going 'like Anacreon, crowned with roses and singing of pleasure.' This was by way of being high praise.

Nineteenth-century historians, shocked by the contemplation of such a merry, pointless life, have been at great pains to emphasize the boredom from which, they say, the whole Court, and the King himself, suffered. No doubt a life devoted to pleasure must sometimes show the reverse side of the medal, and it is quite true that boredom was the enemy, to be vanquished by fair means or foul. But the memoirs of the day, and the accounts of those courtiers who lived through the Revolution and remembered the *Ancien Régime*, do not suggest that it often got the upper hand; on the contrary they speak, one and all, of a life without worries and without remorse, of a perfectly serene laziness of the spirit, of perpetual youth, of happy days out of doors and happy evenings chatting and gambling in the great wonderful palace, its windows opening wide on the fountains, the forest and the Western sky. If ever a house radiated cheerfulness, that house is Versailles; no other building in the world is such a felicitous combination of palace and country home.

The four main pastimes were love, gambling, hunting and the official entertainments. Love was played like a game, or like a comedy by Marivaux; it had, of course, nothing to do with marriage. Children, in those days, were married off in their teens, and these little husbands and wives usually grew up to be very fond of each other, sharing the same interests, absorbed in the family and its fortunes. Even if they did not like each other, which was rare, they could generally manage to get on, since good manners demanded that they should; it was quite unusual for a woman to go back to her father or into a convent because she could not bear to live with her husband. She had a lover, he had a mistress; everything was most friendly.

'I allow you every latitude,' the courtiers used to say to their wives, 'except footmen and Princes of the Blood.'

A husband, finding his wife in bed with her lover: 'Madame! Is this prudent? Supposing somebody else had seen you!'

Mademoiselle de Richelieu and the Comte de Gisors played together when they were very small, and fell in love. When they were of marriageable age they so desperately wanted to marry each other that various sentimental relations tried to help them; it was a perfectly suitable match. But Gisors, though one of the paragons of that age, enormously rich and son of the powerful Maréchal de Belle Isle, had *bourgeois* blood; he was the grandson of Fouquet. The Duc de Richelieu would not hear of such a connexion. He refused his consent to the marriage, saying coldly: 'If they are in love they will find each other in society.'

The *bourgeoisie* of Paris did not see things with the same eye. The financier La Popelinière discovered a revolving fireplace in his wife's bedroom, by which the Duc de Richelieu used to come from the next-door house and visit her. He turned her into the street there and then. The pretty creature went straight off to the army manœuvres which were going on near Paris, found Maréchaux de Saxe and de Lowendal, and persuaded them to take her home and use their influence with her husband. They had just come back from Fontenoy and were at the very height of their glory. But La Popelinière was adamant, his door remained shut. Richelieu gave her a house and an income; she very soon died of cancer. At Versailles such tragic dramas were unheard of; good manners—*bon ton*—prevailed in love as in everything else; the game must be played according to the rules.

Gambling was a more savage pursuit; enormous fortunes were won and lost at the tables and, as in eighteenth-century England, everything was the subject of a bet. At the Queen's table, where they played the dowdy Cavagnole with dice, it was possible to lose 200 *louis* in an evening; at the King's table, where piquet and whist were played, 1000 *louis* and more quite often changed hands, a huge sum in those days.

As for the hunting, this existence would hardly have been possible without it. The men were properly exercised and properly fed; since man is, after all, an animal, he can rather easily be happy under these circumstances. It is the fashion now, among those who have never hunted, to regard it as a dull and cruel sport. Dull it is not, and for cruelty cannot compare with the long, awful journey to the gruesome slaughterhouse, against which no voice is ever raised. A day on horseback in the immeasurable forest, with its rides starring out, each ending in a blue distance, and its varying carpet of leaves and flowers: the smell of earth and horses, the cold rain on a warm face, the distant horn when the hunt seemed lost, the kill by a lake, with wild swans circling overhead, the tunes, unchanged in those woods since Charlemagne, which the hunters play over the dead beast: the gathering

cold and darkness of the ride home, the lighted warmth of the
arrival, the relaxed nerves and physical well-being—these things
once enjoyed can never be forgotten. Louis XV, so delicate as a
child that they hardly expected to rear him, grew up with iron
health; he never felt tired. During the thirty years of his prime he
killed the enormous average of 210 stags a year, without counting
wolves and wild boars. His huntsman, Lasmartre, was a privileged
being who could say what he liked to the King. 'The King treats
me well,' said the Maréchal de Saxe, 'but he doesn't talk more to
me than to Lasmartre.' After killing two stags one day the King
said:

'Lasmartre, are the horses tired?'

'Yes, Sire, they're just about finished.'

'And the hounds?'

'Tired? I should say they were.'

'All right, Lasmartre. I'll be hunting again the day after to-
morrow.' Silence. 'Did you hear me, Lasmartre? The day after
to-morrow.'

'Yes, Sire, I heard you the first time.' Loud aside: 'It's always
the same thing, he asks if the animals are tired, he never thinks of
the men.'

One of his keepers calculated that in a single year he covered
8100 miles on horseback, on foot, or in a calèche. If the hunting
had to be put off, because of hard frost, he would go for a three-
hour gallop, regardless of the horse's legs. He was also fond of
partridge shooting, and was an excellent shot.

The palace entertainments were organized by the Duc de
Richelieu who, as First Gentleman of the Bedchamber, had *Les
Menus* under his direct control; they were always the same and
had hardly varied for fifty years. Twice a week theatre, the
*Comédie Italienne* and the *Comédie Française*, and on special
occasions, such as a royal wedding, or birth, or the celebration
of a victory, there were ballets, balls and fireworks. They were

all well done, but there was no originality and no surprise; except for the balls the King did not enjoy them very much. He was a restless man who loved change and novelty.

Soon after her arrival at Versailles Madame de Pompadour, always thinking how best to amuse him and keep off the yellow colour which meant that he was bored, decided to get up private theatricals among their little set of close friends. She herself, having been taught to sing by Jéliotte of the *Comédie Française* and to speak alexandrines by Crébillon the old dramatist, was well known to be one of the best amateur actresses in France; and she was certainly not averse from showing off her talent to the King. The idea was received with enthusiasm by all her friends, and was indeed a brain-wave.

Everybody enjoys private theatricals. Choosing the play, distributing the parts, the rehearsals, the dressing up, the gossip, the jokes and even the quarrels involved give rise to all sorts of diversions; the whole thing is fun. Though they had never been held at Court before, they were a favourite amusement of the age; when people were exiled from Versailles, or ruined, or for some other sad reason obliged to go and live on their estates, the first thing they always did, even before adding a modicum of comfort to some old, derelict château which had not been lived in for years, was to build a theatre. King Stanislas had a famous theatre at Lunéville, so had Maréchal de Saxe at Chambord and so later on, after his disgrace, had the Duc de Choiseul at Chanteloup. Almost every educated person could act, or play a musical instrument; even in the depth of the provinces enough neighbours could usually be found to form an orchestra capable of playing light opera. When Madame de Pompadour began looking for talent among courtiers of the King's little set, she found that they could nearly all act or dance, some could also sing and play some instrument, and many of them had musical servants.

A tiny theatre, holding an audience of fourteen, was now built, under the supervision of the Marquise, in a gallery which led to the Cabinet des Médailles; it was decorated by Pérot and Boucher, Perronet designed the costumes and Notrelle the wigs. Rehearsals took place at Choisy, in deep secret, even the King not being allowed to attend; and in an incredibly short time the curtain went up on the first of the many plays to be produced in the Théâtre des Petits Cabinets: *Tartuffe* (17th January, 1747). The King was so excited for it that he came home from hunting before having killed his stag; its foot arrived in the middle of the entr'acte. The audience consisted of the King; Mesdames d'Estrades and du Roure; the Maréchal de Saxe; M. de Tournehem, Madame de Pompadour's uncle; her brother Abel; Champcenetz the King's valet, and his son, and one or two other servants.

The Maréchal de Noailles, Prince de Conti, and the Comte de Noailles, governor of Versailles, were among those refused admission. The Comte de Noailles asked if he could have leave to go and hide his tears in Paris; the King was delighted, he said that was a splendid idea and he said afterwards to the Dauphin: 'The Comte de Noailles has taken a hatred for the Court and he's going off to seek oblivion in the arms of his wife.' The Dauphin asked why, and the King replied that it was a secret.

The actors were Mesdames de Pompadour, de Sassenage, de Pons and the tall Duchesse de Brancas, the Ducs d'Ayen, de Nivernais, de Meuse, de la Vallière and M. de Croissy. The Duc de Chaulnes and M. de Sourches with a few musical servants composed the orchestra; no professionals on this occasion, though later on some of the King's musicians took part when operas were given. The whole thing was a resounding success and plans were laid for a season of repertory in the Théâtre des Petits Cabinets.

Madame de Pompadour now issued a set of rules for her troupe, which she and the King drew up together.

1. Nobody may join the society who is not an experienced actor. Beginners are not admitted.

2. It is forbidden to change parts without the consent of all the other members of the society.

3. Each person will state in what capacity he or she is joining.

4. In case of absence the absentee may not choose a substitute, this to be done by the other members of the society.

5. The absentee goes back to his original job on his return.

6. Nobody may refuse a part because it is unflattering or tiring.

These six rules apply to actors and actresses alike.

7. Works to be acted will be chosen by the actresses.

8. They will fix the date of the performance, as well as the number, the day and the hour of the rehearsals.

9. The actors will arrive punctually at the rehearsals, subject to a fine for lateness to be imposed by the actresses.

10. The actresses will be allowed half an hour's grace; if later than that they will be subject to a fine which they themselves will fix.


Madame de Pompadour also laid it down that an author could go to the rehearsals only if his play was being given for the first time. The author of an established play was, however, always invited to the performance.

On January 24th two more plays were given, *Le Préjugé à la Mode* by La Chaussée and *l'Esprit de Contradiction* by Dufresny. After that there was a new play every other week until the 'season' ended on April 17th. In all these plays Madame de Pompadour took the chief woman's part; she was acknowledged to be far better than the other women, though some of the men were up to professional standards. The Duc de Nivernais, in *Le Méchant*, was so much better than Roselli of the *Comédie Française*, that Gresset, the author, asked if Roselli could come and see his interpretation. The original of *Le Méchant* was the Duc d'Ayen; they had great fun with this play and rehearsed it for two months.

While nearly every inhabitant of Versailles was passionately anxious to get somehow, by hook or by crook, an invitation to Madame de Pompadour's theatre, the Marquise herself was longing for the presence of the one person who would not spring forward when she lifted her little finger: the Queen, the dowdy, sleepy Queen, impervious to fashion and charm. She knew all about the theatre because Moncrif was for ever showing her little odds and ends he wrote for it. 'Very nice to be sure,' she said at last, 'and now, Moncrif, that's enough.' She was very polite to Madame de Pompadour, who continued to pay her court punctiliously, although it must often have bored and tired her to do so. The outward appearances were thus perfectly maintained; but the Marquise wanted more than that. She really seems to have wanted, in her affectionate *bourgeois* way, to be looked upon as one of the family. In the end it must be said that she succeeded, but these were early days, and she started off by making a curious mistake. She saw that the Queen's happiness, interest and occupation was in her religion, and she thought a good way to approach her would be by showing an interest in the life of the chapel.

Now Madame de Pompadour was totally irreligious, that is to say she was not one of those who, believing in God, and understanding the protocol with which He is surrounded, are kept away by some weakness of the flesh; she simply did not grasp the meaning of religion. All her life she behaved with an extraordinary denseness where anything to do with the Church was concerned. The first step she took towards a greater intimacy with the Queen was to ask if she could assist in the ceremony, on Maundy Thursday, when the Queen and fifteen ladies of the Court washed the feet of poor little girls. How could she have expected the Queen to allow this? The answer was kind but firm: there were enough ladies already to wash the feet; the Marquise would have the merit of her wish without the inconvenience of its fulfilment. Nothing daunted, Madame de Pompadour had another idea. Why should she not take round the plate on Easter Sunday? (This was a function reserved for particularly holy Duchesses.) She set about this rather differently.

'Everybody tells me,' she said to Madame de Luynes, the Queen's lady-in-waiting, 'that I am expected to take round the plate on Sunday.' Madame de Luynes went with this news to her mistress, who said that she supposed even the King would hardly think Madame de Pompadour a very suitable choice, and quickly named the Duchesse de Castries. Madame de Luynes, a thoroughly nice person, was always smoothing out matters between Madame de Pompadour and the Queen. When the Court was about to leave for Fontainebleau, Madame de Pompadour asked if she could travel in the Queen's coach, a suggestion that was very badly received. It was an enormous honour at Versailles to travel with the King or the Queen. Madame de Luynes, instead of inflaming the Queen against her, as so many people would have, pointed out that Madame de Pompadour would not ask for such a thing unless the King wanted it. She said, privately, to her husband that it must be remembered how much Madame de Pompadour always tried to please the Queen. Finally she almost forced her mistress to say that the coaches were quite full, but that if one of the ladies were to drop out, Madame de Pompadour would be given her place. Eventually this very thing happened; the Queen accepted her company with a good grace, and even invited her to dinner before starting.

The Queen was not ill disposed towards Madame de Pompadour, quite the contrary; she could not, of course, allow her to take part in the religious life at Versailles, but the theatre was a different affair. She now made a little bargain. She had an old friend, M. de la Mothe, a worthy old soldier, who deserved, she thought, to be a Marshal of France. There was no possible objection; the King gave M. de la Mothe his *bâton* and in return the Queen, the new Maréchal, his Maréchale, and the Duc and Duchesse de Luynes went to the next performance in the little theatre. The King himself had chosen the play, *Le Préjugé à la Mode*, not perhaps the very most tactful choice imaginable, as it mocked at conjugal love. But it was the lightest of light comedies; Madame de Pompadour acted a difficult part to perfection, and nobody seems to have been put out. When the play was over the same actors gave a little opera, *Bacchus et Erigone*. The Duc de Luynes notes that Madame de Pompadour was simply excellent in this with a small but lovely voice; next best, though far behind the star, was the tall Duchesse de Brancas. As for M. de Courtenvaux, he could be a dancer at the ballet any day he liked.

The enthusiastic players went from strength to strength; soon they began to long for a bigger stage and more numerous audience. In 1748, while the Court was away at Fontainebleau, a theatre was constructed in the well of the Ambassadors' Staircase which led to the state rooms in the north wing. As this staircase had to be used twice a year for certain diplomatic functions, as well as for a procession of the Cordons Bleu (knights of the St. Esprit), the theatre was made in moveable sections; it could be taken down in fourteen hours and put up again in twelve. There is a gouache by Cochin of this little blue and silver theatre; Madame de Pompadour and the Vicomte de Rohan hold the stage, they are singing in the opera *Acis et Galatée*, the Marquise in a huge skirt of white taffeta embroidered with reeds, shells and fountains, a bodice of palest pink and green gauzy draperies. The King and his friends in the auditorium are all holding copies of the libretto; in the orchestra the Prince de Dombes can be seen, the St. Esprit on his bosom, puffing into a big bassoon. Many ambitious works were given there during the next year, with great success where comedy was concerned, though the King was apt to yawn rather at tragedy. After a play called *Le Prince de*

*Noisy* in which Madame de Pompadour, dressed as Prince Charming—but very decently, not showing more leg than in a riding habit—had played the title role, the King, least demonstrative of men, kissed her in front of everybody and said, 'You are the most delicious woman in France.'

Things were not always so rosy, however. During a performance of *Tancrède* the King received the news that, on his orders most reluctantly given, Prince Charles Edward had been arrested outside the Opéra in Paris and taken to Vincennes.[1] Bonny Prince Charlie was a hero to the French and that evening was quite spoilt for everybody.

Then there was the dreadful day when the Prince de Dombes downed his big bassoon and killed M. de Coigny, one of their very best actors, in a duel. Coigny was the King's greatest friend. He was told the news at his *lever*, immediately cancelled the hunt and went straight to the Marquise; when he came away his eyes were red with weeping. The Prince de Dombes was really not to blame; Coigny had lost a lot of money to him, lost his temper and said 'only a bastard could be so lucky.' This was a bit too near the knuckle, as Dombes was a grandson of Louis XIV and Madame de Montespan. He said nothing at the time but when the party broke up he whispered to Coigny that he would be by the river below Passy at the *point du jour* (daybreak). Forthcoming performances in the little theatre were cancelled, and Madame de Pompadour had migraine for a week.

Soon after this a strong smell of musk in the King's rooms indicated that Son Excellence was back from the wars, with a bâton in his hand, Marshal of France. He was in particularly high favour with the King because he had succeeded in conquering Parma, an establishment that would do very well for Madame Infante,

---

[1] A clause in the Treaty of Aix-la-Chapelle stipulated that the Prince must leave French territory. He refused to go of his own free will and Louis XV was obliged to evict him.

until something better should turn up. She had really wanted a
throne, but anything was better than being merely the wife of a
younger son at the Spanish court, so she and her husband were
quite pleased with this grand duchy. While he was away, the
Marquise had been writing very friendly little notes to Richelieu.
'I look forward so much to your return, do let it be as soon as
possible' and so on; perhaps she thought he would now feel better
disposed towards her. She was soon to be undeceived.

As First Gentleman of the Bedchamber, Richelieu should, by
all the rights of Court usage, have had the Théâtre des Petits
Cabinets directly under his control, first of all because he was
responsible for the palace entertainments and the department of
*Les Menus*, and secondly because the Ambassadors' Staircase was
part of the state rooms, which were also his department. The Duc
d'Aumont, who had been First Gentleman during his absence,
had always been perfectly agreeable when furniture, carriages,
costumes, chandeliers, stage jewellery, and other properties were
borrowed from the warehouse of *Les Menus* by the Marquise
and her producer, the Duc de la Vallière. On one occasion he did
query a bill. Madame de Pompadour went to the King, who sanc-
tioned it at once but remarked, 'Just you wait until Son Excellence
gets back, things will be very different then.' He was perfectly
right. Richelieu had not been in the palace twenty-four hours
before he wrote a strong letter to the King, protesting against
the abuses which M. de la Vallière had introduced while he had
been away. The King did not reply.

Richelieu then struck. He gave orders that no properties were
to be taken from *Les Menus*, that none of their workmen, or
musicians, were to be employed, by anybody whatsoever, without a chit signed by himself. The musicians, who received this
warning on their way to a rehearsal, rushed to his office to ask
for further instructions; they were plainly told that they must
work no more for Madame de Pompadour. M. de la Vallière

then went round to protest; the terrible Duke merely made a
gesture which indicated that, as indeed everybody knew already,
he was very friendly with Madame de la Vallière. The Marquise
now entered the fray. What she said to the King is not known,
but that evening, while his hunting boots were being pulled off by
Son Excellence, the King asked him how many times he had been
to the Bastille? 'Three times, Sire.' That was all, but it was enough.
The Duke was obliged to take the hint and to reverse the orders
he had given.

He said to the Duc de Luynes, who was always so much occupied with questions of Court usage, that of course the offices of
state would lose all their meaning if abuses like this were allowed
to creep in—it had been his duty to protest—he had protested—
Madame de Pompadour was the mistress—no more to be said.
Meanwhile this accomplished courtier had been all the time in the
company of Madame de Pompadour and her troupe, at his very
most delightful, covering them with compliments, laughing,
joking, and telling stories of his campaign. He had been particularly cordial with M. de la Vallière. His manner never altered in
defeat, and nobody not aware of the truth could have guessed
that anything was going on behind the scenes. The King, however, thinking that the Duc de la Vallière had really been rather
badly treated, consoled him with the Cordon Bleu at Candlemas.

The Théâtre des Petits Cabinets lasted for five years, after which
it became too much for Madame de Pompadour and she gave it
up. During this time a total of 122 performances was given of
sixty-one different plays, operas and ballets. They were rehearsed
until they could not be improved, even the most acid critics of
the Marquise being obliged to state that never did any performance
fall below first-class professional standards, and that she herself
was entire perfection in all of them. This venture had two important consequences for her. It consolidated her position at

Court; so mighty a nobleman as the Duc de Richelieu was forced to realize that he had met his match, while the other courtiers had to go on their knees to her if they wanted invitations to the plays. People became perfectly hysterical in their efforts to be given the smallest walk-on part, to be allowed to play in the orchestra or to see the performances; they even bribed Madame du Hausset, her maid, who thus obtained a very good job for her nephew, with the knowledge and amused consent of the Marquise.

On the other hand the great unpopularity with the Parisians, from which she suffered for the rest of her life, began at this time. Hated by the crowd at Versailles because she was a *bourgeoise*, Madame de Pompadour was soon hated by the *bourgeoisie* because of her association with the government, in other words the tax collectors. The theatre was merely a peg on which to hang their grievances. It was said to be an unjustified extravagance; taxes were high, there was a good deal of misery, and ridiculously inflated stories of expenditure were bandied about the capital. The temporary theatre in the staircase was supposed to have cost thousands. It must be remembered, too, that in those days plays and players were considered slightly immoral. The great Molière himself had almost been refused Christian burial because he had once been an actor, many priests would not give them the sacraments—the *Comédie Italienne* had a special dispensation which made the *Comédie Française* very angry—and the pious Dauphin signed himself with the Cross whenever he passed a theatre. D'Angerville says that, in imitation of the Marquise, 'the whole of France now took a taste for the stage, princes and *bourgeois* alike; it penetrated even into the convents and finished by poisoning the morals of quantities of children who were brought up to this profession. In short, it carried corruption to its extreme limits.' It was not true, the taste had existed already, but it was convenient to blame Madame de Pompadour for it. From now on she could not do right in the eyes of the general public.

## Chapter Nine

# ROYAL FAMILY AND POISSON FAMILY

IT was obvious that the sad Dauphin must quickly marry again, and produce an heir to the throne. The baby, *la petite Madame*, who had killed her mother, was useless for the succession and the Dauphin himself an only son. In the autumn of 1746 a list of Princesses was hurriedly made up for the King to study, with the usual embarrassing biological details appended by the French ambassadors to their fathers' courts. Yet another Spanish sister was offered, a little black dwarf this time, but the King rather snubbingly observed that French people abhor incest. The candidate strongly supported by Madame de Pompadour was Marie-Josèphe, fifteen-year-old daughter of Maurice de Saxe's half-brother, the Elector Augustus III, King of Poland. The King and the Marquise both loved Saxe, and the King was deeply indebted to him for all the victories he had won for France. He treated him like a royal cousin, though the Marshal was illegitimate; he had given him the Château of Chambord and had just made him Marshal-General of the French camps and armies.

'M. le Comte de Saxe, I create you Marshal-General of my armies.' Saxe turned to the Comte de Clermont. 'What did the King say?'

'I didn't hear, either. Sire, the Comte de Saxe did not hear what your Majesty did him the honour to say to him.'

'M. le Comte de Saxe,' said the King, raising his voice, 'I create you Marshal-General of my armies, like M. de Turenne. Did you hear me this time?'

'Yes, Sire, and it only remains for me to die like M. de Turenne.' [1]

It would be agreeable to welcome his niece to Versailles as Dauphine; big business, headed by the Pâris, was greatly in favour of the match; last, but not least, there were reasons to suppose that this Princess would be very fecund.

Now Saxony at that time evoked but one idea in the minds of the courtiers at Versailles. It was the country of porcelain, of the factory at Meissen where, some thirty odd years before, *pâte dur* had been invented and which still kept the secret of making it. But for Queen Marie Leczinska it had more lugubrious associations. Augustus III had chased her father, King Stanislas, off the throne of Poland and sat there now in his place, and though, in fact, Stanislas was perfectly happy reigning at Lunéville, the Queen was outraged at the idea of receiving his rival's daughter as her daughter-in-law. However, the King had made up his mind. Madame de Pompadour whom he saw night and day was in favour of the match and the Queen, whom he never saw alone, did not dare raise her voice against it. She merely looked cross. She knew that she had no influence with her husband, and he intimidated her dreadfully. It so happened, too, that there were fewer suitable Princesses on the market than usual, Marie-Josèphe being almost the only Roman Catholic of the right age.

So Richelieu was sent off to Dresden to fetch Marie-Josèphe away. He made a great splash at the impoverished Court with his retinue, his clothes and his carriages, and gave a splendid banquet, pretending not to notice when the guests departed laden with his silver. The Princess was put in charge of the Duchesse de Brancas (not the tall one), who was to be her principal lady-in-waiting, and escorted to Versailles. The King bought the first Dauphine's jewels from *la petite Madame* and gave them to Marie-Josèphe as a wedding present; her own presents to her ladies were chosen

[1] Turenne was killed in action.

by him for her to give, all of them matching those given by her predecessor, a watch to go with an *étui*, and so on. The whole thing was run on nice, sensible lines.

Madame de Brancas said the new Dauphine was a great improvement on the other, whose lady-in-waiting she had also been; Marie-Josèphe bubbled over with high spirits, and was not all the time on her dignity. She was neither pretty nor elegant, very German; the old people at the Court said her curtsey put them in mind of Madame, the Regent's mother. But she had a charming, tactful character; for such a young girl her behaviour with the Dauphin was extraordinary. She understood and fully sympathized with his grief, revived as he went through the same ceremonies, two years, almost to the day, after those which had preceded such perfect love and happiness. When they were publicly put to bed together in the same room, with the same furniture, as that which he had shared with his first wife—the rooms for *Madame la future Dauphine* not being ready yet—he covered his face with the bedclothes and sobbed. The good little Pépa simply said: 'Don't stop crying, your tears don't offend me, on the contrary they show me what I can expect if ever I should succeed in winning your love.' She did succeed; they were very happy and had eight children, three of whom were Kings of France. They could hardly have been more united. When *la petite Madame* died, at the age of two, they wept for her together; years later they were both seen to be in floods of tears at a requiem mass for the first Dauphine. But he never forgot his first wife, and left instructions that his heart was to be buried with hers.

As for the Queen, she was soon won over. She noticed that the Dauphine always wore the miniature of a man set in diamonds on a bracelet. 'Is that your father?' she asked one day. The Dauphine unclasped it to show her; it was a portrait of King Stanislas. The Queen and her father took the child to their hearts and she was like a daughter to both of them.

The ball which was given at Versailles, in honour of this second marriage, was less splendid and more select than the ball of the clipped yew trees, where there had been too many people who had not behaved very well. Not only had there been the incident of the Spanish cook; the King heard that most of the oranges from his buffets had re-appeared the next day on the Paris market; it really seemed to be getting too easy to hire a coach and the suitable clothes and drive down from Paris. This time, therefore, people were invited, and Madame de Pompadour made out all the lists for the Parisians. The courtiers noticed that every day, in one way or another, she was becoming more powerful. Great amusement, at this ball, was caused by a certain yellow domino, who stood by the buffet, eating and drinking, hour after hour. Nobody could imagine how any human stomach could hold so much, until it was discovered that the Swiss guards were putting on this domino in turns. There was, as before, a ball in Paris. During both these evenings Madame de Pompadour watched the King closely; she knew that many pretty women counted on meeting him. At the Paris ball people only had to follow the direction of her eyes to see which domino was the King. But he seemed quite as much in love as she did; very soon they both unmasked, and he sat at her feet. They made a picture of radiant happiness.

The King adored his children, especially the daughters. Between him and the Dauphin relations were apt to be rather strained. The jealousy which monarchs often feel for their heirs came between them; besides, they were too near in age and too different in character to be great friends. The Dauphin was a prig, he disapproved of his father's morals and mode of life, and made his disapproval felt. Like his mother, whom he tenderly loved, he was sleepy and rather a bore; he enjoyed neither the theatre, nor dancing, nor hunting, shooting only rather, and society least of all. When asked what he did like doing he replied: 'I like vegetating.' The King once inquired how he intended to amuse himself during the Carnival. 'I shall go to bed at ten instead of eleven.' Perhaps there was something wrong with his glands —fat with the unnatural fatness of his son Louis XVIII, he suddenly, at the age of thirty-six, became very thin and died.

Men with such a different view of life could hardly be expected to understand each other, or to enjoy each other's company for long, but there was affection all the same. When the Dauphin was taken ill with smallpox in 1752, the King, though he had never had this most dreaded of all diseases—of which, years later, he died—dashed back to Versailles from Compiègne and was hardly out of his son's room during the crisis. He sat up with him night after night. A certain Dr. Pousse was brought from Paris, a specialist in smallpox, and amused them all with his way of talking. 'I don't know how I am supposed to address you,' he said to the King, 'but I'll tell you something, you're a good Papa and I like that. Don't forget we're all your children and share your grief, but don't be downhearted, your son will be restored to you.'

To the Dauphine, not knowing who she was, in her plain cotton dress, 'You're the best little nurse I ever saw, what's your name, my lass?' When he was told he cried: 'There's an example for me to hold up to all those fashionable ladies who won't go near their husbands when they have the smallpox.' She replied that whereas it would be very easy to find another Dauphine, the Dauphin was irreplaceable. On the seventeenth day Dr. Pousse took the King by the buttonhole and said: 'Monseigneur is out of danger now. He has no more need of me, and I'm off.' The King said: 'Very well, but first you must dine.' When he sat down at the table he found, in his napkin, an order giving him fifteen hundred *livres* a year for life. The Dauphin recovered, but the Parisians were not delighted. He was known to be governed by the Jesuits and many people dreaded his reign which was sure, they thought, to bring a period of religious intolerance; they preferred his jolly cousin the Duc d'Orléans whom they saw every day in Paris. The fact that the Dauphin now had a little boy was quite discounted, these royal babies died like flies, and, in fact, neither this child, his next brother nor his elder sister lived to be grown up.

The Dauphine, chosen very largely because her family had such a wonderful record of fecundity, had worried everybody very much at first by showing no signs of a baby. Every month the whole Court held its breath and every month hopes were blighted. Then she began to have miscarriages at a very early stage, a fortnight, three weeks at the most. Her doctors kept her in bed, would not let her go to Compiègne and Fontainebleau, for fear she should become pregnant and have to stay on indefinitely, and still this bouncingly healthy girl continued to miscarry. At last, in 1750, a daughter arrived, Marie-Zéphirine, as self-willed and naughty as a little dragoon; and after that, regularly every autumn, Marie-Josèphe produced an *enfant de France*, greatly to the delight of the King and the Marquise, whose letters are seldom without some allusion to the Dauphine's health.

'The Dauphine, I am thankful to say, is keeping to her *chaise longue*.' 'The Dauphine is certainly three months pregnant now, we can really begin to have hopes, if there is no accident.' 'Madame la Dauphine has passed four months, you can imagine my joy.' '. . . but this is a very small misfortune, a real one is the daughter which has just been born to Madame la Dauphine, but as, at the eleventh day, she is in very good health, she will give us a prince next year. We must console ourselves with this reflexion and try not even to think of *la petite Madame* [the new baby]. I couldn't bring myself to look at her until to-day.' 'We go to Compiègne on Friday for six weeks, leaving Madame la Dauphine here, very well, with a child that jumps about like anything. I hope to God he will arrive safely and be a boy. I can tell you, and you will believe me, that the sight of all these girls dries me up. The one we have got is quite well again now, but we should have died of fright if she had been a boy.'

The first boy was born, with one pain, in about ten minutes; very inconvenient as it was absolutely vital that there should be witnesses of the birth. The doctor, who was sleeping in the Dauphine's room, told her she must hold everything, while the Dauphin rushed out in his nightshirt to find somebody. 'Well then hurry up,' she said, 'it's kicking me.' A sleepy Swiss guard was very much surprised when the Dauphin seized him by the arm, said: 'Quick, go in there and see my wife having a baby,' and went on to look for one more witness.

The King was playing cards at Trianon; a man galloped down from Versailles: 'A boy, a boy!' Was he drunk? they wondered. The news was confirmed and the King, overcome with happiness, felt giddy and had to be half carried to the only coach available, that of the Prince de Conti. He cried over the little Duc de Bourgogne, who was tactful enough to look very much like him, and stayed till five in the morning talking to the Dauphine. Then he ordered a Te Deum before going to bed.

The Dauphine never knew whether these babies were boys or girls until they were brought to her with, or without, the *cordon bleu*, a little blue ribbon from which hung a tiny St. Esprit, first made for the sons of Henri IV. Out of her first five children four were boys. The Parisians thought the younger ones received the most affected names: Duc d'Aquitaine, Duc de Berry, Comte de Provence and Comte d'Artois, instead of the customary Bretagne and d'Anjou. 'It didn't do d'Aquitaine much good,' they said—he died at five months old.

Louis XV was one of those fathers who never want their daughters to marry. The eldest, Madame Infante, did so, for urgent reasons of State, when she was thirteen; neither she nor her father was really happy until she was back again at Versailles. She returned in 1749, aged twenty-two, a grown-up lady with a little Infanta of eight at her skirts; the King hardly recognized her, she was far prettier, more intelligent, more a woman of the world than her sisters, whom she found very babyish. Unfortunately she was ambitious and never stopped plaguing her father for a throne. He was so delighted to have her with him again that he would have given her anything in his power; he gave her equal honours with her mother, greatly to the latter's displeasure, but the throne never materialized and she had to be content with Parma. To-day the Parma Bourbons descend from Louis XV, and, through his son-in-law the Infant Philip, in a direct male line from Louis XIV, but they have never put forward a claim to the French throne because of the oath taken by the Duc d'Anjou when he became King of Spain. Through them, the blood of Louis XV flows in the veins of nearly all the royal families of Europe. Madame Infante was a great deal at Versailles after she became Duchess of Parma, and Madame de Pompadour used to complain that she saw very much less of the King when she was there.

Madame Henriette, the twin of Madame Infante, was in love with the Duc de Chartres (later Duc d'Orléans) and he with her, but the King would not allow them to marry for fear of giving too much power to the house of Orléans. He made a great mistake; if Chartres had married her, horrible Philippe-Egalité would never have been born. In spite of his love for the Regent, and the fact that he always got on very well with Chartres, the King felt the traditional Bourbon distrust for the Orléans family. There is little doubt that if the Dauphin had died without an heir, he would have encouraged the Spanish Bourbons to put forward a claim to the throne of France, illegal as it would have been. Sad, and for ever ill, Madame Henriette died just before the Dauphin's smallpox in 1752; she had been the King's favourite and his grief at her death was intense.

Then Adélaïde became the adored of her father; she lived, and always had lived, for him alone. At six years old she had refused to be parted from him, and was the only daughter not to be brought up in a convent. She was eleven when war broke out with England; they found her leaving Versailles with a few *louis* in a little bag. 'I am going to make the English lords sleep with me in turns, which they will be honoured to do, and bring their heads to Papa.' She was rather like a furious boy, very passionate and attractive, but nothing ever turned out quite right for her.

After Madame Adélaïde came Mesdames Victoire, Sophie and Louise, not very interesting characters; Mesdames Adélaïde and Victoire survived the Revolution and died in exile. There was no question of any of them marrying. The magic of Versailles worked as strongly upon the royal family as it did upon the nobles; to leave its precincts seemed the most dreadful of fates, no crown on earth could compensate for it. A child of France, as they were called, would never have been allowed to marry a subject. The King went to Madame de Pompadour one day in a great rage because he thought he had noticed that a certain young man was in love with Madame Adélaïde who, at seventeen, was exceedingly pretty. This young man soon found himself back on his estates. Madame de Pompadour told her maid that no death would be cruel enough, in the King's view, for somebody who seduced one of his daughters.

To all outward appearances, the Marquise was on excellent terms with these girls, but they really wanted to get their father away from her. As they grew up they began to have a good deal of influence with him, and but for Madame de Pompadour would have been very powerful indeed. Bigoted, and, like their mother and brother, led by the Jesuits, they were almost more shocked by her friendship with the *philosophes* than by her relationship with their father. Among themselves they called her Pom-pom, not an unfriendly little name, and probably were charmed by her when she was there; nevertheless they intrigued against her whenever they saw an opportunity. As for her, with her usual warmth, she encouraged the King to see more and more of his daughters, always arranged for one or other of them to join the voyages, and sat them next to him at meals. She spoke and wrote as if she loved them all dearly. In any case they soon found out that it was useless to cross swords with the Marquise; the King always took her side in the last resort. They had their real revenge after she was dead, when they moved into her two favourite houses and altered them out of all recognition.

Like the King, Madame de Pompadour loved her own family. She was very lucky in her brother. The Marquis de Marigny, a charming and clever man, entirely devoid of ambition, was the exact opposite of the grasping relations who have so often blackened favourites such as Madame de Pompadour in the eyes of posterity. He always refused honours until he felt he had earned them; greatly to her annoyance he always refused the heiresses to whom she hoped to marry him.

'He writes to me,' she said, angrily, to her maid one day, having just read a letter from him, 'because he doesn't dare say it to my face. I had arranged a marriage for him with a certain nobleman's daughter; he really seemed quite in favour of it and I had given my word to the family. Now he tells me he has heard that the father and mother are arrogant, and the daughter spoilt, that she knows all about the proposed marriage and has spoken of it in terms of the utmost contempt, and that she despises both of us, me even more than him. He says he knows that this is all quite true. Yes—well, perhaps, but these people will be my deadly enemies from now on; he should have thought of it sooner.' She was very angry indeed with Marigny. However, she arranged another good marriage for the little girl, whose conduct in a very short time forced her to admit that her brother had been quite right.

Shy, modest and unassuming, Marigny saw all the dangers of his position and was fully conscious of its ridiculous side. Indeed this seems to have preyed on his mind almost too much and to have made him too surly and grumpy to the courtiers, who positively detested him. They were furious enough when he was made a Marquis, but his St. Esprit was almost more than they could endure. 'Here comes Marinière, with his Cordon Bleu.' Though devoted to the King, he never cared for Versailles, he was a real Parisian and his life and pleasures were centred in the capital. Very rightly and wisely he refused various ministries proposed to him by his sister, who, as she became more and more involved in politics, would have liked to have his support. He pointed out that it would be sheer folly for him to be in charge of a government department; the moment anything went wrong she would be doubly blamed. All he wanted was to inherit the post which Tournehem occupied, Intendant of the King's Buildings; he felt, and rightly, that he would make a success of this job. Indeed, he made a resounding success of it; Marigny's administration is an important chapter in the history of French art.

In 1749, Madame de Pompadour, realizing that a talented and energetic young man should be given something better to do than kick his heels at the Court, conceived the idea of sending him to study art in Italy. It was clever of her to think of it, and rather original, for unlike the English at that time, Frenchmen seldom travelled; Croÿ says that in all his life he only knew two well-bred men who had been abroad for pleasure (though every artist who could do so, went sooner or later to Italy). She chose, as companions for her brother, the artist and engraver Cochin, the architect Soufflot and the Abbé Leblanc, an art critic, famous in his day; the four of them set off, primed with good advice from her and followed by more good advice which arrived by every post.

'Don't imagine that because I am young my advice is worthless. After living here for four and a half years, I have as much experience as a woman of forty.' She begged him not to make jokes about the various royalties he would meet, or at any rate not to write them to her, as their letters would surely be opened. 'Be polite and nice to everybody' was the burden of her song. Poisson also wrote saying: 'Listen to your sister, she may be young but she is very sensible.' Madame de Pompadour wrote to the Duc de Nivernais, now French ambassador in Rome, where his chief occupation seems to have been trying to keep the works of French writers off the Index. For some unknown reason she always called him *petit époux* (little husband). 'My brother leaves in about six weeks—I ask your friendship for him—he deserves that of anybody who appreciates good qualities. . . . He is not at all stupid, but he is too frank, so truthful that sometimes he seems unsympathetic. Curiously enough, this virtue does not pay, at Court. I have suffered from that, and have made a resolution never to tell anybody the truth as long as I live—I only hope I can keep it. My brother is going with a certain Soufflot of Lyons, a very gifted architect, Cochin whom you know, and think the Abbé Leblanc. Good night, *petit époux*.'

Nivernais replied: '. . . One thing is lucky for him [Marigny]: they love frankness here, rather as we love that stuff from India which we can't make at home. So I guess he will have a great success. I can't say the same for poor Abbé Leblanc; French abbés are not liked in Rome, where they are treated as an enormous joke.' He ended this letter with a P.S. saying that the King ought to go to Rome for Holy Year (1751); after all, there were precedents as Charlemagne and Charles VIII had both done so.

Marigny was received everywhere in Italy, saw all the reigning Princes, had a great success with the women and made an excellent impression. People put themselves out for him to any extent; Madame de Pompadour writes that this would be quite understandable in *ce pays-ci* where they might need her help one day, but was most unexpected and gratifying abroad. But the object of this tour was not to see reigning Princes and flirt with Italian beauties; it was to become conversant with classical art.

French architecture had been very little dented by either the baroque or the rococo, and it was now moving to a new and even greater severity of line. Madame de Pompadour liked everything that was new and she foresaw that furniture and interior decoration would slowly but surely follow the architecture; she told her brother to bear this constantly in mind and to study all the classical remains that he could find. Cochin says that the Italian journey of M. de Marigny and his companions marked a turning point in French art; the turning point in fact from the style of Louis XV, all curves and arabesques, to what we call the style of Louis XVI, but which is also that of a long part of the reign of Louis XV, all straight lines and angles. From the acanthus leaf to the laurel. It is a pity that Madame de Pompadour did not live long enough to direct this new trend, and that it should have fallen into the incompetent hands of the uneducated Madame du Barry and feather-brained Queen Marie Antoinette.

Towards the end of the tour, Madame de Pompadour wrote, 'They say that M. de Tournehem is going to resign when you return, but I hope not. I would do everything in my power to stop him; for one thing it would kill him and then you are really too young, not yet twenty-five, and although you are beginning to know a great deal I think you should be at least twenty-eight or thirty before taking on such a job.' Hardly, however, had he returned than Tournehem died; so the problem resolved itself and Marigny became director of the King's buildings. He found that Tournehem had left a flourishing charge. He had put order into the finances, introduced a system of inventories, reformed many abuses, and founded a museum in Paris by opening the royal collections in the Luxembourg to the public. Thanks to

M. de Tournehem's probity and hard work, Marigny was able to develop his new department unhampered by administrative worries.

Poisson's old age was very happy, owing to his daughter. He thoroughly enjoyed being a country squire, with enough money to indulge the family passion for building. Madame de Pompadour thought of many little ways in which to please him, and wrote to him regularly; she and her daughter Alexandrine were the light of his life. He hardly ever went to Versailles, except to see her act, but he often accompanied the Court to Fontainebleau and Compiègne. In Paris he and M. de Tournehem lived together, and Madame de Baschi kept house for them; when Poisson was at Marigny, M. de Tournehem constantly sent him news of Reinette and Alexandrine.

This little 'Fan-fan' was as pretty and charming as possible. Her mother adored her and kept her more and more at Versailles as she grew from a baby into a little girl. She was loved by the whole family as much as Madame de Pompadour herself had been loved when she was little. Her uncle, Marigny, was devoted to her and old Poisson was quite silly about her, as can be seen from his daughter's letters to him—they also show us exactly what sort of a man he was. 'I believe that Alexandrine has quite supplanted Reinette in your heart, but as I love her very much I must forgive her. I am sending you her letters as I see you like to have them.'

'I had Fan-fan to-day at la Muette—I even dined with her; she is very well. I have nothing to add to what I have already told you; I am far poorer than when I was in Paris. Never have I asked for what has been given me, and the expenditure on my houses has worried me very much, but all this amuses the Master, so no more to be said. If I had ever wanted to be rich, the money that has gone on all those things would have brought me a considerable income, but I have never wanted it. I defy fate to

make me unhappy—only through my feelings can I be hurt. . . .
M. de Monmartel has some money of mine which you are
welcome to. . . . I can only offer what I have got. I am worried
about a writing table and a big Vincennes vase which left a fortnight ago by carriage to Marigny. What can have become of
them. . . ? Love your daughter as much as she loves you.'

'I am very sorry, dear father, that you ask for Vincennes for
M. de Malvoisin [a cousin of Poisson's]. I can't understand what
can have come over you to want to put there a man of twenty-
five, who only has six years' service, however intelligent he may
be. . . . Certainly I'm not going to lend myself to such an injustice. Here is Alexandrine's letter, with my profound respect
and tender love.'

'You are so right not to come here [Versailles]. If you knew
*ce pays-ci* as I do you would detest it even more.'

'I'll try and get a present for Fan-fan, for you to give when
you arrive—but never give her money, I beg.'

'She seems to be getting very plain, not that I care—so long
as she isn't really hideous I should prefer her not to be a great
beauty. It only makes enemies of the whole female sex which,
with their friends, amounts to three-quarters of the world's
inhabitants.'

In a letter to Crébillon, who looked after Alexandrine's education, the Marquise said: 'I don't want her to seem too clever.
Molière says that we women are only intended to sew and spin
—I don't agree with that, either, but I think the learned look and
know-all manner simply ridiculous.'

Fan-fan, like a royal princess, was never addressed by her
surname but always as Madame Alexandrine. As she was evidently going to be an enormous heiress, and very influential,
since the King was known to be fond of her, many families would
have been glad to welcome her as a daughter-in-law; but her
mother flew high. Too high.

One day, at Choisy, two little children aged about eight and eleven sat in the fig-house eating figs and brioches, having their tea in fact; they were Alexandrine and the 'demi-Louis,' son of Louis XV and Madame de Vintimille. Madame de Pompadour brought the King to see this pretty sight; he was evidently in one of his sulky tempers. Madame de Pompadour said: 'Do look at that little boy!'

'Why?' said the King.

'Well, isn't he the very image of his father?'

'Really! I had no idea you were so friendly with M. de Vintimille.'

Very ill-advisedly, after this rebuff, the Marquise went on to say what a charming couple the two children would make. The King gave her a freezing look and the subject was never mentioned again.

'So like him,' she said afterwards, to her maid, adding that she had only wished for this marriage because the boy was the King's son. 'That's why I would have preferred him to all the little dukes at the Court. My grandchildren would have had something of me and something of him, it would have made me so happy.'

Her next move was quite as silly. She suggested to M. de Richelieu, of all people, that his son, the Duc de Fronsac, might marry Alexandrine. Richelieu very cleverly got out of it by saying that his son had the honour, through his mother, of belonging to the house of Lorraine and that he would therefore be obliged to consult the princes of that family before making any matrimonial plans for the boy. Madame de Pompadour once more had to take a hint; she began to realize that, while she could expect a good marriage for her daughter, the very grandest *parties* of all were not within her reach. In the end she affianced her to the little Duc de Picquigny, son of her great friend the Duc de Chaulnes (*mon cochon*, she always called him).

They were to be married when Fan-fan was thirteen. Alas, at this point Fate stepped in and settled the matter. Alexandrine was seized with 'convulsions'—appendicitis almost certainly—at the convent where she was being educated, and died before her mother could get to her. She was ten years old (1754). Madame de Pompadour was so prostrated with grief that, the news coming at a critical moment for her, the doctors thought that she might herself collapse and die. The blow did kill old Poisson, who died four days later. Marigny, in spite of the fact that he was now the heir to his sister's vast estate, was also beside himself with misery.

The King, though he was, understandably, more worried for the mother than grieved about the daughter, was kindness and solicitude itself; he sat by Madame de Pompadour's bed hour after hour and hardly left her for days. She rewarded him by pulling herself together as soon as she was physically capable of doing so, and resuming life as if nothing whatever had happened. In a few weeks she seemed quite unlike a bereaved mother. But four months later, at a performance, by the *Comédie Française*, of *Les Troyennes*, she fainted dead away and could not be brought round for a long time; nobody could think why, until it was realized that a mother, in the play, had lost her daughter at that moment.

The death of Alexandrine was a crushing blow from which Madame de Pompadour never fully recovered. She felt that she had nothing to look forward to any more, that the future could only offer her old age and death. She longed more than ever for Marigny to found a family which would be an interest and a comfort to her and to whom she could leave her collections. But he wanted a love match—years later he made one, with disastrous results. Like many childless women, Madame de Pompadour now turned more and more to the minor but not unrewarding love of dogs and various other pet animals.

## Chapter Ten

## POWER

THE King's mistress was a traditionally unpopular figure in France. She was also a convenient scapegoat. The French could thus love their monarch, while laying his more unpopular actions at her door. (Marie Antoinette, who doubled the role of wife and titular mistress, suffered in her turn from this long established attitude.)

After the Peace of Aix la Chapelle, in 1748, Madame de Pompadour became more unpopular every day. The public was displeased by the treaty and indeed, considering the splendid victories of French arms during the past years, it did seem rather unprofitable. The only advantage it brought to France was a not very exalted establishment for Madame Infante whose husband received the duchy of Parma. 'As stupid as the Peace,' said the Parisians, and blamed Madame de Pompadour.

Only those who have known what we call now a bad press can realize what a perpetual source of irritation it is, nearly always, to its victim. Nowadays the victim can at least answer back, with a dignified letter to *The Times*, or a less dignified libel suit, or he can hire a publicity agent. But the bad press of the eighteenth century was impossible to combat, taking, as it did, the form of horrid little poems and epigrams passed from mouth to mouth, posters, pamphlets and leaflets, all anonymous. Hundreds of these were directed at Madame de Pompadour, they were called the Poissonades; dull and dirty, they are untranslatable, since they nearly all depend on a play of words round her maiden name. Most of them originated at Court, with courtiers too stupid to realize that in thus attacking the monarch they were casting opprobrium on their own way of life. M. Berryer, the chief of police, a devoted friend of Madame de Pompadour, was crossing the state rooms at Versailles one day when he was rudely stopped by a group of courtiers who asked him how it was he could not run to earth the authors of the libels. 'You ought to know Paris better,' they said. He gave them a sharp look and said he knew Paris like the palm of his hand, but was not so much at home at Versailles. The Parisians lapped up the Poissonades, added to them and eagerly distributed them; the King was not spared and the two names were bandied about with evil intent. Nothing they could do was right. If they entertained they were wasting money, if they did not it was her fault because she wanted to prevent him from meeting other women. When they built the house at Bellevue, they were abused by half the public for spending too much, and by the other half for building such a wretched little house, smaller than that of a *fermier général*.

Each taxpayer felt that her houses, furniture and works of art were paid for out of his own pocket, and to make matters worse, her taste was for small things of an impermanent nature. Instead of great monuments like those of Louis XIV, the King's money was being frittered away on such toys as little wooden pavilions in the forest, built and furnished with amazing elegance, surrounded with large groves of exotic trees, and aviaries of tropical birds, visited once or twice and then taken down again so that the next year it was impossible to see where they had been. Croÿ describes a visit to Trianon with the King, who showed him the hot-houses, the rare plants, the hens (which he specially liked), the charming pavilion, the flower and the vegetable gardens; all arranged so prettily. Croÿ is full of admiration, but deplores the fact that Madame de Pompadour should have given the King 'an unfortunate taste for expensive little things which cannot last.' This view was shared by the public. Madame de Pompadour excelled at an art which the majority of human beings thoroughly despise because it is unprofitable and ephemeral: the art of living.

When the Marquise first arrived at Versailles she had four implacable enemies there, the Duc de Richelieu, the brothers d'Argenson (the Marquis and the Comte), and the Comte de Maurepas. The last three were ministers, of *bourgeois* antecedents, sons of ministers in the government of Louis XIV. The Marquis d'Argenson, already out of favour, was sent away in 1747, more through the influence of Madame Infante than that of Madame de Pompadour. He was not disgraced, since he was allowed to resign, but he left the Court and would never have been heard of again had he not kept a diary. Unfortunately for Madame de Pompadour, since it is largely devoted to envenoming her memory, this diary is far the wittiest and best written of the memoirs of her contemporaries. However, d'Argenson overdoes it and the reader ends by hardly believing a word he says. He is one of those diarists who are fond of prophesying and whose prophecies never seem to come true. The King is getting tired of her, she has completely lost her looks: old, yellow, faded and withered, her teeth have gone black, her neck is all scales, her bosom a terrible sight, she is spitting blood: the King cannot bear to go near her, she disgusts him, he will send her away and go to live with his family. Everything she touches turns to ruin, and so on. At the same time the other diarists, who, after all, lived at Versailles and saw her every day, entirely contradict him; they record that never has she been prettier, gayer, or the King more in love, and everything she does is delicious and delightful.

D'Argenson, scribbling furiously away in the country, was no menace to Madame de Pompadour in her lifetime, but the other two politicians were. Maurepas was the first to show his claws. He was a minister of thirty-one years' standing, at this time Minister of the Marine, and he had enormous influence with the

King, who had, of course, known him from a child. He was a most entertaining, lively fellow, who roared with laughter, especially at his own jokes; except for the Duc de Richelieu, he amused the King more than anybody. Writing in his journal the best account we have of Madame de Pompadour's presentation at Court, he adds: 'She is excessively common, a *bourgeoise* out of her proper place, who will displace everybody if she is not soon herself displaced.'

It was his aim to see that this should happen, as quickly as possible. But, so far from her being displaced, he found her daily becoming more powerful. She was nearly always present when he saw the King; she would not hesitate to burst in, when they were working together, with some such request as the cancellation of a *lettre de cachet* issued by Maurepas. Should he venture an objection, the King always took her side: 'Do what Madame suggests, please.' None of the mistresses had liked Maurepas but none had dared to treat him in such a way. 'M. de Maurepas,' she said, on one occasion, 'you are turning the King yellow. Good day to you, M. de Maurepas.' The King said nothing, and Maurepas was obliged to gather up his papers and go.

His revenge was to heap ridicule on her, to imitate her *bourgeois* ways as soon as her back was turned, and to invent Poissonades. He was an accomplished rhymester; all the most spiteful and beastly of these were attributed to his pen. Madame de Pompadour was determined to get rid of him, but Maurepas, quite well aware of this, was not at all alarmed; he thought himself indispensable to the King. This was a misapprehension under which each of Louis XV's ministers suffered in turn; it is very curious to see how little they seem to have understood the circumstances of their predecessors' exits. The King was too shy, he hated any form of embarrassment too much, ever to hint that somebody was displeasing him. He would let matters go on until, having had enough, he would strike with a dreadful swiftness; a letter of dismissal and banishment, couched in freezing terms, would be delivered to the unsuspecting offender.

In 1749, more and more hateful verses were being whispered round the Court until finally Madame de Pompadour, sitting down to supper, found, in her napkin, the famous quatrain:

> Par vos façons nobles et franches,
> Iris, vous enchantez nos cœurs;
> Sur nos pas vous semez des fleurs
> Mais ce ne sont que des fleurs blanches.

The disgusting implication[1] of this rhyme, whether true or not, was perfectly clear to all who read it and the Marquise, usually rather philosophical about such things, was thoroughly upset. Dr. Quesnay went to the King and said the whole affair was preying on her mind and making her ill; indeed she now had a miscarriage, followed by one of her attacks of fever. She told the King that she was thoroughly frightened, Maurepas would murder her, she said, as, some thought, he had murdered Madame de Châteauroux. But the King still hesitated to dismiss him. He was fond of Maurepas, old friend of all his life; he enjoyed working with him, and thought him good at his work. Above all, he loved his jokes. Madame de Pompadour made a temporary alliance with Richelieu over this affair; Son Excellence hated the minister even more than he hated the mistress and for the same jealous reasons.

Together they composed a memorandum, which they gave to the King, accusing M. de Maurepas of allowing the Navy to become dangerously weak. They had not entirely invented this; as early as 1745 the Duc de Luynes says that many people considered Maurepas responsible for the fall of Louisburg,[2] whose garrison he was supposed to have kept short of ammunition. He

---

[1] That Madame de Pompadour suffered from *fluor albus*.
[2] In Nova Scotia. Louisburg was razed to the ground by the English.

was also accused of an act of gross negligence—it was said that three ships of the Compagnie des Indes were captured by the English, because Maurepas had omitted to tell them the route which could safely have been taken.

Of course he answered this memorandum with the plausibility of an old hand at the political game; nothing had been his fault. The money, he added—with a dig at Madame de Pompadour —which should have been used for building ships, seemed to have gone into other channels. One morning, the Marquise ordered her sedan chair and, accompanied by Madame d'Estrades, she went to call on him. 'Nobody shall say that I send for the King's ministers.' Then, very sharply, 'When will you find out who it is that writes these poems?' 'As soon as I do find out, Madame, I shall of course inform His Majesty.' 'You are not very respectful, Monsieur, to the King's mistresses.' 'On the contrary, Madame, I have always respected them whoever they may be.'

The Court was naturally buzzing with the news of this un-accustomed morning call, and that evening, at a party, somebody said to Maurepas that he seemed to have had an interesting visitor. 'Yes,' he replied carelessly, for all to hear, 'the Marquise. It won't do her any good, I'm not lucky to the mistresses. I seem to remem-ber that Madame de Mailly came to see me two days before her sister took her place, and of course everybody knows that I poisoned Madame de Châteauroux. I bring them all bad luck.' These rash words were immediately reported to the private apartments; Maurepas had gone too far. Next morning at the King's *lever* he was in wonderful form, never had he talked more brilliantly and never had the King laughed so much at his sallies. He announced that he was going to Paris that afternoon for a wedding.

'Enjoy yourself,' said the King, as they parted. He himself was going to Madame de Pompadour's little house at La Celle, near St. Cloud, with a few friends, including Richelieu. The next morning at eight o'clock Son Excellence was seen leaving for Paris, in such tremendous spirits that the onlookers wondered if some misfortune had not befallen M. de Maurepas. Also at eight o'clock the Comte d'Argenson, who had received a note from La Celle in the middle of the night, went to wake up Maurepas, sound asleep after his wedding party. One look at d'Argenson's face told the Minister what had happened. The wretched man, who lived but for society, politics and the life at Court, rubbed his eyes and read the following note: 'M. le Comte de Maurepas, having promised to tell you myself when I have no further use for your services, I request you herewith to resign your ministry. As your estate at Pontchartrain[1] is too near, I request you to retire to Bourges during this week, without having seen anybody but close relations. Send your resignation to M. de Saint Florentin. Louis.'

Smiling, imperturbable as ever, Maurepas got up, dressed and went his way. He knew his master well enough to know that this was final. Ministers who lost their jobs at that Court were always exiled, since the King did not care to see their gloomy, reproachful faces, with an implied, 'I told you so', when things went wrong. Nobody had ever been recalled. Maurepas, luckier than most, did return to Versailles; some twenty-five years later Louis XVI made him Prime Minister and was not well-advised in doing so.

The Duc de Nivernais, Madame de Pompadour's *petit époux*, was married to Maurepas' sister, and a few months later (1749) he wrote from Rome to the Marquise: '. . . May I be allowed to describe his condition, without society, with nothing to occupy him, in a country which is literally a desert, where the air is unhealthy most of the year and where the roads are impassable from November to May. . . . You know quite well how delicate Madame de Maurepas is; not a single day that she doesn't suffer either from colic of the stomach or from sharp pains in the head,

[1] A few miles from Versailles.

where she very likely has a growth such as killed her father. Should she get a fever, she would certainly be dead before a doctor could arrive from Paris. She and her husband have this prospect ever before them; it goes to my heart to think of it; surely I can touch yours, and that of the King, always so good and understanding. All we ask, and it seems not unreasonable, is that His Majesty should allow him to live on his estate at Pontchartrain, to be understood that Paris would be out of bounds—his punishment would still be terrible enough . . .' (Two more pages on these lines.)

The Marquise merely replied that this letter did not surprise her at all; it was what she would have expected from such a nice person. In fact the King had been more thoughtful and merciful than he might have been in this matter. He had chosen Bourges because Maurepas' greatest friend and close relation, the Cardinal de la Rochefoucauld, was Archbishop there, and the Maurepas went to live with him. Four years later they were allowed to return to Pontchartrain, both in perfect health.

In September, 1749, the King decided to inspect his fleet at Havre and to take Madame de Pompadour with him. His popularity among the Normans was still as great as it had been at the time of Fontenoy and they do not seem to have been at all put out by the presence of a mistress instead of a wife; a double line of people waited to cheer them the whole way between Rouen and Havre. The only slight set-back was when the Bishop of Rouen, the Queen's Chaplain, indicated, by a respectful silence, that he would prefer not to have Madame de Pompadour under his roof for the night. They were obliged to make other arrangements. The account of this journey shows what enormous physical endurance Louis XV expected of his friends. The party left Crécy in the morning, Mesdames de Pompadour, du Roure, de Brancas and d'Estrades in a berlin, the King and the Duc d'Ayen *tête-à-tête* in a smaller carriage. They took riding horses and some hounds with them and hunted most of the way. That evening they arrived at the Château de Navarre, where the Duc de Bouillon gave a big party. All next day the King hunted in the forest; after supper they got back into their coaches and travelled through the night, arriving at Rouen at eight in the morning. They did not stop, but went straight on, through cheering crowds, to Havre, where they arrived at 6 p.m.

After an enthusiastic reception, the governor took them up a tower to look at the sea, which most of the party had never seen in their lives. A bitter wind soon drove them back to the Hôtel de Ville, where supper for twenty-eight was prepared. Next morning the King got up early to go to church while Madame de Pompadour received presents and compliments from the municipality, exactly as if she had herself been royal. All that day there were ceremonies, lasting well into the night, when two hundred ships were illuminated in the harbour. Next morning the party left for Versailles, only stopping once on the way.

Except with the Normans this journey was very unpopular; it was supposed to have cost a fortune and the King was blamed for taking his mistress with him so openly.

From now on Louis XV shut himself up in his houses and hardly ever left them again, never even going to Paris unless absolutely obliged to. He felt himself criticized unjustly, and mis-understood, and a serious riot which broke out in Paris confirmed him in this feeling. There were various causes for discontent. The Peace of Aix la Chapelle, which had been signed the year before, 1748, had brought no relief from taxation. Corn was scarce and prices were high. The immediate reason for the uprising, however, was the disappearance of a little boy. Waifs and strays, together with prostitutes and other undesirables, were rounded up from time to time by the police and shipped off to colonize Canada; the story went round that the police received so much a head, and Parisian parents lived in terror that their children would be picked up by mistake, or even kidnapped. The small boy of certain respectable citizens disappeared mysteriously; the frantic mother roused her neighbours; finally a whole quarter of the town rose in fury. Howling against Madame de Pompadour, the mob pursued Berryer, who was, justly, considered as her creature, to his house, threatening to kill him and burn it down. With great presence of mind he threw them a policeman, who was torn to pieces while Berryer opened all his doors and windows. The rioters, suspecting a trap, beat a hasty retreat.

Of course, neither Berryer nor his masters believed a word of the kidnapping story, and they were all outraged by the accusation. The King refused to drive through Paris when next he went to Compiègne—'Can't see why I should go to Paris to be called Herod'—a new road was made for him across the plain of St. Denis; it is still known as the *Chemin de la Révolte*. He suffered when his people behaved, as it seemed to him, so unreasonably. He felt that he and they were united by a religious link; he loved them, he lived for them, and like a father with naughty children he was vexed. But he was as far from understanding the root of the trouble as he was from knowing how it could be cured.

He had been brought up to consider that France was his property in the same way as an estate was the property of its owner. Taine, writing in 1875, says that the King would have thought it as surprising and unfair to be put on a civil list, as a modern millionaire if the State took away part of his income. A huge proportion of the national revenue was spent on the royal household. This had been regarded as a natural order of things by his subjects while taxes were low, but France had been at war for seven years, taxes were high, those who paid them thought they were not collected fairly and there was a great deal of murmuring. Unfortunately, like so many of the rulers of France, Louis XV did not understand money at all. When he was younger he came back from Paris one day so horrified by the poverty and famine he had seen there, that he immediately dismissed eighty gardeners. Then it was pointed out to him that these men and their families would die of starvation, so he took them back again. He had the irritating impression that he could never do right.

As for Madame de Pompadour, who loved Paris so much, she almost gave up going there. When she did so, it was at the risk of an embarrassing incident. If she went to the Opéra she would be greeted with ironical cheers, too loud, and lasting too long, to sound quite real; if she went to the convent to see her little girl, her carriage would be covered with mud; and on one occasion when she went to dine with M. de Gontaut, such terrifying crowds gathered that he was obliged to hurry her off by the back door. But none of this in any way affected her rise to power: after the exile of Maurepas and the journey to Havre she was regarded at Court as paramount. Only God or another woman, it was felt, could now bring a term to her ascendancy; no man could hope to do so.

Her enemies bided their time and bided it in vain, for it never came. Henceforward the King, though very faithful to his old friends, made no new ones except through the Marquise; favours and advancement could only be obtained through her. The courtiers assumed a new attitude towards her as she did towards them. Her staircase was thronged with people who wanted her to do something for them; she received them kindly and patiently and always tried to help them if she possibly could.

Marmontel describes calling on her, at her *toilette*, with Duclos and the Abbé de Bernis. 'Bonjour, Duclos, bonjour, Abbé,' with an affectionate tap on his cheek, and then, in a lower, more serious tone of voice, 'bonjour, Marmontel.' He was, at the time, a penniless, unknown, unsuccessful young writer; he took her a manuscript which she promised to read. When he returned for it she got up on seeing him, and leaving the crowd of courtiers standing there, she led him into another room. They talked for a few minutes and she gave him the manuscript covered with pencilled comments. Back among the courtiers, Marmontel saw that the effect of all this on them had been prodigious. Everybody pressed forward to shake his hand, and one nobleman, whom he scarcely knew, said: 'Surely you're not going to cut your old friends?'

As in the Queen's bedroom there was no chair for her visitors, who were therefore obliged to stand, whatever their rank, even if they were Princes of the Blood. In the whole history of France no other commoner had ever dared to behave thus, and yet there only seem to have been two protests: the Prince de Conti dumped down on her bed one morning, saying 'That's a good mattress,' and the Marquis de Souvré perched on the arm of her chair while talking to her. 'I didn't see anywhere else to sit.' But these daring actions were not repeated, and the Marquise got her way in this as in most other things. She began to study Court usage of the previous reign and modelled herself on Madame de Montespan, sitting in the former mistress' box at the theatre and in her place in the chapel. It was noticed that she spoke of 'we', meaning herself and the King.

'We shall not see you for several weeks,' she said to the Ambassadors on the eve of a voyage. 'For I suppose you will hardly come all the way to Compiègne to find us.' Guests at her country houses were obliged to provide themselves with uniforms as at the King's little houses. Her retinue of fifty-eight servants included two gentlemen, decorated with the order of St. Louis, and ladies of quality. She built the Hôtel des Réservoirs, in Versailles, to house them and as an overflow for her collections; it was almost an annex to the palace and joined to it by a covered passage. All these signs of power came gradually; gradually the courtiers understood that there were now two Queens of France within the walls of Versailles, and that it was not the wife of the King who reigned.

## Chapter Eleven

# FRIENDS AND TABLE TALK

VOLTAIRE, busy and consequential, with two posts at Court, King's historian and gentleman in ordinary, with his room over the Prince de Conti's kitchen and the public privy; and with his great friend in such an exalted condition, might have been thought to have reached a harbour where he could spend a most agreeable old age. Versailles was not a bad place in which to work. Marmontel, to whom Madame de Pompadour had given a sinecure in Marigny's department and a little lodging, so that he could be sheltered from material worries, says that he spent there the happiest and most profitable years of his life. There was a splendid library (happily still intact) second only to that of the rue de Richelieu in Paris. So great was the crowd hanging round King and Court that it was easy to be left alone, forgotten for weeks at a time. But Voltaire, as usual, gave the ladder under his feet a good sharp kick. He wrote an exceedingly tactless poem in which he said that Madame de Pompadour was an embellishment to *la Cour, Parnasse et Cythère* and charged her and the King to keep what they had each conquered. This was followed, after the victory of Berg op Zoom in 1747, by:

> *Et vous et Berg op Zoom vous étiez invincibles*
> *Vous n'avez cédé qu'à mon roi*
> *Il vole dans vos bras du sein de la victoire*
> *Le prix de ses travaux n'est que dans votre cœur*
> *Rien ne peut augmenter sa gloire*
> *Et vous augmentez son bonheur.*

It was too much for the King's real family; Queen, Dauphin and Mesdames were outraged. The King was none too pleased, and the Marquise, whatever she may really have felt, had to pretend to be very much annoyed. The atmosphere at Versailles turned so threatening that Voltaire thought he had better make himself scarce. He packed up his things and went off to Lunéville, where King Stanislas, always on the look out for entertainers, received him with open arms. Perhaps Madame de Pompadour breathed a sigh of relief; perhaps she thought she had heard the last of him for a while.

Somebody told her that Crébillon, her old friend and teacher, was living in terrible want, starving to death really, in the Marais, surrounded by the dogs he loved so much. 'Crébillon, in misery?' she cried, and immediately rushed to the rescue; she gave him a pension, asked him to supervise Alexandrine's education and arranged for an edition of his collected works to be published by the royal printing press. He came down to Versailles to thank her, and found that she was ill in bed; however, she insisted on receiving him.

As he was bending over to kiss her hand, in came the King—'Madame, I am undone,' cried the old man, 'the King has surprised us together.' The King immediately took a great fancy to him, and backed up Madame de Pompadour when she said that he ought to write a last act to *Catalina*, a play which he had begun many years ago and had never finished. She saw that this would do more to raise his morale than any pension. So he went off and finished it. Madame de Pompadour gave a little party at which he read it out loud, and then, through the King's influence, she had it produced at the *Comédie Française*.

When Voltaire, at Lunéville, heard all this he could not contain his jealous fury—of course, he said, the Marquise had done the whole thing on purpose to make him miserable. He worked himself into a passion, and would gladly have killed her. As he was never very good at keeping his feelings to himself, his enemies in Paris soon heard of them; unlike Madame de Pompadour they really were delighted to seize an opportunity of torturing him. Led by Piron, they leagued together to hail *Catalina* as a masterpiece. Now *Catalina*, as it happened, was a very bad play, and furthermore was written in an old-fashioned idiom which sounded affected and absurd on the modern stage. Madame de Pompadour was perfectly aware of this; she looked forward to the first night with considerable misgivings. The audience, thanks to her, was a galaxy of rank and fashion, and probably, like all Parisian first-night audiences, more inclined to be interested in itself than in the play—but what of the critics? The Marquise went up from her house at St. Cloud. The King put her into her carriage at three in the afternoon, and then entertained a party of men friends. At ten o'clock he heard wheels on the cobble-stones, ran downstairs and out into the courtyard crying: 'Well, so have we won our case? Is it a success?' It had been a huge success.

'Maybe,' said Voltaire, when he heard the news, 'but there'll never be a second performance.' He was quite wrong and had to endure the fact that there were twenty performances, which for those days was an enormous run. 'Never will I forgive the Marquise for supporting that old madman.'

Spurred on by rage, he wrote *Sémiramis* simply in order to make Crébillon's *Sémiramis* look ridiculous. It was put on at the *Comédie Française*, and Voltaire came to Paris from Lunéville for the first night. Total failure. The verses were, naturally, a hundred times better than Crébillon's, but the crowd scenes were almost impossible to produce successfully. 'Make way for the ghost,' in an audible hiss from the prompter's box, was not a happy prelude to a speech. Furthermore the theatre was full of Voltaire's ill-wishers filling the air with loud, catching yawns. When this agony was over, the wretched man hid himself in a near-by café and listened to the remarks of the customers who, one and all, made a mock of his play. He sat up the rest of the night re-writing great chunks of it; in the end it was a success and ran for fifteen nights.

But this was not all. In those days, parodies of well-known plays were very popular; it came to his ears that a parody of *Sémiramis* had been written, and was about to be acted before the Court at Fontainebleau. He flew into a misery, seized his pen and wrote to, of all people, the Queen. 'Madame, I throw myself at Your Majesty's feet and beseech Your Majesty, by the goodness and greatness of your soul, not to deliver me to my enemies,' etc. The Queen, who detested Voltaire and regarded him as the anti-Christ, the instigator of everything that was most horrible in France, replied, very coldly, through Madame de Luynes, that parodies were quite usual and she could see no reason whatever to stop this one. He then forgave Madame de Pompadour for *Catalina* and wrote to her. She, always concerned to save his feelings whenever she could, stopped the parody at Fontainebleau and, even more important, in Paris.

'If I had not known that you were ill,' she wrote, 'I should have realized it from your second letter. I see that you are torturing yourself over the hateful things people have said and done to you, but really you should be used to this by now, you must remember that it is the inevitable lot of great men; they are always run down during their lives and admired when they are dead. Think of Racine and Corneille; you are no worse treated than they were. I am quite sure you have done nothing to injure Crébillon. Like you, he has a talent which I love and respect. I have taken your side against all who accuse you, I know you are not capable of such infamous behaviour. You are quite right when you say that I am pursued by libels, but I treat all these horrors with the utmost contempt. . . . Adieu, take care of yourself, don't go off after the King of Prussia however sublime his soul may be; now that you know the great qualities of our Master, you ought not to think of leaving him and I for one will never forgive you if you do.'

He did, however, and it might have been expected that, in the dust and fury of his encounters with that worthy antagonist, any grievances against his compatriots would have been forgotten for a time. Not at all. The more miserable he was in Germany, the more he blamed Madame de Pompadour for his self-imposed exile. She ought to have forced the King to like him, to have made him more welcome at Versailles; then he would have stayed there and none of this would ever have happened. So he vented his bad temper on the Marquise in the following terms:

> *Telle plutôt cette heureuse grisette*
> *Que la nature ainsi que l'art forma*
> *Pour la b . . . l ou bien pour l'Opéra.*
> *Qu'une maman avisée et discrète*
> *Au noble lit d'un fermier éleva*
> *Et que l'Amour d'une main plus alerte*
> *Sous un monarque entre deux draps plaça.*

After this there were no communications between them for some years. Even so he continued to draw his pension. Few women would have been so magnanimous, but Madame de Pompadour knew her own worth, she suffered neither from an inferiority nor a superiority complex, she saw herself as she was and on the whole approved of what she saw. So she went through life with a calm self-assurance, which increased as she grew older. Only one thing could frighten or upset her, and that was the idea that she might lose the King.

'Here come my little cats,' she cried, after a political discussion with the King, during which he had said, as he often did, that his Magistrates were republicans at heart but that the system would last out his lifetime. 'They wouldn't understand such serious talk—you, Sire, have the hunting to distract you, I have them.' The little cats were Mesdames d'Amblimont and d'Esparbés;

Madame d'Amblimont was also known as the little heroine since she had once repulsed the advances of the King. Madame de Pompadour made him reward her with a diamond necklace. The King now began to talk about Lasmartre, his huntsman, who was a character. As more people came in he would begin again for their benefit, Madame de Pompadour encouraging him to do so, and always listening with the same attention as the first time she had heard the story.

Her confidential maid, Madame du Hausset, amused herself by writing down these things she heard, while perched up in her little listening gallery or during the course of her duties. Madame de Pompadour liked her to know everything that was going on and told her to come and go as she pleased. 'The King and I trust you completely, we go on talking as if you were a pet dog or cat.' Uneducated, she scribbled down a jumble of facts and scenes without any sequence, but she had the gift of catching the tone of a dialogue; everything she wrote had life. She was what was called a lady of quality, that is of the minor nobility, and there are reasons to think that she and Madame de Pompadour may have known each other as children. She must have been very poor to accept such a position but it is evident that she thoroughly enjoyed it. Madame de Pompadour looked after her dependants and they loved her.

After his sister's death Marigny was found, by a friend, burning some papers. He held up a packet and said: 'This is the journal of a maid my sister had, a very estimable person, but it's all rubbish.' The friend, who had a passion for anecdotes, asked if he could take it away. Marigny gave it to him; in due course he passed it on to a Mr. Crawfurd of Kilwinnik, a Scotsman who lived in France, collected objects of art and was friendly with Madame du Deffand, Queen Marie Antoinette and Fersen. He edited it, and published it in 1809, but the original manuscript has disappeared. Of course the authenticity of this document has been questioned; it certainly seems rather strange that Marigny should have been so offhand with something which so nearly concerned his sister. But Marigny had a curious character, not the least sentimental; he sold her most intimate souvenirs as soon as she was dead, although there is no doubt that he loved her deeply. The memoirs have the ring of truth, and if they were forged, or added to, it must have been by somebody who knew the Court from the inside, since they are often corroborated in detail by memoirs which were published many years after they were. It really seems easier to believe that Madame du Hausset herself wrote them.

Madame du Hausset was once involved in a terrifying drama, when the King appeared to be dying in Madame de Pompadour's bed. The Marquise came for her in the middle of the night. He was panting and half unconscious with one of his attacks of indigestion. They threw water over him and gave him Hoffmann's drops, a medicine to which the Marquise was greatly addicted, and then Madame du Hausset fetched Dr. Quesnay from his lodging further down the staircase. By the time he arrived the worst was over, but he said that if the King had been sixty it would have been a serious affair. Presently he helped the King back to his own bedroom and nobody was ever the wiser.

Next morning the King sent a little note to Madame de Pompadour: 'My dearest friend must have been very much alarmed, but let her be reassured, I am better, as the doctor will tell you [sic].' When the emotion was over the two women could not help saying to each other how extremely awkward it would have been if the King had died there, though they had been quite in order when they called Dr. Quesnay, as he was one of the royal physicians. But still——! The same thought must have occurred to the King; he sent the maid and the doctor presents of money, and to Madame de Pompadour a beautiful clock, and a snuff box with his portrait on the lid.

Madame du Hausset nursed the Marquise during all her many

illnesses. Her bad health was a great drawback to happiness; as she got older there was hardly a week without a day or two in bed. Whether she was really consumptive, as has so often been said, seems open to doubt; the life she led would have been enough to kill a healthy woman, and would surely have killed a consumptive before the age of forty-three. Her weak spot was her throat, she was for ever having feverish sore throats; from early childhood she was liable to colds and asthma. She kept her room very hot, which the King also liked, and had a fire during most of the summer; her favourite attitude was standing by it, one arm on the chimney piece and her hands in a muff. Like everybody who feels the cold, she often suffered from it more in the summer than in winter. She wrote once from Marly, in June, 'frightfully hot in the *salons* and cold everywhere else, more coughs and sneezes than in November.' Dr. Quesnay understood her constitution and while he was looking after her she kept pretty well. Apart from the fact that he thought everything should be treated by bleeding, he had sensible ideas about general health. Sometimes, however, she consulted quacks who made her do eccentric things, like lifting heavy weights, and then her health would go to pieces.

Quesnay was a friend of the *philosophes* and contributed to the *Encyclopédie*, articles on Evidence and on Farming. His political views were very pronounced; he and the Marquis de Mirabeau (father of the famous Mirabeau) were leaders of a school of economists called the Physiocrats, of which Turgot was a member. They were in favour of free trade and a 'back to the land' movement; deists, they believed that the laws of nature are those of God and that, since man is naturally good, he can easily be persuaded that honesty is the best policy; he should be governed as little as possible. Quesnay, who was a country-man born and bred, thought all the evils in France came from the oppression and underpayment of the agricultural classes which drove them off the land into the towns; France should and could live by exporting agricultural produce. The Physiocrats favoured a single tax. The King was very fond of Quesnay, called him *Le Penseur*, and himself designed and bestowed on him a coat of arms with the flower *pensée* (pansy) as his crest. His book, *Le Tableau Economique*, was printed at the royal press. But Quesnay's economic principles, summed up, as they were, by *laisser faire, laisser passer*, were perhaps not very useful to the King who was already too much inclined to do both.

One day Madame de Pompadour said to Quesnay: 'Why do you seem so frightened of the King? He is a good man.'

'Madame, I only left my village at the age of forty and it is difficult for me to get used to the world. When I'm with the King I say to myself, "This man can have my head chopped off." It upsets me.'

'But the King is good, don't you think of that?'

'Yes, reason tells me so; but I can't help it, he frightens me.'

It has sometimes been said that the French Revolution was cooked up in Quesnay's little *entresol* and he certainly entertained people who expressed very daring opinions, knowing that their words would never go beyond his four walls. All the intellectuals who went to see Madame de Pompadour stopped on their way up or down the staircase for a word with the doctor, and she herself would sometimes come there and join them for a chat; they felt more at their ease than in her room, with the King making his sudden appearances and disappearances. Marigny was there a great deal, and Madame du Hausset who, one day, heard a Magistrate utter the petrifying words: 'This country can only be regenerated by some great interior upheaval, but woe to those who find themselves involved, the French people won't go to it with gloves on.' She trembled, but Marigny, who was also there, told her not to worry. 'All these people', he said, 'are perfectly well-intentioned and they are on the right lines, I'm sure. The trouble is they don't know where to stop.' Quesnay and his friends were quite harmless, in fact the more advanced *philosophes* were intensely scornful of the Physiocrats.

Dr. Quesnay said about Marigny: 'He is too little known, one never hears people speak of his wit and his knowledge, nor yet of what he has done for art—nobody has done so much, since Colbert. He is an excellent man, but people only see him as the favourite's brother, and because he is fat they quite unjustly think of him as heavy and dull.'

Quesnay introduced the Comte de Buffon, the naturalist, to Madame de Pompadour and she and the King liked him very much. They both loved animals and had a great many pets, monkeys, dogs, birds of every kind. The King had a big white angora cat and kept pigeons, hens and rabbits on the roof above his apartment at Versailles. They had a farm at Trianon and there was a menagerie, the other side of the canal, which had once been the toy of his mother, the Duchesse de Bourgogne. One day, as he came out of chapel, a time when presentations were made, M. de Maurepas presented two young lions to the King, and on another occasion some ostriches; he wanted to buy a little rhinoceros, but the man it belonged to made a good living by showing it and asked too much money. Buffon was in trouble with the Jesuits for saying that animals had souls. He said so in his article on animals in the first volume of the *Encyclopédie* when it appeared in 1752 and this was one reason for the Church's objection to that work. (Another was that the miracles of Æsculapius, Greek god of medicine, should be mentioned in the same book as those of Jesus Christ.) Buffon finally severed his connexion with the *Encyclopédie* in order to remain on good terms with the King, whom he loved.

Madame de Pompadour supported the *Encyclopédistes* against the Jesuits and Archbishop de Beaumont by all the means in her power; the Queen, the Dauphin and Mesdames of course pulled in the other direction, and played upon the superstitious side of the King's nature. When Madame Henriette died they said it was God's vengeance on him for allowing this sacrilegious work to appear in his Kingdom; this was the sort of thing he half believed, in moments of emotional stress.

Soon after the *Encyclopédie* had been confiscated there was a supper party at Trianon. The Duc de la Vallière was saying that he wondered what gunpowder was made of. 'It seems so funny that we spend our time killing partridges, and being killed ourselves on the frontier, and really we have no idea how it happens.' Madame de Pompadour, seeing her opportunity, quickly went on: 'Yes, and face powder? What is that made of? Now if you had not confiscated the *Encyclopédie*, Sire, we could have found out in a moment.' The King sent to his library for a copy, and presently footmen staggered in under the heavy volumes; the party was kept amused for the rest of the evening looking up gunpowder, rouge and so on. After this subscribers were allowed to have their copies, though it was still not on sale in the bookshops.

But towards the end of her life the Marquise began to have doubts about the *philosophes*. 'What has come over our nation?' she wrote during the defeats of the Seven Years War. 'The *parlements*, *encyclopédistes* and so on have changed it utterly. When all principles have gone by the board, when neither King nor God are recognized, a country becomes nature's pariah.' All the years she had spent at Court had made her more royalist than the King.

He came up her little secret staircase at all hours, to tell her the news, to have a word with her, as a modern lover would telephone, or for a long session of chat. She never went out, for fear he might come and find her not there; he appeared and vanished again without warning, to the embarrassment of her friends who would suddenly find him in their midst; upon which they would retire unless specially asked not to.

One day he came to tell how, going at an unusual hour to his bedroom, he found a strange man there. The poor fellow, terrified, threw himself at the King's feet, begging to be searched at once, and explaining that he had lost his way in the palace. He was an honest baker, known to the household, and his story was evidently quite true. The King, as soon as all this was proved, gave him fifty *louis* and told him to forget about it, but Madame de Pompadour could not forget; she was appalled to think that anybody could find his way, unhindered, to the private apartments. When she told her brother the story he merely said: 'That's funny, I would have betted anything against the fifty *louis*.'

But the King was always generous to Madame de Pompadour and anybody connected with her. 'Who was it I saw leaving your room as I came in?' 'A poor relation of mine, Sire.' 'Did she come to beg?' 'Oh no, only to thank me for something I had done for her.' 'Well, since she's your relation I would like to give her a small annuity, as from to-morrow.' He once gave Madame de Pompadour six *louis* for being brave when Dr. Quesnay bled her.

The King never could bear Frederick the Great, even when they were allies in the field. Arriving on one occasion with an open letter in his hand he said, sarcastically, 'The King of Prussia is a great man, he loves culture and, like Louis XIV, he wants all Europe to echo with his munificence towards learned foreigners.' Madame de Pompadour, and Marigny, who was with her, waited for what would come next. 'Now listen to this,' he read from the letter. '"There is in Paris a man whose fortune is not equal to his talents. . . . I hope that he will accept this pension and thus give me the pleasure of having obliged a man who not only has a beautiful nature but is also sublimely gifted."' At this point in came Gontaut and d'Ayen; the King began all over again, adding: 'the Foreign Office wants to know whether I will give my permission for this sublime genius to accept the money. Now I ask you all to guess the sum which is involved.' They variously guessed six, eight, and ten thousand *livres*. 'Nobody has guessed twelve hundred *livres*,' said the King, delighted. 'Really,' said the Duc d'Ayen, 'it doesn't seem very much for such sublime talents!' The man of genius in question was d'Alembert. Madame de Pompadour very sensibly advised the King to give double the annuity himself and withhold permission for Frederick's, but he felt that he ought not to reward somebody so irreligious as d'Alembert. He allowed the King of Prussia's annuity, however.

Louis XV had an extremely morbid side to his nature, which some thought was the result of that terrible week when, at the age of two, he had lost father, mother and brother. The modern psychologist might say that this explanation is not so far-fetched. He was very fond of talking about death beds and horrifying medical details over which in those days no veil of decency was ever drawn; the whole Court knew when the King or Queen had taken a purge and every aspect of the health of women was openly discussed by all.

'Have you decided where you are going to be buried?' he once asked the old Marquis de Souvré.

'At your feet, Sire,' was the tactless reply.

When the King was in these dark and morbid moods he used to ask Madame de Pompadour not to make him laugh. One day, driving to Choisy, his coach broke down, and he got into that of the Marquise, who was alone with her little friend the Maréchale de Mirepoix. He saw some crosses against the sky, on a nearby hill, and saying that he supposed there must be a graveyard he sent one of his outriders to see if there were any new graves. The man came back saying that there were three graves, freshly dug. 'Why, it's enough to make one's mouth water,' cried the Maréchale, gaily. But the King looked sad and thoughtful.

This little Maréchale was a great comfort to Madame de Pompadour. She and the tall Duchesse de Brancas were her closest friends; the King, too, was very fond of them. The

Maréchale, born Beauvau, was first married to the Prince de Lixin, a Prince of the House of Lorraine; he was killed by Richelieu, in a duel. Then she gave up her rank, in order to marry, for love, the Marquis (later Duc) de Mirepoix. The courtiers thought that this disinterested action marked her as eccentric indeed. Mirepoix was a soldier; not even very rich. Their life was a perpetual honeymoon until, in 1757, he died suddenly on a journey to Provence. The Maréchale was the sister of the Marquise de Boufflers, one of the great charmers of the age, whom we do not meet very much at Versailles because she lived in Lorraine and was the mistress of King Stanislas. Both sisters were excessively gay and treated life as an enormous joke; their contemporaries said they never grew old, since it was for ever springtime in their hearts. But whereas Madame de Mirepoix loved nobody but the Maréchal, Madame de Boufflers was extremely unfaithful, not only to her husband but also to King Stanislas.

The Maréchale understood the King perfectly, better, perhaps, than Madame de Pompadour, since she was not in love with him, and when he was difficult, or seemed to be attracted to other women, this practical Frenchwoman, who saw life clearly as it is, was always able to reassure her friend. 'He's used to you, he doesn't have to explain himself when he's with you. If you disappeared and somebody younger and more beautiful were suddenly to be found in your place I dare say he wouldn't give you another thought, but he'll never be bothered to make a change himself. Princes, above all people, are creatures of habit.'

The King was very difficult: centre of the universe from such an early age, he could hardly have avoided being selfish and spoilt. Sometimes even the Marquise could do nothing with him. Soon after her arrival at Versailles she gave a *fête-champêtre* for him at Montretout, a little house at St. Cloud, which she embellished, called her dear Tretout and very soon abandoned for the nearby La Celle. A small number of his favourite friends were invited, the June night was hot and delicious, she looked perfectly lovely in a dark blue dress embroidered with all the stars of the milky way; everything augured well. The party began with a wonderful supper on the terrace, to the sound of music. When that was finished, the Queen of the Night sang a song in honour of her guest; then she held out a white hand to him. The King, who liked sitting on at the supper table, looked the other way; she insisted, however, and led him, preceded by the orchestra, to a little wood. The whole party, wreathed in smiles, advanced two by two as in a graceful minuet; but the King stumped along looking very cross indeed. Who is this shepherd, sitting surrounded by his flock? Why, none other than M. de la Salle! Amazed to see so great a King in so rustic a haunt the honest shepherd recited some lines in his honour; they fell flat. A troupe of villagers now appeared, and one of them handed the King a mask and domino. He did not bother to put them on, never attempted to conceal his yawns and soon went grumpily off to bed.

Needless to say, there was a good deal of crowing over this fiasco at Versailles, among those who had not been invited. The Queen, who, like many meek and holy people, had a catty side to her nature, could not resist dotting the i's. She pretended to be quite upset about it all and scolded her husband for not being more appreciative of Madame de Pompadour's kind efforts to amuse him.

Very soon, however, the Marquise knew exactly what sort of entertainment he did like, and such a distressing occurrence does not seem to have been repeated. When she gave rustic fêtes they really were rustic, and she and the King very much enjoyed wedding parties for youths and maidens who lived on her various estates. She would marry off several couples at a time, with a feast and country songs and dances; she liked to give dowries and trousseaux to poor girls who otherwise would not have been able to marry.

But the best way to amuse the King was with any sort of building project. 'After the King's Mass,' says Croÿ, 'we went to the Marquise. The King came and fetched her to walk in the gardens, hot-houses and menagerie at Trianon. As the Duc d'Ayen and I were chatting about gardens, a hobby we share, the King asked what we were saying. The Duc d'Ayen said we were talking about country places, and that I had a charming one near Condé which was becoming quite well known. . . . The King asked me about it; I explained that I had a forest and wanted to rebuild my house in a clearing where four rides met at right angles, that I was not sure about the design for it because I wanted a *salon* in the middle which would look out in each direction, with nice bedrooms at the four corners. . . . The King was very fond of building and plans. He took me to see his pretty pavilion in the garden at Trianon and observed that I ought to build something on those lines. . . . He ordered M. Gabriel to give me two plans they had made together, then he asked for pencil and paper and I made a sketch of the site. He put down his own ideas and asked M. Gabriel to go over them with him. In the end it lasted an hour or more and I was quite embarrassed. That evening he talked of it again, and the next day. . . . By dinner time we had visited all the hens, and collected the fresh eggs, and stifled in the hot-houses, which were very interesting, then we went back to Trianon, for luncheon [*déjeuner*] with the King.'

After luncheon they walked to the Hermitage, Madame de Pompadour's little house on the edge of the park, and went over the gardens, hot-houses and menageries of that pretty place. On the way they saw some partridges; the King said to d'Ayen, 'Take the gun from that keeper and shoot a cock.' D'Ayen took the gun and shot a hen, and this amused the King very much. After this day spent together the King would always ask Croÿ how the plans for his house were going, and even referred to himself as M. de Croÿ's architect.

## Chapter Twelve

## TASTES AND INTERESTS

MADAME de Pompadour was one of those people who like to acquire houses, expend energy, taste and knowledge in embellishing them, live in them for a while, and then go on to something new. Her first house of her very own was Crécy, which she always loved and in whose neighbouring village she took a particular interest; then came Montretout, quickly exchanged for the slightly larger La Celle, and then the Hermitage at Versailles. This little rustic one-storied pavilion was to her what the Petit Trianon later became to Queen Marie Antoinette; she used it as a summer house and spent happy days there alone with the King. 'A certain Hermitage,' she wrote to Madame de Lutzelbourg, 'near the Gate of the Dragon, where I pass half my life. It is sixteen yards by ten, nothing above, so you see how grand it must be; but I can be alone there, or with the King and a few others, so I am happy.' Mademoiselle Langlois, of the Musée de Versailles, has recently discovered this little house which was supposed to have disappeared; Mesdames had it after Madame de Pompadour's death and disguised it by adding a storey; it is now a convent. The great point of the Hermitage was its wonderful garden, all arranged for scent so that one heavenly smell led to another; it could be visited blindfold for the scent alone. Here she had fifty orange trees, lemons, oleanders single and double, myrtle, olives, yellow jasmin and lilac from Judea, and pomegranates, all in straight avenues with trellised palisades leading to a bower of roses surrounding a marble Apollo. Shrubs and flowers were brought to Madame de Pompadour from all parts of the French empire, chosen for the scent; she specially loved myrtle, tuberoses, jasmin and gardenias. Labour was so cheap that flowers in the gardens were renewed every day, as we renew them now in a room; in the greenhouses at Trianon there were two million pots for bedding out.

The Hermitage was very simply decorated, the hangings were all of cotton and the furniture of painted wood; it was meant to be rustic, a farm house. It was such a success that she soon built two others, one at Compiègne designed by Gabriel, which has utterly disappeared, pulled down nobody even knows when or by whose orders, and one at Fontainebleau. The Fontainebleau Hermitage belongs now to the Vicomte de Noailles and is the only habitation of Madame de Pompadour's which she could visit to-day without grief. She never much liked her rooms in the palace there, and lived a great deal in this little house. The King would pretend he was going out hunting, leave the palace early in the morning booted and spurred, and spend the whole day with her, sometimes cooking their supper himself. People who liked to carp at her love of building used to say that she only had this Hermitage in order to offer the King a boiled egg from time to time. She had here one of the farmyards of which she was so fond, cows, goats and hens, and a donkey, whose milk was supposed to be particularly good for her.

The Réservoirs at Versailles (architect Lassurance) was only intended to be an overflow from her rooms in the palace, she never seems to have slept there. It is still called the Hôtel des Réservoirs, and still bears her coat-of-arms, but it has been enlarged and completely spoilt.

The only house of any size that Madame de Pompadour built was Bellevue (1750), all her other châteaux already existed when she bought them and were altered by her. Bellevue was the finest flower, inside and out, of eighteenth-century domestic architecture; its destruction was a terrible loss to France. (The royal houses which disappeared during the Revolution were not pulled down, burnt or looted by a furious mob. The government, hard put to it for money, to keep off the invading Austrians and Prussians, sold them all to speculators who disposed of them piecemeal; Chantilly and the Bastille were used as quarries for many years. It was at this time that rich English collectors acquired the treasures of French art which so greatly embellish our museums and country houses.) Bellevue was built on that wooded bank which hangs over the Seine between Sèvres and Meudon, and a beautiful view indeed it must have had, of the clean, sparkling and unspoilt city of Paris, with no blocks of flats, no *Electricité de France*, above all no rusty Eiffel Tower, to dwarf the domes and spires of the many churches. She employed her favourite architect, Lassurance, and, once the designs were approved, she left him to get on in his own way; when it was finished she stepped in and added her, entirely personal, touches. She had a horror of common or banal objects, or ones that were often copied, with fashionable motifs; if a piece of furniture was to please her it must be unique of its sort; the same applied to all her upholstery and hangings, always specially woven for her.

By order of the King, Bellevue had only nine windows on the front overlooking the river; marble busts decorated its otherwise simple façade. Inside were sculptures and vases by Pigalle, Falconnet and Adam, the panelling was by Verberckt, and painted decorations by Van Loo and Boucher. While the works were in progress, Madame de Pompadour wrote to d'Argenson. 'I have an enormous favour to ask. Boucher has been deprived of his *entrées* at the Opéra. Now it happens that he is engaged on the paintings at Bellevue, so he must be kept in a good temper—I'm sure you would hate to find a crippled or cock-eyed nymph in your pretty room . . .' The favour was granted and Boucher's *entrées* were restored to him. Boucher was, as it were, official painter to Madame de Pompadour, a position which, he said, he greatly preferred to that of Van Loo who was official painter to the Court.

The gallery at Bellevue was entirely designed by Madame de Pompadour herself; here Boucher's paintings were linked together with garlands of carved wood by Verberckt. The walls of all her rooms were either bluish-white and gold, or painted in bright pastel colours by members of the Martin family. The horrible 'gris Trianon', a dreary, yellowish grey, which now spoils so many French houses, was invented by Louis Philippe; nobody in the eighteenth century would have thought of using such a depressing colour to paint their rooms. As always, at her houses, the garden was a dream of beauty, terraces, bosquets, avenues of Judas trees, lilac and poplars, leading to cascades and statues. It was at Bellevue that she filled the garden with china flowers from Vincennes, which smelt like real ones, and quite took in the King with them.

The party to inaugurate her new house was a fiasco, though not because of the King's bad temper or lack of interest. She had worn herself out over every tiny detail, but it was one of those occasions on which nothing seems to go quite right. The uniforms for the guests were a present from her to them, purple velvet coats and off-white satin waistcoats, and the women's dresses of satin to match. They merely had to have them embroidered at their own expense. Unfortunately they clashed with the green liveries of her servants. She had arranged a fireworks display in the garden, but a message came from Paris that a hostile crowd was gathering on the Plaine de Grenelle, the other side of the river, so she hastily cancelled that. The November weather was bad, with a high wind; it got worse towards the evening, and the fires began to smoke. In the end the food had to be transported to a cottage she had built in the garden, variously called the Taudis, Babiole or Brimborian. When this disastrous evening was over, the Marquise retired to bed with a temperature, bitterly disappointed that a party so carefully prepared should have ended so badly. But it did not prove to have been a bad omen for the house and she was always very happy there.

Her next acquisition (1753) was the Hôtel d'Evreux which we know as the Elysée. When Madame de Pompadour bought it from the Comte d'Evreux, Pineau was already engaged upon the panelling; she let him go on with what he was doing, and occupied herself with the garden and furniture. There were the usual complaints of her extravagance—the curtains for each window were supposed to have cost five thousand *louis*. She took a big bite into the Champs Elysées for her kitchen garden, and would have taken a bigger had there not been a public outcry; then she made Marigny cut down all the trees between her garden and the Invalides of which she thus had an uninterrupted view. Probably it amused her to decorate a really grand town house; it was a palace by the time she had finished with it, with the royal coat of arms and enlaced L's everywhere. But she hardly ever slept there.

In 1757 she sold Bellevue to the King and took Champs from the Duc de la Vallière. She spent thousands on it, although it did not belong to her. It has recently been given to the French State by its owners and is used as a country house for the Prime Minister; it has been spoilt by restoration after suffering damage from the Germans in 1870, but a great deal of the original decoration remains, including a room painted by Huet, his last work before he died. The King disliked Champs and they used it very little. She also took a house from the Duc de Gesvres, St. Ouen, and made alterations to that. Finally she bought Ménars, on the Loire, but she only went there twice, at the end of her life; she left it to her brother and it became his home.

'The Palace of Ménars,' writes Mr. Joseph Jekyll to his sister-in-law, after a visit there in 1775, 'built by the late Marchioness of Pompadour on the banks of the Loire, at the distance of two leagues from here, and now in the possession of her brother, is one of the first in point of splendour in this kingdom, as you may conceive from its foundress, who, as the favourite of a great king, had the means, and joined to an exterior the most exquisite, that constitutional love of beauty which produces taste and order.

'There had been a prohibition of seeing the apartments in consequence of some impertinences similar to those committed in the Queen's Palace at London. Mr. Rockliff and myself were informed of this by the *suisses* at the gate. Sap was impossible, and I changed the manœuvre to an assault. I inquired for the Marquis, and announced some English gentlemen of Blois who begged to kiss his hand. We found him in the gout and a nightgown, the latter sparkling with the Cross of the Holy Ghost. I blundered out, "How fortunate we were in having an occasion of paying our court to M. le Marquis de Marigny, on begging permission to see the most elegant château in France, which was the *universal topic* of travellers in *London*." The reply to this was in an excess of politeness; and had I not urged the gout he would have stumped about the house with us. "This, gentlemen," said he, "is my library. Here is an edition of Terence, printed and given me by Walpole of Strawberry Hill. These chairs are English. How beautiful is your manufacture of horsehair for the bottoms! This is the Hall of Kings. There are the portraits of Louis XV, Christian of Denmark, and Gustave of Sweden, given me by their own hands." I observed that "there was a panel vacant for George III, and that if Monsieur would honour London with a winter's residence he would not fail of filling it." "I do not despair of seeing London," replied Monsieur. "I was once so near paying you a visit that my house was hired there, and the wine even laid into my cellars, when my sister, the late Marchioness of Pompadour, sent for me abruptly to Versailles. 'Monsieur, my brother,' said she, 'sell your house at London, and all your affairs there. In less than three months we shall have their Hawke and Boscawen thundering on our coasts.' Amongst the infinity of fine objects you will see at Ménars, don't overlook the hydraulique machine I have lately constructed on an improved plan of your affair at Chelsea. The first agent in mine is water, and it is a masterpiece of mechanics that would do honour even to an English artist." '

All these houses were furnished and embellished with a perfection of taste and attention to detail which can be realized by a perusal of her account with Lazare Duvaux, the retailer who found the necessary objects, or had them made, or re-mounted, and then sold them to her. On the eleventh of December, 1751, he sent her, at the Hermitage:

A little ormolu lantern, with lacquer trellis, decorated with flowers of Vincennes china. 336 *livres*.

Two screens of massive amaranthus wood. 48 *livres*.

Two small Dresden candlesticks. 48 *livres*.

Two *pots pourris* of India work, decorated with ormolu. 72 *livres*.

A figure in white Vincennes. A Chinese sunshade. 9 *livres*.

A dove cote on a column, with pigeons on the roof and a terrace with two figures and other pigeons. 168 *livres*.

And a whole farmyard of china animals, which she was for ever ordering; her rooms must have been full of them. At least once a week, and during some months, almost every other day, such an assortment was dispatched by Duvaux to one or other of her residences.

Not only did she do up houses for herself, she was continually suggesting alterations and improvements to the King's; Choisy and la Muette were always being pulled about by workmen, not to speak of Versailles.

The Marquise and her brother controlled all the artists in France, and were so tactful and knowledgeable that none of this touchy breed of men seems to have objected one single moment to their rule; on the contrary, when it came to an end, they were united in deploring the anarchy which succeeded it. La Tour, the pastellist, was the only one who showed any intransigeance. He was an eccentric who, when he wanted to go to St. Cloud from Paris, would take off his clothes and have himself towed up the river by a passing barge. He made a great fuss before he would consent to paint the Marquise at all, but he did consent, only making a condition that nobody was to come in during the sittings. One day the King appeared. La Tour pretended not to recognize him, packed up his things and grumbled off, 'You told me the sittings would not be interrupted.' Later, when he was painting the King, he tried to make a little political propaganda.

'Your Majesty realizes that we have no navy?'

The King, who would not have put up with such an impertinence from most people, merely replied: 'Oh surely—what about those ships M. Vernet is for ever painting?' He offered him the order of St. Michel, which conferred nobility on its possessor, but La Tour refused, saying that he wanted only to have nobility of sentiment and no other pre-eminence than that of talent.

When Marigny became *Intendant des Bâtiments*, he followed the excellent example set by M. de Tournehem and took an artist as his private secretary. He inherited Coypel from him, when Coypel retired he replaced him first by Lépicie and then, almost at once, by his old friend Cochin. Le Chevalier Cochin was a delightful man, embued, as was Marigny, with a positively religious love of art. Their correspondence is most satisfactory reading, it shows two good and clever men, in perfect accord with each other, absorbed in their work. They really ran the artists, found them lodgings and materials to work with, got orders for them, saw that they were paid, arranged the times of sittings, suggested subjects and were always at hand to help and encourage them. The result was that a happier community of artists has seldom existed. Cochin never says a disagreeable word about anybody. 'Chardin, whose integrity none can doubt— Parrocel, loved and esteemed by all—Bouchardon, whose career has been so glorious—a man of real merit, such as Vernet—the rare gifts of M. Tocqué' and so on. Neither he nor Marigny could endure the Comte de Caylus, the collector of antiques, but even in their private letters to each other they extol his enormous culture.

The most lasting of all Madame de Pompadour's achievements and the most profitable to France, both in money and in prestige, is the factory at Sèvres. She loved china in the same way that she loved flowers, and filled her rooms with it, more and more china, holding more and more flowers. From the Far East, India, Japan, Korea and China it was brought to her and the other amateurs, as well as from Saxony. She saw that much foreign currency was expended in this way and was careful to patronize the French factories at St. Cloud and Chantilly, and particularly that at Vincennes.

In 1754, Croÿ, supping with the King, arrived late and sat down at a little table in the window with M. de Lameth; the King was very kind to him, sent him various titbits and generally looked after him. When the meal was over the King made all his guests unpack a beautiful white, blue and gold dinner service from Vincennes, one of the first masterpieces of the china which was to surpass that of Dresden. Croÿ then heard that the King had given Madame de Pompadour the whole village of Sèvres, just below her house at Bellevue, where she was going to install the china factory, transferred from Vincennes, so that she would have it under her own eye. Here it prospered greatly, many artists and sculptors of the day worked for it; the wonderful colours, *Rose Pompadour*, *Bleu du Roi*, *Gros Bleu* and apple green were invented; the shapes were highly original, sometimes more reminiscent of silver than of porcelain; while the *biscuit* figures, by Pajou, Pigalle, Clodian, Falconnet, Caffieri and so on, have never been surpassed. To French taste, its products were superior to those of the Meissen factory. Once a year a sale of this china was held at Versailles in a room in the King's apartments, and the courtiers knew that it pleased him enormously when they bought; he sometimes acted as salesman himself. Beautiful as they admitted it to be, they thought it too expensive—twenty-eight *louis* for a sugar bowl and cream jug, twenty-five *louis* for a flower vase. Like most other things patronized by the Marquise it would have been an excellent investment at such prices.

A curious and charming craft, much liked by Madame de Pompadour, was the engraving of precious stones. A jeweller from Marseilles called Jacques Guay exercised his great talent in this medium. For years Madame de Pompadour commissioned most of his output and she left her collection to the King; it is now at the Bibliothèque Nationale. Nearly all the outstanding events of their life together are recorded in these tiny engravings: Portrait of Louis XV (onyx in three colours), Victory of Fontenoy (cornelian), Apollo (the King) crowning the spirit of Painting and Sculpture (cornelian), Madame de Pompadour's dog, Mimi (agate onyx), etc. There were seventy of them altogether, and Madame de Pompadour did a series of engravings from them. She was fond of engraving in *eau forte*, fonder of it than she was good at it; the famous copy of Rodogune, printed in her apartment, under her eyes, with *au Nord* on the title page, has a frontispiece engraved by her after Boucher.

Madame de Pompadour's books were sold the year after her death; the catalogue exists, a very revealing document, and one to drive a bibliophile mad with desire. It is clear that she read her books and did not simply have them as a wallpaper to her rooms; the books of somebody who reads are an infallible guide to the owner's mentality, and hers are a very individual assortment. In all there were 3525 volumes, roughly divided into the following categories:

87 translations from the classics.
25 French, Italian and Spanish grammars and dictionaries.
844 French poetry.
718 novels, including: *Manon Lescaut*; *La Princesse de Clèves*; *La Princesse de Montpensier*; *Histoire Amoureuse de la Cour*

*d'Angleterre* par le Comte de Hamilton; *Robinson Crusoe*; *Perkin, Faux Duc d'Yorck*; *Anecdotes Secrètes et Galantes sur la Cour d'Angleterre*; *l'Histoire de Cleveland, Fils Naturel de Cromwell*; *Milord Stanley, ou le Criminel Vertueux*; *Tom Jones*; *Roderick Random*; *Moll Flanders*; and *Amelia* (all translated).

52 fairy stories, including those of Perrault.

42 religious history.

738 history and biography.

235 music.

Only 5 books of sermons, including those of Bourdaloue, Massillon and Fénelon.

215 philosophy.

75 lives of writers.

Withdrawn from the sale, by Marigny, was *Représentations de M. le Lt. Général de Police de Paris sur les Courtisanes à la Mode et les Demoiselles de Bon Ton, par une Demoiselle de Bon Ton.*

These books were all bound in calf, or red, blue or citron morocco gilt, with the castles and the griffins of her coat of arms. She had a great love of beautiful morocco, and after her death several choice skins, ready for working, were found among her belongings.

Madame de Pompadour never seems to have sold any of the objects which belonged to her. They accumulated in their thousands, and filled all her many houses to overflowing; after her death Marigny was obliged to take two big houses in Paris which, as well as the Elysée and the Réservoirs, contained her goods until the sale of them began. Furniture, china, statues, pictures, books, plants, jewels, linen, silver, carriages, horses, yards and hundreds of yards of stuff, trunks full of dresses, cellars full of wine; the inventory of all this, divided into nearly three thousand lots, very few lots containing less than a dozen objects, took two lawyers more than a year to make. Few human beings since the world began can have owned so many beautiful things.

## Chapter Thirteen

# FROM LOVE TO FRIENDSHIP

THE years 1751–2 saw a change in Madame de Pompadour's relationship with the King, the outward and visible sign of which was that she moved into a new apartment, positively royal in its dimensions, on the ground floor of the north wing. At the same time we are invited to believe that she gave up sleeping with him. This fact is accepted by all the historians, and all her contemporaries, and is supported by a wealth of evidence, including Madame de Pompadour's own protestations on the subject. It is nothing if not unusual for a woman, no longer in her first youth, to want everybody to think that her lover has turned into her friend; and yet the Marquise announced the fact, she gave it out as it might be a marriage, or a birth, or some other interesting family event. If she did not actually send *lettres de faire part* to all her acquaintances, she did to the Pope, written in her own hand. Her friends at Court, primed, no doubt, by her, told everybody. At Bellevue, she put a statue of herself as *Amitié* in a bosquet hitherto dedicated to *l'Amour*—the Queen, on seeing it, could not repress a catty smile.

But was it true? The funny thing is that nobody ever seems to have asked that question, either at the time or subsequently. Madame de Pompadour was a very honest person, honesty and truth were the foundation of her character; in all her years at the Court she was never known to have told a lie. She was perfectly incapable of dissimulating her feelings, she had not a vestige of the sort of vanity which makes people pretend not to mind when things are going against them. So categorical a statement, coming from her, is a weighty piece of evidence.

The courtiers, valuable witnesses in a case like this, accepted the *amitié* with interest, but without question. The French pride themselves on second sight where love is concerned (to this day the Parisians know, or believe they know, the very minute two people have stopped sleeping together); all were agreed that friendship had now taken the place of love. They recalled that the King had already lived platonically with one of his mistresses, Madame de Mailly. At the beginning of their affair he only went to bed with her now and then, followed by a quick dash to confession. Certain historians explain everything by saying that, as indicated in Maurepas' poem, Madame de Pompadour had developed a complaint which made sexual relations impossible; the only evidence for this comes from gossip put about by her enemies who, as soon as it suited them to do so, did not hesitate to accuse her of being the mistress of the Duc de Choiseul. We do know that making love had never afforded her much pleasure, that it tired her and that she often had miscarriages. Some think that Dr. Quesnay positively ordered her to give it up. Unfortunately, Madame du Hausset throws no light at all on this most fascinating subject.

It must, however, be observed that the relationship between two human beings is seldom as cut and dried as other human beings like to imagine; the very blaze of publicity in which she left the King's bed throws a certain shadow of doubt. And Madame de Pompadour's new bedroom, like her old one, had a secret staircase leading to the King's.

As for the King, in his early forties, he was becoming rather middle-aged; M. de Croÿ describes him as riding heavily and not looking very well. He was more and more restless, moving off to a different house every week; in 1750 he only spent fifty days at Versailles. He seemed less passionate, neither as easily amused nor

6*

as easily bored as he used to be. He was gambling more than ever. A story, told to Dufort de Cheverny by the King's servants, is not without significance in this context. A certain rich widow of the Paris *bourgeoisie*, beautiful, elegant, young and well-educated, thought that she would like to replace the Marquise. She made friends with Lebel, who seemed to fall in with her scheme and promised to introduce her to the King. She was to go to Versailles on a certain evening, when a little supper would be arranged in the private apartments. The young woman dressed herself up, as may be imagined, in her very best, and went down to Versailles, calling first on some friends in the palace so that she would have a reason to give if anybody should see her coach in the Cour Royale. Punctually at 11.30 p.m., as arranged, she went to Lebel's room; he complimented her on her looks and her exactitude, but said she might have to wait a little while. Then, greatly to her dismay, he showed her into the King's bedroom, where the bed was turned down ready for the night, and left her; it was not at all what she had expected. She began to feel more and more embarrassed as the minutes went by, and she waited there nearly two hours. At last in came the King, who spoke to her exactly as if she were a prostitute, and behaved not much better. Accustomed as she was to being treated with the usual deep respect accorded to women at that time, she was very much put out, but of course it was now too late to withdraw, or enter into explanations.

'I must say you are a great deal prettier than I had expected you to be,' said the King, 'you seem altogether most attractive. Get into bed and I'll come back presently.' And off he went to his public *coucher*. Now it so happened that she had never in her life undressed herself without the help of a maid; her clothes were, of course, all done up down the back, with hundreds of hooks, very difficult to manipulate alone. However, she struggled out of them as best she could, and got into bed, where she waited another hour. At last the King returned, this time in his nightshirt. He joined her in the bed, looked at her and said: 'You are certainly very beautiful, but you know it's now three in the morning, and I'm not as young as I was; I don't think I shall be able to do you justice. I would like to keep you here all night, but it's really not possible and I think the best thing will be for you to go back to Paris. Put on your clothes and I'll see you past the sentries.'

Now if this lady had never undressed herself, still less had she ever dressed herself alone; under the eye of the King she managed somehow, and then he escorted her out into the dark, deserted palace. Of course, as soon as he had left her in its maze of passages, she was completely lost, and wandered about for ages before she came to her friends' flat. She cooked up some story about a carriage accident and spent the few remaining hours of night lying furiously on their sofa.

It is quite clear that what the King did not want was another Madame de Pompadour; he had already got one, he loved her, was used to her and she suited him perfectly. His mistresses, from now until after her death, were pretty little lower-class girls who did their work with no fuss, made no demands on him, had no influential relations or angry husbands, who did not insist upon their children being ennobled and who were content to retire with a modest dowry. These prostitutes, found for him by Lebel, were kept in the Parc aux Cerfs, a small villa in the town of Versailles. Occasionally they were lodged in an attic in the palace itself. They took no other part in the King's life. The courtiers always said that, if Madame de Pompadour had lived, Madame du Barry, good-natured, gorgeous, illiterate and common beyond belief, would have been treated like this; the King only established her in the palace with him because he was so lonely. Many of the inhabitants of the Parc aux Cerfs had no idea that their lover was the King; they were told that he was a rich Pole, a relation of the Queen's, indeed they were only told as much because he sometimes arrived in a great hurry, still wearing his

Cordon Bleu. They came and went in a fairly quick succession. It is said that the King's doctor warned him that he was making love too often. 'But you told me I could, as much as I wanted to, so long as I used no aphrodisiacs.' 'Ah! Sire! Change is the greatest aphrodisiac of all!'

The first and most famous occupant of the Parc aux Cerfs, who lasted there longer than any, was an Irish girl, Louise O'Murphy, commonly known as *La Morphil* or *La Morphise*. She was one of five or six sisters who, in spite of the fact that several of them were pock-marked, were all prostitutes. When their father, an Irish cobbler, was told that Louise was now the King's mistress, he exclaimed: 'Ah me, among all my girls not one is virtuous.' A ravishing beauty, Boucher's favourite model, we can still see her lovely round, angelic face in many of his compositions, nymph, goddess, saint and shepherdess (more sheep than shepherdess, Michelet says unkindly); the Queen saw it every day of her life among the Holy Family in her private chapel. As the first appearance of *La Morphil* coincided with Madame de Pompadour's move into the new flat, a great deal of interest was taken in her; at one moment she was expected to supplant the Marquise. However, when Alexandrine died, Lord Albemarle, the English Ambassador, reported: 'The affliction this unhappy accident has thrown her mother in is almost inexpressible. . . . The tender attachment His Most Christian Majesty has shown her on this occasion has plainly proved that her favour is not diminished whatever hopes her enemies may have raised upon the French King's *fancy* for Mlle Murphy.'

*La Morphil* never appeared at Court, though the Duc d'Ayen was allowed to meet her as a great favour, but went quite openly about her occasions in the town of Versailles, simply dressed and pretty as a peach; she always went to the Parish Church on Sunday. She inhabited the Parc aux Cerfs for several years and had one or two babies; her downfall was caused by saying to the

King: 'What terms are you on now with the old lady?' meaning
Madame de Pompadour. He gave her one of his freezing looks,
and she never saw him again. She was married off, with a good
dowry, to an officer from Auvergne who was soon afterwards
killed at the battle of Rosbach; their son, General Beaufranchet,
was present at the execution of Louis XVI.

Nineteenth-century historians, so easily shocked that it is impossible not to suspect them of hypocrisy, pretend to think that
Madame de Pompadour differed in no way from the prostitutes
of the Parc aux Cerfs and that furthermore she acted as manageress
of this establishment, procuring the girls for it and making all the
arrangements. According to them, she was not only a whore but
also a procuress. The truth is that she accepted the Parc aux Cerfs
as a necessity, but had nothing whatever to do with it. However,
she did prefer its inhabitants to any other sort of rival; these
uneducated children, she very well knew, would never endanger
her position in the King's heart. 'It's his heart I want,' she said,
over and over again. She was too honest not to see the facts as they
were, and she spoke quite openly on the subject.

'The King does pick up the most extraordinary expressions,'
she said to Madame du Hausset, 'for instance "*il y a gros*"' (meaning a big bet, probably.)

'He picks them up from those young ladies,' said the maid.
Madame de Pompadour laughed, and said, '*Il y a gros.*'

No doubt Carlyle, Lord Macaulay, Michelet, the Duc de
Broglie and so on would have found even this shocking enough;
but they had never been in love with Louis XV. Given all the
circumstances it is hard to see how else she could have behaved.

We only know of one occasion when she was actively concerned with these pleasures of the King. She sent for Madame du
Hausset, who found her alone with him, and said: 'I want you to
spend a few days at a house in the Avenue de St. Cloud, where
you will find a young woman about to have a baby. You must

take charge of the household; preside, like a goddess in a fable, over the birth; be present at the christening and give the names of the father and mother.'

Here the King began to laugh, saying: 'The father is a very good sort of fellow.' 'Loved by all,' said Madame de Pompadour, 'and adored by those who know him.' She took a diamond aigrette out of a little cupboard, and showed it to the King; 'I thought it should not be too grand.' 'How good you are,' he said, kissing her. Her eyes filled with tears and she laid her hand on his heart, saying: 'That's what I want'; whereupon they all began to cry. Presently the King spoke of god-parents for the baby, saying: 'Better get two people out of the street, so as not to attract attention, and give them a few *livres*.'

'Oh, give them a *louis*,' said the Marquise, 'or it will really seem too little.' The King said: 'Do you remember the cab driver? I wanted to give him a *louis* but the Duc d'Ayen said we should be recognized if I did.' Perhaps they had another little cry after this touching reminiscence. He then gave fifty *louis* to Madame du Hausset, saying: 'Look after the mother, won't you, she's a good girl, though not particularly brilliant.'

Madame du Hausset went off to the address she had been given, and here she found one of the King's men servants, already known to her, the 'abbesse' or matron in charge, a nurse, three old servants and a between maid. The expectant mother, pretty and well-dressed, was very much pleased with Madame de Pompadour's aigrette. When the child, a boy, was born, it was taken away and its mother was told that it was a girl, and dead. But later on it seems to have been given back to her. Madame du Hausset says that these children received a good income, which they inherited from each other, most of them dying young; seven or eight, she adds, had already died.

After the French Revolution, when the Monarchy was being blackened in every possible way, fabulous stories were told about the Parc aux Cerfs. It was said to have been a harem fit for a sultan, the scene of orgies without name, and to have cost the country millions. In fact, it was a modest little private brothel, run on humane and practical lines.

Madame de Pompadour's new apartment, where she now established herself and lived for the rest of her life, had once belonged to Madame de Montespan. When that magnificent mistress of Louis XIV left the Court, it had passed to their second son, the Comte de Toulouse, and it was still inhabited by his widow. The Toulouse family were by far the most human of all Louis XV's relations, and Madame de Toulouse, born a Noailles and married for love, was the nearest thing to a mother he had ever known. She was the only woman at Versailles who could go and see him without being announced; she even had the key to his study where the most secret papers were kept.

Now there was a general re-shuffle of lodgings. Madame de Toulouse moved into the flat of her son, the Duc de Penthièvre, and his wife. The Penthièvres were given that of the Duc d'Orléans, who had just died. The Duc d'Ayen got Madame de Pompadour's old flat on the second floor.

Everybody seems to have been delighted by the new arrangement, except the King's daughters, Mesdames Adélaïde and Victoire, who, now that they were grown up, had wanted the Toulouse apartment for themselves. Some said that Madame de Pompadour had been very clever in preventing this. Had the King got into the habit of going down one staircase to see his daughters they might have stopped him going up another to see his mistress. In this matter the Queen surprised the Court by taking Madame de Pompadour's side against Mesdames. She was jealous, and not very fond of them; it was the Dauphin whom she loved so much. Unfortunately for Versailles, the King was determined to have the Princesses near his own rooms; he pulled down the beautiful Ambassadors' Staircase, designed by le Vau, with frescoes by Lebrun, and built an apartment for them in its place.

Madame de Pompadour's ground floor apartment has been entirely destroyed. When Louis Philippe turned Versailles into a museum he altered the shapes of these rooms, took down the panelling and stored it in the cellar. Madame de Pompadour, who hated Prussians so much, would not have been surprised to learn that all the carving done for her by Verberckt ended up in stoves to keep the German soldiers warm in 1870. One of her rooms was panelled in red lacquer by the Martins; she liked it better than any she had ever had. Altogether the work took a year. Among other things the drains had to be entirely renewed; a huge marble bath, old-fashioned even in Madame de Montespan's day, dating from the time when two or three people liked bathing together, was removed and made into a fountain at the Hermitage. Twenty-two men could hardly lift it. (They were always tinkering about with the bathrooms at Versailles—there were 250 altogether in the palace—and on one occasion when the Queen's was out of commission for some reason, she sent a message asking if she could use one of the King's; this was immediately accorded.)

Madame de Pompadour had set her heart upon moving into her new flat after the voyage to Fontainebleau in 1751, and she bullied and teased M. de Tournehem to have it ready for her by then. He in his turn bullied and teased the foreman; their letters still exist and evoke all the difficulties of trying to get workmen out of a house, all the horrors of a move. 'Much more to be done than we expected; floors and chimneys are in a bad state; the carpenter never sends anything when he says he will; none of the built-in cupboards have come, so the painters cannot get on with their work.' Who has not had these things to contend with? Only—the carpenter was Verberckt and the painters were the Martins. Madame de Pompadour sent M. de Gontaut to see how it was getting on, but his report cannot have been very encouraging. In the end, she only moved in after Christmas. Then she complained that she could hear everything that went on in the State apartments overhead, so while she was at Compiègne the flooring was taken up and stuffed with gun cotton and flock. M. de Tournehem's last job as *Intendant des Bâtiments* was to arrange this palatial apartment for his niece; he died just before she moved into it.

The clique at Versailles whose avowed aim was to get rid of Madame de Pompadour were furious to see her so splendidly housed in a semi-royal apartment; and this against all their calculations. For 1751, Holy Year, was by way of being a difficult time for the Marquise, and her enemies had long centred their hopes on it. A wave of religious hysteria swept the land; the Jesuits thundered in the pulpits against immorality; in Paris the penitents heard Mass in sixty different churches, and were supposed to take part in at least five processions; the Dauphin and his sisters, buried in devotion, prayed night and day for the soul of their father. No doubt the Queen prayed too, but her prayers may have been modified by a certain spirit of realism. 'Madame de Pompadour had fever yesterday and was bled,' she wrote to Madame de Luynes at this time. 'I was terribly frightened, and not only, I must confess, from charitable motives.'

There was a great deal of speculation as to whether the King would, or would not, *faire son jubilé*, in other words, communicate at Easter; and the efforts of all the priests at the Court were directed at making him do so. Their hopes rose when he announced that he would not leave Versailles at all during Lent, and even altered his hunting days in order to hear the sermons. He particularly appreciated those of Père Griffet, which were well-composed and only lasted three-quarters of an hour.

At the end of Lent, while this moral offensive was at its height, Madame de Mailly died. After her sister had driven her from the

Court, she had lived only for God and good works, had worn a hair shirt and had mortified the flesh in every possible way. She was exactly the King's age, forty-one; he became very thoughtful on hearing of her death and wanted to hear all the holy details of her latter years. These things, coming together at a time when Madame de Pompadour said herself that she had lost her physical hold over him, were considered to be very dangerous for her, and the courtiers awaited developments with a breathless interest. Nothing whatever happened. The Queen performed her Easter duties one day, the Dauphin and the Dauphine on another and then the Princesses; but the King did not.

As soon as Lent was over, the little voyages began again as usual; the King and the Marquise collected the eggs and visited the goats, they gambled, he hunted and together they planned the decoration of her new rooms. There was rather an unsuccessful season of the private theatre at Bellevue. The Duc de la Vallière was not too sure of his words; but on the other hand M. de la Salle sang charmingly and was rewarded with the governorship of a province—a piece of news very badly received by various Marshals of France who would have liked the job.

A more serious occupation was the project for the Ecole Militaire. This was entirely Madame de Pompadour's idea, to show the soldiers that the King took a true interest in them and their welfare. The old and disabled had already been provided for at Les Invalides by Louis XIV; now, within a stone's throw, his descendant would create an establishment for theirs. The cradle and the grave of heroes, side by side. Five hundred boys, sons of officers whose families had a claim to nobility, were to be taken at the age of eight and given a general education, to include Latin and foreign languages. At eighteen, they would receive commissions in the army. Madame de Pompadour had arranged the financial side of her scheme with Pâris-Duverney who put up the money for it; he was to be repaid by the profits on a lottery and a tax on playing cards. The King approved the plan, and it now remained for M. Gabriel to do his part. He was given a studio over the Réservoir at Versailles; here he made an enormous model of the school, which was to be built on the Plaine de Grenelle, with its grounds extending to the river. Very soon, stone brought by the Oise and wood by the Marne came floating down the Seine, to be unloaded and dumped on the future Champ de Mars. Building proceeded apace, and in five years the first batch of little boys was housed there. The whole project was only completed in 1770; in 1784 the name of Buonaparte, Napoleon, appeared on the register, as having arrived for his first term, aged fifteen. Owing to money troubles the Ecole Militaire was only one-third of its intended size, but even so, nobody would ever be able to say again that Louis XV had not left a durable monument to posterity.

## Chapter Fourteen

# THE *AFFAIRE* CHOISEUL-ROMANET

THE Church having failed to separate King and Marquise, in spite of the spiritual power so impressively displayed during Holy Year, Madame de Pompadour's enemies saw that their only hope now lay in another woman. A pretty face, cleverly manœuvred, must do their work for them. Her chief enemy, the most dangerous and the most determined, was still the Comte d'Argenson, and he was seconded by Madame d'Estrades.

This cousin and bosom friend whom Madame de Pompadour had brought with her to Versailles now began to show her true colours; she was not very nice. She seems to have been eaten up with jealousy. In spite of daily acts of kindness and countless privileges received at the hands of the Marquise the horrible little creature turned on her friend almost from the beginning. First of all, though excessively plain, with her pendulous cheeks, she tried to worm herself into the King's bed. One night at Choisy, when Madame de Pompadour was ill upstairs, the King got very drunk—a thing which seldom happened—and Madame d'Estrades had him to herself for an hour or two. He never could remember afterwards what had occurred but she did not fail to tell the Marquise that she had been obliged to fight for her honour.

After this Madame d'Estrades began to plot with d'Argenson against Madame de Pompadour, carrying tales, making trouble, dangerous as only an intimate friend can be. She became d'Argenson's mistress and soon she was the most powerful woman in

France, except for the Marquise herself; those who, like the Prince de Croÿ, had *affaires* to prosecute were obliged to be very assiduous in their attentions to her. Some people liked her, Croÿ for one. She was clever and amusing, and knew the Court inside out; her love for d'Argenson was certainly quite genuine. But nothing can excuse her behaviour to Madame de Pompadour.

The Marquise continued to trust her, even after the episode at Choisy, and never believed those who uttered words of warning. She made the King appoint her lady-in-waiting to Madame Adélaïde, a post which brought a good income and greatly increased her importance at Versailles. In 1752, when the Court barometer was still registering stormy days ahead for the Marquise, Madame d'Estrades and d'Argenson saw a chance of getting rid of her. If they could do so they thought that their influence with the King would be so great that they would really be the rulers of France.

Some years before, Madame d'Estrades had arranged a marriage between a young cousin of her own, a Mademoiselle Romanet, and a member of the aristocratic Choiseul family. Madame de Pompadour, to whom the most remote family connexions, even the cousin of a cousin of her husband, were always dear, had arranged a wedding party for the young people at Bellevue. She had lent them the house for their honeymoon, had given them sumptuous presents, and thereafter had been kindness itself to them. Entirely owing to her they became members of the King's little set, often went on the voyages, were invited to the supper parties and so on; they had far more fun than most young couples at the Court.

The bride, an extremely pretty little prattler, hardly out of her nursery, amused the King, and Croÿ says several times in his journal that it was perhaps not very wise of Madame de Pompadour to throw them together quite so much. A great deal of amorous ragging went on, and Madame de Choiseul was heard to say that never would she leave her husband, except, of course, for the King. She was not the first to have expressed this sentiment. In fact the King was very much taken with her. She kept him on a string and kept Madame d'Estrades informed of her progress, hour by hour. Madame d'Estrades knew him well enough to know exactly how he should be managed; and she conducted this vicarious affair brilliantly. She told the little girl what she must do, adding that it was essential for her to make Madame de Pompadour's exile a first condition of surrender. Things reached a climax during the autumn voyage to Fontainebleau. The King had twisted his knee on a dark staircase leading to Madame de Choiseul's room, without any reward; he was getting cross and impatient, the time had clearly come for the angel to fall.

While the angel was thought to be engaged in doing so, Madame d'Estrades and d'Argenson were waiting impatiently in the Minister's room. Dr. Quesnay, and Dubois, d'Argenson's secretary who described the scene to Marmontel, also happened to be there. At last the door burst open, in came Madame de Choiseul, very much rumpled, no doubt at all as to what had been happening to her, and flung herself into Madame d'Estrades' arms. 'Yes, yes, I am loved, he is happy, she is to be sent away.' All were delighted, except Dr. Quesnay.

D'Argenson said to him: 'But, Doctor, this will make no difference whatever to you—you will stay on at the Court.' 'Me, M. le Comte?' said the doctor shortly, as he got up to go, 'I stick to Madame de Pompadour, fair or foul,' and he left the room. D'Argenson looked rather worried, but Madame d'Estrades said: 'He'll never give us away, I know him too well to think that.' She was quite right, Quesnay could be counted on never to give anybody away. But all the same, their plans were defeated.

A new character now came into Madame de Pompadour's life, who was soon to play an enormous part in it. This was the Comte de Stainville, another member of the Choiseul family (known to history as the Duc de Choiseul, which he became in 1758). He was the brother-in-law of M. de Gontaut, Madame de Pompadour's friend from Etioles days, who was for ever telling these two how well they would get on; indeed given their characters it seemed that they must rejoice in each other's company. Greatly to Gontaut's disappointment, however, they at first particularly disliked each other. Stainville went but seldom to Versailles, he was a Parisian by inclination and a soldier by profession; he paid his court to the King when duty obliged him to do so, and not more.

It so happened that he was at Fontainebleau during this fateful voyage, and had observed the conduct of his young cousin with a great deal of disgust; he was proud of his family name and had no wish to see it dragged in the mud. One of the greatest lady killers of the century, he was on semi-flirtatious terms with Madame de Choiseul and she, either to make herself more interesting in his eyes, or because she was not quite certain of her next move, took him into her confidence and showed him a letter from the King. It was very long, left no doubt as to their relationship and was full of promises to send away Madame de Pompadour. Madame de Choiseul assumed that Stainville would be only too delighted to see her installed as titular mistress; few cousins at that Court would have objected to a relationship so greatly to the advantage of the family concerned. When he asked if he could keep the letter until next day, to think it over, the little goose consented.

Stainville's motives in this matter are rather mysterious. Was he really so much preoccupied with the honour of the Choiseuls? Was he himself in love with the young lady? Or did he see that the opportunity of a lifetime had come his way? With Madame de Choiseul installed as the King's mistress he would have had every opportunity of feathering his nest. But money was of less interest to him than to most people, since his wife was one of the richest women in France. If he had already turned his thoughts to power he may have considered that his silly little cousin would never be much help in achieving that. Be it as it may, he put the letter into his pocket and went off to find M. de Gontaut, who, like everybody else by then, could talk of nothing but the *affaire* Choiseul-Romanet. Madame de Pompadour, he said, was in a perfectly frantic state of mind over it, and the faithful fellow was very much distressed on her account. His brother-in-law let fall a great many mysterious hints; he had it in his power, he said, to put an end to her anxiety; but as he and the Marquise were on the worst of terms, it really rather amused him to sit back and watch the situation develop, knowing all the time that he had but to say a word . . .

'Well then, say it!' cried Gontaut, beside himself. But Stainville had to be pressed much harder; Madame de Pompadour must be made to realize to the full the value of his intervention, should he decide to intervene. Only after Gontaut had brought him a series of imploring messages from her, did he allow himself to be conducted to her room. They found her in tears, and she was not very much consoled by what Stainville had to tell her, which was that Madame de Choiseul was expecting a baby, and her husband was taking her away from the Court in a few weeks' time. At last he thought that the moment had come to produce his trump card, the letter. When the Marquise read this, tears gave way to temper and she flew into a great rage.

Madame de Pompadour was one of those rare women who know exactly when, and how, to make a scene. When the King went to her room that evening as usual, for a little chat before working with his Ministers, a tempest broke over his head for which he was quite unprepared and against which he had no defence. But when he saw his letter in the hands of the Marquise, and heard how it had come there, he in his turn flew into a rage with Madame de Choiseul. He stormed off to find her; the poor little wretch and her husband were obliged to leave Fontainebleau that very night. Six months later she died, having a baby; she was only nineteen.

D'Argenson and Madame d'Estrades were disgusted by the failure of their plans, and even more disgusted when, a few days later, the King bestowed on Madame de Pompadour the rank and enormous privileges of a Duchess. With her usual good taste she still called herself Marquise, but assumed the ducal coronet and mantle on her coat of arms, dressed her men servants in scarlet, and sat on a stool in the presence of the Queen. She was presented, on her new rank, by the Princesse de Conti as before; and, as before, Madame d'Estrades accompanied her when she made her curtseys to the King and the Queen.

For Stainville this episode was the beginning of a meteoric career. Madame de Pompadour realized that, after all, she liked him very much indeed; he thought her perfectly remarkable. They became intimate friends in a very short time, Gontaut saying he had always known that they were made for each other. Not unnaturally, however, after what had happened, the King could not bear the sight of Stainville. Stainville complained of this to the Marquise who said: 'Nonsense, he likes you very much,' and asked him to supper. But after supper he won a large sum of money from the King, which did not help matters at all. At last Madame de Pompadour, realizing that Stainville was quite right, had it out with the King, saying that if he was against him because of what had happened at Fontainebleau she must take it that he was against her, too, since Stainville's intervention in this matter had been entirely to her advantage. She then asked him to send Stainville as Ambassador to Rome, and, rather grumpily, he did so.

Madame de Pompadour knew quite well that Madame d'Estrades and the hated d'Argenson had been behind Madame de Choiseul, encouraging her in her intrigue for all they were worth.

She longed for an excuse to get rid of her cousin. It was not so easy. The King was used to her; he liked her company and her wonderful talent for gossiping; she formed part of his little circle. He had no proof that she was a treacherous friend. For three years more Madame de Pompadour had to see her all day and every day and try to behave as if none of this had happened.

At last, however, Madame d'Estrades went too far. She abstracted a memorandum on the political situation, in the King's writing, from the table by Madame de Pompadour's bed. She alone could have done it as the only other people who had been in the room were Madame d'Amblimont, who could have had no possible interest in the paper, and M. de Gontaut who was above suspicion. While the King was still annoyed over this, Madame de Pompadour went to see Madame Adélaïde and asked if Madame d'Estrades had not become rather a bore. Madame Adélaïde had, in fact, never liked her much, though chiefly because she was put in her household by the Marquise. She intimated to her father that she would be glad to see the last of her and have a different lady-in-waiting, less pretentious and better born. The King gave way at last, and the blow fell, as usual, without warning.

During a visit to La Muette, when it had poured with rain for several days and the two women were seen to be very much on each other's nerves, Madame d'Estrades said to Madame de Pompadour that she had one or two things to do in Paris, and asked what time she should be back for supper. 'The usual time, Comtesse.' She had not gone very far before her carriage was stopped and she was handed a note from the King. It banished her from the Court and intimated that her room would be given to M. de Tessé; but stated that she would retain her salary as lady-in-waiting and be permitted to live in her house at Passy.

While she was reading this, Madame de Pompadour came by in her coach. It must regretfully be stated that she hung out of the window to relish the scene.

## Chapter Fifteen

## POLITICS AT HOME

MADAME de Pompadour's excursion into politics will not give much satisfaction to the feminist. Although she was prettier, better educated, and had a more natural motive for her activities, she was no more successful than those ladies who adorn to-day the *Chambre des Députés*, nor had she any more influence than they over the general trend of events. To her, as to most women, politics were a question of personalities; if she liked somebody he could do no wrong—a good friend was sure to make a good general, a man who could write Latin verses, and amuse the King, a good minister. Political problems in themselves were of no interest to her, her talents did not lie in that direction. Marigny, who was in almost every way her male counterpart, never would touch the various ministries she was for ever pressing upon him; he knew his own limitations too well. She was not driven to this unsuitable career by a longing for power but by her love for the King. He was by now immersed in the intricate, delicate and dangerous politics of the day, and spent most of his thought on them. The Marquise could no longer distract him with frivolities. She could only continue at his side, a true companion and helpmeet, by turning herself into his private secretary; with her usual energy she proceeded to do so.

France was governed, at this time, by a *Conseil d'Etat* composed of a varying number of ministers and one or two Princes of the Blood; it worked at Versailles, under the presidency of the King. Hitherto the Prince de Conti, his favourite cousin, an able and ambitious man, had acted as the King's private secretary. The ministers had no power of their own; they were advisers, counsellors to the King, and appointed by him. As there was no Prime Minister the man who had the strongest personality, or in whom the King had the most confidence, led this cabinet. In time of war the War Minister and the Foreign Minister were particularly important; in time of peace the *Garde des Sceaux*, whose functions were those of our Lord Chancellor, and the Controller General. They often doubled their charges; Machault, for instance, was Minister of the Marine as well as *Garde des Sceaux*, and they sometimes exchanged jobs. They stayed in the *Conseil* at the King's pleasure, usually for many years. When Maurepas was disgraced, he had been Minister for thirty-one years, Orry for fifteen. A certain M. Silhouette, whose ministry (of finance) lasted less than a year, gave his name to something shadowy and fleeting, a mere outline. (He was really sent away for boring the King. The first day of his office he came primed with facts and figures; the King only asked him if the panelling in his study at Versailles was gilded. The poor man, who had not noticed, was so taken aback that he was struck dumb. The King went off with a resigned shrug and Madame de Pompadour said: 'You should have answered—said yes or no—he wouldn't go and see for himself. Now it will take me a week to bring him round to you again.')

The *Conseil* appointed thirty *intendants* who governed the provinces and collected the direct taxes; their powers were so great that they could make or mar the happiness of the thousands under their sway. They always belonged to the *noblesse de robe*, the *noblesse d'épée* would have despised such a job, though the titular head of each province was a *noble d'épée*. Besides the *Conseil d'Etat* there were the *Etats Généraux* and the *Parlements*. The *Etats* had not been summoned since 1614, but had never been suppressed and were therefore still a part of the Constitution.

They represented the Clergy, Nobility and Commoners, but neither the number and qualifications of their electors, nor their procedure and their powers, had ever been precisely determined. The *Parlements*, whose organization had hardly changed since the fourteenth century, sat in 14 important towns; the most powerful of them sat at Paris, in the *Palais de Justice*. These *Parlements* bore but little relation to ours, since their members were not elected, and their powers were judicial, not legislative, but they always had an eye on Westminster and as the English Parliament became more powerful, so they became more pretentious, until finally they persuaded themselves that they represented the nation. In fact, if they represented anything at all, it was the King rather than the people. The Paris *Parlement* was the supreme court of justice, its members, the *noblesse de robe*, were magistrates, and their office was hereditary; though it could also, in certain circumstances, be disposed of for money. Princes of the Blood, peers of the realm and bishops could also sit in the *Palais de Justice*, but it was not the custom for them to do so. Apart from their judicial functions, the Magistrates had certain political rights, they could refuse to register laws passed by the *Conseil d'Etat*, and they alone could register and legalize the taxes. The Magistrates were like one large family; indeed they were very much intermarried, and they were nearly all Jansenists. They were proud and self-important and despised every other section of the community, though they had a certain respect for Louis XV.

Meanwhile the country was really run by its Civil Servants (in those days a royal bureaucracy), for whose excellence France has always been noted. They were busily transforming the ports, the harbours and all communications. In 1744 the mines were nationalized, that is to say everything under the ground was declared to be the property of the King. Their exploitation was left in private hands, but was regulated by a very enlightened *code des mines*, enforced by regular visits from inspectors.

France in the nineteenth century was far ahead of all other countries as regards nationalization because of the enormous wealth o
her Kings; so much of the country's land and industry had belonged to them and had then passed into the hands of the Repub-
lic. If to-day it is possible to be in a deep forest twenty minutes
away from Paris it is because these were all royal forests in the first
place, and have never been at the mercy of the private owner. The
Sèvres, Gobelins, Aubusson and Savonnerie factories all belonged
to the King and were subsequently nationalized.

The troubles between Church and State which are sure to be
endemic in a non-Protestant but highly individualistic country
were then, as now, the curse of French political life; then,
as now, they occupied too much attention at a time when
public energy should have been concentrated on more important
matters. In 1749, Machault, who had succeeded Maurepas, saw
that money was badly needed to build more ships. Backed up by
the King, he decided to levy a tax, called *le vingtième*, a sort of
income tax of five per cent, to be paid by all classes including the
clergy. He also asked for a declaration of property.

The clergy, richer than any other section of the community, did
not care for the prospect of paying the tax and still less for that of
declaring their revenues. Their system of tax-paying was that they
made presents to the State from time to time, the amount fixed
by themselves; it was against their conscience to do more. They
spoke a great deal about their divine immunity. Every year the
Secretary of State and the Archbishop of Paris would meet to
discuss this matter; the Secretary of State exposing in energetic
terms the King's financial needs and difficulties, to which the
Archbishop would ripost with a heartrending account of the
desperate position in which the Church found itself. Machault,
however, attacked with rather more vigour and determination
than his predecessors; public opinion seemed to be on his side and
the clergy saw the moment coming when it would be impossible

to avoid paying taxes any longer. With a perfect indifference to any call of patriotism, they made a diversion by stirring up as much trouble as they could, against the ministers, against the *Parlement*, against the Protestants, and above all against the Jansenists.

Jansenism proper had practically died out under the persecutions of Louis XIV. The plough had been driven over the ruins of Port Royal, the inhabitants of its graveyard had been dug up, hacked into suitable joints and removed to some spot where there was no danger that they would attract pilgrims. In 1713 the Jesuits completed their victory by procuring a Papal Bull, Unigenitus, condemning 101 propositions in a popular book of devotion as Jansenist and therefore heretical. The result was that many people, who had never suspected the fact before, found themselves labelled Jansenist. At the beginning of the reign of Louis XV, a popular kind of Jansenism had evolved, anathema to the Court and the fashionable world—dowdy and ridiculous, with its nuns mewing like cats and barking like dogs, its convulsionists and flagellationists, eaters of earth and swallowers of live coals. The King regarded it with a great distaste while the Queen felt so violently against it that she was nicknamed Unigenita.

The Jesuits were determined to establish control of the Church in France; the great Magistrates of the *Parlements*, who considered themselves guardians of this Church's liberties, were equally determined to prevent them from doing so. It was this struggle between the Jesuits and a neo-Jansenist section, supported by the *Parlements*, which the clergy now saw fit to exacerbate. They refused the sacraments, including extreme unction, to anybody unable to produce a certificate stating that he had confessed to a qualified priest. Confession to priests of the lower clergy suspected of Jansenism was not accepted as valid. Those dying without *billets de confession* were refused extreme unction. Their relations would then apply to the *Parlement de Paris* which would issue an order for the arrest of the priest who had refused. The Archbishop of Paris would then appeal to the King who in his turn would issue an order quashing that of the *Parlement*.

A bitter quarrel now broke out between *Parlement* and the Church. The Magistrates alleged that it was part of their police duties to ensure that citizens duly received the sacraments. The Church itself was given over to the old arguments, which had been thrashed out time without number in the course of a hundred years, between Jesuit and Jansenist. 'The country,' says Mgr. Knox, 'that had once been so rich in saints and mystics was now condemned to dissipate its energies in controversy . . . which weakened [the Church's] influence and left her ill-prepared to face the crisis of the Revolution.' The importance attached to this affair may be judged by the fact that Maupéou, senior President of the *Parlement*, wrote to the King: 'Your *Parlement* has never been brought to the steps of your throne by a matter of such gravity...'

The King was now obliged to make up his mind whether to support his Church or his Magistrates. So far he had always managed to avoid taking sides between them; but a grave situation was developing. In Paris there were riots, priests were beaten up or forced at pistol point to take the sacraments to dying Jansenists. A nun called Sœur Perpetuée was said to be paid by the *Parlement* to die slowly and ostentatiously, while an argument raged as to whether she should, or should not, receive extreme unction. At last the King had her shut up in a convent and no more was heard of her. People began to fear a civil war, the dreaded word Fronde was heard again, and it began to look as if the rivers of ink which had already flowed over Unigenitus were going to turn into rivers of blood. On the whole the King leant towards the Jesuits, though he was far from approving everything they did. His family was blindly on their side. Madame de Pompadour, with her philosophical upbringing, should have provided a counter weight, but the years at Court had not been without their effect on her; the word *Parlement* seemed to strike rather a dubious note, evoking Cromwell, and dreadful republicanism. Besides she knew quite well that the Magistrates disapproved of her extravagance, at a time when public funds were low and there was talk of a new tax. Let it not be thought that the *Parlements* were any more anxious to pay the *vingtième* than was the Church.

Finally the King came down on the side of the Church and exiled the *Grand' Chambre* (the highest court) of the *Parlement* to Pontoise (May 1753). He said that in the future he himself would be the arbiter as regarded sacraments. The place of the *Grand' Chambre* was taken by a *chambre de vacations* composed of *Conseillers d'Etat* and *Maîtres des Requêtes*; but this lacked the authority of the *Parlement*.

At Pontoise *Messieurs les Présidents* kept great state. They never went out except in coaches-and-six; they entertained each other and the whole neighbourhood lavishly. After some months, the inconvenience of the King's action began to be felt. Nobody could go to law. Perhaps this did not matter very much, people often settled out of court, but there were other consequences. The Magistrates were putting out a very convincing propaganda in which they represented themselves as the defenders of public liberty. The winter was a hard one; all the humble but literate men who depended on the Palais de Justice for a livelihood were unemployed and consequently in great distress. They stirred up trouble among the masses. The police were afraid to interfere in the cafés and on the streets where insurrection was openly being planned. 'Burn Versailles' was heard and other revolutionary slogans. The Prince de Conti, who, as he lived in Paris, was more in touch with public opinion than the King, saw the necessity of recalling the *Grand' Chambre*, and, if possible, of raising something in the way of taxes from the clergy. The King seemed to be on the point of recalling it, but then he changed his mind and issued further *lettres de cachet* sending some of its members to Soissons and some to other provincial towns. This was a very severe measure; the Magistrates were now debarred from holding any meetings. It was not until September 1754 that the King decided to reinstate his *Parlement*, which returned to Paris, amid scenes of wild rejoicing, the same week that Louis XVI was born.

The King enjoined a ban of silence on the subject of the recent controversy, and the prelates were advised to lie low for a bit. But the Archbishop of Paris, Christophe de Beaumont, was not an accommodating man. When the King appointed him, in 1745, he did not at first want to accept. In those days he was said to have a sweet, and even timid, nature; if so he had hardened up considerably. He was the most implacable enemy of the *Encyclopédie* and hated Madame de Pompadour so much that he said he would like to see her burnt; he refused her permission to reserve the sacraments in her chapel at the Elysée. Very soon he broke the King's ban of silence and refused extreme unction to yet another old dying Jansenist.

The King, taking no notice of his family, who filled the palace with their moans and groans, exiled the Archbishop to his country house, 3rd December, 1754. Three days later *Parlement* registered taxes to the tune of a hundred million *livres*.

'That,' they said, 'is the end of the Bull.'

'Unfortunately, though,' said the King, as he once more imposed silence on the subject, 'the Bull happens to be the law of the land.'

The sacraments continued to be refused; the next victim of note was the Duchess of Perth. However it transpired that her husband had been one of the convulsionists of St. Médard, a church which had been shut by the King when the convulsions there were forbidden in 1732.

> *De par le Roi, défense à Dieu*
> *De faire miracle en ce lieu.*[1]

[1] 'By order of the King, God is forbidden to perform miracles on this spot.' Written up by some wag on the church door.

So the case of the Duchess was allowed to drop, but others came up almost every day and in every part of the country. Between the years 1751-6, Barbier, the Parisian notary and diarist, who always reported Parliamentary doings in his journal, has nothing to record but the intensely dreary details of this squabble. Not a thought is given to foreign or colonial affairs; all of every page is devoted to the Bull, the refusal of sacraments, *remontrances* from *Parlement* to King, his replies, burning of books by the public executioners, and pastoral letters. Even the Duc de Luynes turns his attention from details of court usage to those of Jansenist death beds.

All the Bishops were not as intransigent as Christophe de Beaumont, and in May 1755 the Assembly of the Clergy met in Paris to decide once and for all whether non-submission to the Bull necessarily meant separation from the Church. The Bishops were divided on the question and the King resolved to ask the Pope for a ruling. This delicate matter was entrusted to Stainville, now Ambassador in Rome; it was his first big political opportunity and one of which he made the most. He received his instructions from Versailles via the Marquise, with whom he was in constant correspondence.

'I madly love the Holy Father,' she wrote, 'and I hope my prayers are efficacious as I pray for him every day. What he said about the *billets de confession* is worthy of a pastor who wishes for peace. . . . *They* seem to be satisfied with your services. M. de Machault is thin and altered. I am doing all I can to be instructed about the well-being of the State.' In the intervals of thanking for cameos and asking for a piece of the True Cross, and the price of a rose diamond in which to set it—finally she put it in a crystal heart with a cross of rose diamonds—she explained to him that he must somehow get a statement out of the Pope which would, without repudiating the previous Bull, uphold the freedom of the French Church.

Benedict XIV was an enlightened and scholarly man, very much admired by Voltaire. He had already written to Cardinal de Tencin suggesting that the French clergy might occupy itself with useful and edifying works rather than spend its time squabbling over *ragazzate*. He and Stainville were on excellent, even joking terms, and understood each other perfectly. On one occasion when Stainville, always very emphatic, was laying down the law, the Pope rose from his throne, and pointing to it he said, 'Perhaps you would like to sit here?' Between them they drew up an encyclical, which limited the refusal of the sacraments, but maintained that the Bishops had an ultimate right to refuse. 'In order to avoid a scandal, the priest must warn the dying, suspected of Jansenism, that they will be damned, and then give them communion at their own risk and peril.'

This encyclical displeased the extremists on both sides; neither *Parlement* nor the Jesuits wanted to accept it. On 13th December, 1756, the King, however, went to the *Palais de Justice*, which he was legally entitled to do, and registered the encyclical. He also registered an edict of submission to himself by which he removed certain powers from the two courts known as *Enquêtes* and *Requêtes*. Their members immediately went on strike as a protest. The encyclical served its purpose, as far as Jansenist death beds were concerned, and from now on they ceased to occupy the attention of the whole country. The King had scored a distinct triumph. He was satisfied with the part played by Stainville and sent him the order of the St. Esprit.

'I madly love the Holy Father.' While Madame de Pompadour was busy learning the affairs of state, she turned her attention to another interest of the King's, in which it seemed desirable that she should share. During the early days of her life with him, she had studied the story of Madame de Montespan, Louis XIV's superb mistress, mother of his children; now she concentrated on that of Madame de Maintenon, the barren but enormously powerful wife of his old age. She read all the biographies of her that she could find, and subscribed to a new one that was being written. The author was advised, if he wished to please his patroness, not to make too much of Louis XIV's affairs with younger and prettier women. The Duc de St. Simon died in 1755 and the manuscript of his memoirs passed into the royal archives; she had all the passages about Madame de Maintenon copied out for her. In those days the history of preceding reigns was not easy of access; most of the relevant letters and diaries were still unpublished, and the *Gazette de France* was a very rudimentary news sheet (the Versailles correspondent was always one of the King's musicians). We, to-day, know much more about the seventeenth century than anybody knew in the eighteenth. Madame Geoffrin, admittedly not very well educated, thought that Henri IV was the son of Henri III until she read Président Hénault's *History of France*.

Madame de Pompadour made one little mistake about her predecessor. She saw pictures of that hideous old face all over the palace; she knew that Madame de Maintenon was forty-nine when she married Louis XIV, and far too priggish to have been his mistress before that, and she therefore assumed her hold over the King to have been purely intellectual and religious. She must have forgotten to take the Bourbon temperament into account. We know that when Madame de Maintenon was seventy-five and the King seventy she told her confessor that it tired her very much to make love with him twice a day and asked whether she was obliged to go on doing so. The confessor wrote and put the question to his Bishop, who, of course, replied that as a wife she must submit. However, religion and a community of interests had, in fact, been the chief link between Madame de Maintenon and Louis XIV, and it was one which Madame de Pompadour wished to strengthen between herself and her King. She decided that she must become devout so that she and he could have a holy old age together; once again she demonstrated her perfect incomprehension of the Roman Catholic religion.

She began by going a great deal to the Convent of St. Louis, and interesting herself in the young women of poor, but noble, families who were educated there. She also became a regular visitor to St. Cyr so full of august memories, founded by Madame de Maintenon, and the scene of her death. Here the nuns fell under her charm, and the Mother Superior spoke of her as 'that Vestal.' She ordered a beautiful Book of Hours, illuminated by Boucher, with a Turris Davidica strangely reminiscent of the three towers on her own coat of arms. Lazare Duvaux, who supplied her with bibelots, was called in to mend her crucifix. Among such items on her account with him as a seal in the form of a negro's head, decorated with rubies and diamonds, a transparent blind in Italian taffetas, painted with bouquets and garlands, a chocolate box in rock crystal, we find a vessel for holy water in Vincennes china, decorated with cherubs, on black velvet with a gilded frame and destined for the Holy Father whom she loved so madly. She fasted in Lent, which she had never done before, spoke of giving up rouge, which would indeed have been considered a sign of piety; she prayed very often at the tomb of Alexandrine, and her conversation was full of such clichés as 'revealed religion,' 'a Christian life,' 'a state of Grace.' She read holy books and wished that Voltaire would translate the Psalms, went every day now to the chapel, sitting downstairs among the ordinary people instead of in her semi-royal box in the gallery, and stayed on long after the service was over, plunged in interminable adoration. Most extraordinary of all, she had the secret staircase between her room and the King's walled up.

This spectacular piety was the talk of the Court. The Duc de la Vallière wrote to Voltaire: 'A ray of grace has fallen, but there is no intoxication. A few little changes bear witness to it. We have given up going to the play, we fast three times a week during Lent . . . the few moments we can spare for reading are devoted to holy works. Otherwise, charming as ever and quite as powerful, we lead the same life with the same friends, of whom I flatter myself that I am one.'

The Abbé de Bernis saw fit to talk to her like a Nanny: 'I told her straight out that not one soul was going to be taken in by this play acting, everybody would say she was nothing but a hypocrite and that as it wasn't real she would soon be tired of it; that she looks stupid enough now, nothing to what she will when she gives it all up again—she wasn't pleased.'

Was it play acting? The most reliable witnesses, Croÿ and Luynes, were not sure. Luynes says she was a sick woman, and that ill health often brings people to God. He says, several times, that no doubt she really wanted to be converted and hoped that grace would come to her if she prayed fervently enough. Croÿ, though puzzled and seeing all the various contradictions, thought there was something in it because of her extremely honest character; he often says that he never knew her to tell a lie about anything. The most likely explanation is that she longed to be converted but was incapable of it. Since the death of her child she had been very unhappy; she saw people all round her deriving consolation from their religion. She also thought it would bring her a new and even closer union with the King; no effort was too great to achieve this and she set about it with determination. Of course an element of frivolity crept in; Madame de Pompadour could never banish that from any of her activities.

Père de Sacy, a Jesuit, was now sent for. The Marquise explained to him that she wished to make a general confession and go to communion. He replied that this would be difficult. The order to which he belonged had not forgotten that, very soon after they had accorded all these spiritual comforts to Louis XIV, the Comte de Toulouse was born. The royal confessor on that occasion had been the laughing stock of the palace. But, she said, there was nothing wicked any more between her and the King—see the blocked-up staircase—nothing but friendship, chaste and pure. The father then said that, the scandal of her relationship with the King having been so open, there was only one thing for her to do; she must leave Versailles and go back to her husband. Otherwise the Church would be unable to believe that her conversion was genuine.

Madame de Pompadour, knowing that she was rather safe, wrote to d'Etioles and offered to go back to him. The poor man must have shuddered at the idea. He was living the intensely agreeable life of a rich *fermier général*; he had a mistress he loved and boon companions; this merry company would have found the presence of a repentant, unrouged Madame de Pompadour at their suppers nothing if not embarrassing. He replied that he wished her all the good in the world but did not think they could live together again after so long. She showed the letter to Père de Sacy; hardly her fault if her husband refused to take her back? He said that in any case she must leave the Court. She explained patiently that the King would never allow her to do such a thing, it was out of the question. (In this she is corroborated by Luynes who said that even if she had really wanted to leave Versailles the King would never have allowed it; that she did speak of it at one moment and he had been very much upset and refused to hear the subject mentioned.) The father would have to find some other solution.

But he was already in trouble with stricter members of his order. This curious penitent, who still appeared with her face painted, who still received the King at all hours of the day—the secret staircase was not the only one in the north wing—was hardly bringing credit on the Company of Jesus. He must give up his visits. The Marquise, on her side, began to look for somebody more lenient. At last her friend Berryer found her a priest, who said that she might confess, and go to communion, but that she must do so in private. This was not exactly what she wanted; however, she supposed it was better than nothing. 'A great consolation', she said rather drearily, 'to my soul.'

She was going through a difficult and depressing time altogether. During the last months of 1755, little more than a year after the death of Alexandrine, the King had been very much taken with a Court beauty, the Marquise de Coislin, a member of the fatal Mailly family (cousin of his three mistresses). Madame du Hausset describes Madame de Pompadour, at Marley, coming in, flinging down her muff and saying: 'I never saw such insolence as that of Madame de Coislin—I was playing *brelan* with her this evening—you can't imagine what I suffered. Everybody was watching us, Madame de Coislin said two or three times, looking at me, "I take the lot"—truly I thought I should faint when she said, triumphantly: "I've a hand full of Kings." I only wish you could have seen her curtsey when she left me.' 'And the King?' said Madame du Hausset, 'how did he seem?' 'You don't know the King, my dear—if he was going to put her in my room this very night he'd still be cold to her and friendly to me in public—that's how he was brought up, for by nature he is good and frank.'

In the end Madame de Coislin overplayed her hand, asked for too many favours and frightened the King off. She gave herself like a whore, and like a whore she was abandoned. She lived to be a hundred. As an old lady her chief topic of conversation was her affair with Louis XV; she let it be understood that she had played the parts of Mesdames de Pompadour and du Barry rolled into one and that she alone had counted in his life.

As always after these alarms, Madame de Pompadour not only kept her position but improved it. She was now appointed supernumerary lady-in-waiting to the Queen, a post reserved for the highest in the land. Confession and communion, however public, could have set no more of a seal on her piety than this, the good

Queen would never have accepted her if she had not been sure of it. In fact, when the King first asked her to take Madame de Pompadour into her household, she had refused straight out because the lady was fraudulently separated from her husband and unable to communicate. Now it was the lady's husband who was guilty of refusing to take her back, the onus of their separation was henceforth on him. She had communicated. The Queen gave way, though without much enthusiasm. 'I have a King in heaven who gives me courage to bear my sufferings, and a King on earth whom I obey in all things.'

So, on Sunday 8th February, 1756, the Marquise was declared lady-in-waiting amid waves of gossip and speculation, to the fury of d'Argenson and the giggles of Voltaire: '*Qui vult decipi decipiatur.*' None of her previous advancements, neither her marquisate, nor her duchy, nor even her brother's Cordon Bleu ('an insult to the high nobility'), had caused anything like such a sensation. A wild rumour ran round Versailles that the Marquise had given up rouge. It was too much. True, she now received the Ambassadors sitting at her embroidery instead of at her dressing-table. True, she had taken to a little cap of fine white lace in the morning. But when she waited on the Queen for the first time, performing her duties as if she had never done anything else all her life, she was seen to be in full fig and made up more than usual.

As for the King, he showed no signs of being very near a holy old age. He paid regular visits to the Parc aux Cerfs and at the same time d'Argenson noted, with disgust, that he seemed more in love with Madame de Pompadour than ever. Croÿ describes a supper party in a new dining-room from which could be seen the King's study, his famous clock, his writing table, covered with documents, books and instruments everywhere, and masses of flowers. The Marquise looking quite lovely and a little bit fatter, very gay. No change to be observed except that, though it was a Saturday, she only ate fish.

The King brought the Duc d'Orléans to her flat and enjoined them both to make up a long-standing quarrel; they kissed and promised to be friends. It seemed as though she had nothing more to desire. She had, however, one more objective in mind; she wanted to get rid of d'Argenson. The hatred which they felt for each other made it impossible for them to work together and she was determined now to share the King's political life with him. For, while, at Versailles, the courtiers could only talk about whether the Marquise had or had not given up rouge, and while, in Paris, the Magistrates were absorbed in their squabble with the Archbishop, many grave matters were afoot in the world.

## Chapter Sixteen

# POLITICS ABROAD

UNITED Europe has seldom been so nearly realized as it was after the Peace of Aix la Chapelle, in 1748. The King of England was a German, the King of Spain was French. The Empress of Austria was married to a Lorrainer with a French mother, the King of France was half Italian and his Dauphin was half Polish with a German wife. Scottish and French architects were at work in Russia and Germany, Italian cabinet-makers in France, French painters in Rome, Venetian painters in London, Dutch painters in Paris. Internationalism even extended to the armies of the day. During the last campaign of the War of the Austrian Succession in 1747—a campaign marked by the French victories of Berg op Zoom and Roucoux—it so happened that none of the generals engaged was a native of the country for which he fought. The French commander-in-chief was Maréchal de Saxe. Berg op Zoom was taken for France by Maréchal de Lowendal, a Danish Protestant, who amazed his new compatriots by having three wives, all alive. (The current Madame de Lowendal was presented at Versailles and could hardly have aroused more interest if she had been a giraffe.) The general commanding the English soldiers at Roucoux, Field Marshal Lord Ligonnier, was an emigrated Huguenot born at Castries, in the South of France. He was taken prisoner and Louis XV gave a dinner party for him at which he asked whether it would not now be possible to make peace. He had asked this after every campaign of late, but the English, in their rampaging mood, had hitherto refused to listen. 'What cruel neighbours we have there,' the King used often to say.

However, next year the peace was signed. It left Europe divided by alliances into two halves, the Austrian Empire, Russia, England, Holland and Sardinia, against France, Spain, the two Sicilies, Prussia and Sweden; since it would clearly be an unprofitable venture for one of these halves to make war on the other, a long peace might have ensued, had it not been for a new factor. America and Asia were now entering into the calculations of statesmen. The English, who were determined to possess as vast an Empire in these continents as possible, were very anxious to keep their only rivals, the French, fully occupied in Europe while they acquired it.

Englishmen and Frenchmen were already fighting an undeclared war on the high seas, in India and in Canada. In June, 1755, three French ships, the *Alcide*, the *Lys* and the *Royal Dauphin*, became detached, in a fog, from a fleet sailing to Quebec, and ran into the English fleet, also going about its occasions in the Atlantic. The English guns immediately opened fire; the Captain of the *Alcide*, an armed merchantman, who had been at sea for some months, thought that war must have broken out while he was away. He took his megaphone and shouted to the Captain of the *Dunkirk*: 'Are we at peace, or at war?' The Jolly Jack Tar took his megaphone and replied: 'At peace, at peace,' and without bothering to lower it he added: 'Fire.' The *Royal Dauphin*, a man-o'-war, got away, but the other two ships were taken.

The news of this event arrived in France while the Court was at Compiègne. The courtiers imagined that everything would be all right and that London would make amends by handing back the *Lys* and the *Alcide*, but Louis XV was not so optimistic. He immediately gave orders that all building on his houses was to stop, and countermanded the little voyages for the rest of that year. The Maréchal de Mirepoix, French Ambassador in London, saw the full gravity of the affair, and left at once. He loved England and was dreadfully cast down; he gave little parting presents of wine to all his English friends. Lord Albemarle, for many years Ambassador to Versailles, had loved France; it was perhaps fortunate that he had just died of an apoplexy aged fifty-two—*Milord Albemarle aimait son plaisir*. Small and fat, very Dutch, with a wife who, though born a Lennox, seemed even more Dutch than he, he had a French mistress called Lolotte. 'Do not praise the stars, Lolotte, when you know quite well I cannot give them to you.' He had been a great friend of the King, and of Madame de Pompadour who used to send him china flowers and other little gifts. How often do diplomatic friendships end in sad disappointment! Relations between the intellectuals and the aristocracy of the two countries were perfect; the *philosophes* loved and admired, even if they did not always understand, English institutions, while Englishmen of taste and learning derived half their pleasure in life from the civilization of France. The war had nothing to do with sentiment, it was caused by a direct conflict of interests, unfortunately inevitable in the circumstances.

It is curious to note, in the memoirs of the day, that when the French contemplated war with England they did not envisage a war at sea; their thoughts always turned to an offensive against Hanover. But the King was most anxious to avoid it; negotiations dragged on for several months, during which time the two navies were fighting whenever they met; in the end it was the English who made the declaration: 'We declare war on France who has so unrighteously begun it' (May, 1756).

Meanwhile, Starhemberg, the Austrian Ambassador to Versailles, was instructed, by his Empress, to sound the Prince de Conti, and see if, by any chance, an alliance with her would now be acceptable to Louis XV. Starhemberg told her that the Prince de Conti had lost a great deal of his influence with the King; the real private secretary now was Madame de Pompadour, and in his view it would be better to approach her. There was a rule at Versailles that no Ambassador ever saw the King alone, so an intermediary had to be found. None of the ministers would be any good, Starhemberg knew that they were all pro-Prussian, and would be categorically against his suggestions.

The Abbé de Bernis now reappears on the scene. Forgotten were the days when his greatest ambition had been an attic in the Tuileries. In 1752 he had been appointed, through the influence of the Marquise, Ambassador to Venice and in 1755 he was promoted to Madrid. He stayed at Versailles during his holiday between the two posts, and found Madame de Pompadour very much occupied with public affairs. She showed him various memoranda she had addressed to the King, who always preferred to conduct any serious business by letter rather than by word of mouth. Bernis was surprised to find her comments remarkably well expressed and full of good sense; he urged her to go on.

Could she not make up her quarrel with d'Argenson? he asked. She said no, that was not possible; they would never be able to work together, even if she could have forgotten the treachery and insults of years, because there was no trust between them. This was the gravest mistake of her whole career. D'Argenson may not have had a very nice character, but he was a professional politician of experience and ability. Because Madame de Pompadour was unable to get on with him the destiny of France fell, at this critical moment, into the incompetent hands of Babet la Bouquetière.

Early in September, 1755, Madame de Pompadour sent a note asking Bernis to come and see her on a matter of importance. The little fellow trotted round at once; never in a thousand years, he said afterwards, would he have guessed what it was to be about. The Marquise showed him a letter from Starhemberg asking for a private interview; he had secret propositions from the Empress which he would like to lay before her. He also asked that the King should delegate a minister to be present at the interview, to report these propositions to him and to transmit the answer. Now although Bernis behaved, from the beginning, as if he thoroughly approved of the Austrian alliance—he was, in fact, one of its chief promoters—he pretends, in his memoirs, that on reading this letter he suddenly became endowed with second sight. Certainly everything that he says he said happened precisely. If the King were suddenly to shift his alliances the whole political system of Europe would go up in a general conflagration (it did). The first result would be war with Prussia (it was). This war would be intensely unpopular in France; the King had no generals capable of conducting it; and his finances were not in a state to support a Continental as well as a Colonial war (sadly true).

At this juncture the King himself appeared in Madame de Pompadour's room and asked the Abbé what he made of Starhemberg's letter. Bernis, still according to his own account, repeated the arguments which he had just put to the Marquise. The King, very much displeased, said: 'You are all the same, all enemies of the Queen of Hungary.' The Abbé said that on the contrary he had the greatest admiration for the Empress; he then respectfully advised the King to speak to his ministers. Useless, said the King. The whole *Conseil* was pro-Prussian. The fact is that the King was determined to make the Austrian alliance. For years he had wanted it; he had the greatest personal admiration for Maria Theresa and the greatest personal loathing for le Marquis de Brandenbourg (Frederick) and he liked the idea of a Roman Catholic block.

'Very well,' he said to Bernis, 'then we are to send M. de Starhemberg away with empty compliments and without a hearing?' The Abbé said that there could be no harm in listening to what Starhemberg had to say; only it was obvious that the reply must be carefully considered. In the end Bernis, armed with a written statement from the King giving him full powers to negotiate, went to see Starhemberg. They made an appointment for the following day with Madame de Pompadour at Brimborian, her summer house under the terrace at Bellevue.

In a bustle of self-importance, Madame de Pompadour set forth from Versailles. She, Bernis and the Ambassador went by different roads; arrived at Bellevue they sent away their coaches and their servants and proceeded alone, on foot, to the meeting place. Brimborian, the little frivolous summer house, intended for hours of lazy gossip, was indeed a suitable locale for this scene from musical comedy.

Of course Madame de Pompadour should never have lent herself to the affair at all. But how many women in her place would have had the strength of mind to refuse? It brought her too many different satisfactions. She was trusted to conduct a matter of vital importance by the lover in whose serious interests she longed to share. She was recognized as a weighty figure of European diplomacy by the virtuous Empress. Frederick the Great would learn that she was something more than a kept woman; the hated d'Argenson would burst with anger when he found out her new rôle. She thought she understood the European situation as well as anybody; it never crossed her mind that she and Bernis might be as putty in the hands of a clever professional diplomat.

The blue and gold boudoir, with panelling by Verberckt, was just big enough to accommodate the three of them, and here Starhemberg set forth the Empress's proposals for an alliance: Austrian neutrality in the event of war with England; the French to be allowed to occupy Ostend; the Austrian Netherlands to be given to Madame Infante and her husband in exchange for Parma; a mutual security clause engaging each country to come to the assistance of the other if attacked, with 18,000 foot soldiers

and 6,000 cavalry. Having read out this memoir, which was more
or less what the Marquise and Bernis had expected, Starhemberg
went on to disclose a piece of information which they had not
expected at all. Frederick, whose treaty of alliance with France
was supposedly about to be renewed, was in fact negotiating,
secretly, with London.

The Marquise had picked up an ABC of political lore, which
laid it down that foreign politics must be founded on a system of
alliances. Should one alliance seem shaky, another must be sub-
stituted. Starhemberg's news, therefore, if true, seemed to make
the Austrian alliance an urgent necessity. But had she brought to
this problem the original intelligence with which she ordered
objects of art, or laid out her gardens, always eschewing that
which seemed obvious in her search for that which was exactly
right, she might have seen a different solution. The wisest course
for France might have been to stand alone in Europe. Frederick
and the Empress were absorbed by their own quarrel; France,
allied to either of them, was certain to be drawn into it. At the
same time, neither was the least likely to attack her. Madame de
Pompadour did not see this; nor did many another politician, and
it must be said that the pros and cons of this affair have been
argued ever since.

Madame de Pompadour and Bernis hurried back to Versailles
and conferred with the King. He took the matter more calmly
than they did, and behaved with a certain prudence. He wrote a
friendly but non-committal reply to Maria Theresa and sent the
Duc de Nivernais on a special embassy to Berlin, ostensibly to
renew the treaty of alliance with Frederick, but really to see how
the land lay.

Frederick, one side of whose curious nature so revered everything French, fell as he was intended to fall, under the spell of
Nivernais. Nobody could have been more certain to please. He
was not only a rich, powerful and handsome Duke, but also a

man of letters, member of the Académie française. Unfortunately, just as Frederick was enjoying the company of this charmer, the English papers spoiled the party by publishing the Treaty of Westminster. It engaged the English and the Prussians to oppose any foreign troops invading Germany, and was virtually therefore a pact between two German princes, the King of Prussia and the Elector of Hanover. Curious, however, that Frederick should choose the moment when he was about to renew his alliance with France to sign an agreement with her enemy. When questioned by Nivernais about this new development, he looked thoroughly uncomfortable, though he said that it was purely defensive and that he was still quite ready to sign the French alliance. Nivernais replied by packing up and going home. Frederick still seemed to think that he could have his cake and eat it. He and his brother sent loving messages to the Marquise and begged for copies of her portrait by La Tour, which was being exhibited at the Louvre. 'Flatter her in every way,' he wrote to his Ambassador, and the poor German went regularly to do so. He bored her very much; finally she pleaded her religious duties as an excuse for not receiving him.

The Austrians now put it about Versailles that England was trying to arrange an alliance with Maria Theresa. The King regarded this as a matter of such gravity that he could no longer continue negotiating through the medium of two amateurs, a priest and a woman. He took Bernis into the *Conseil d'Etat* and told him to inform the other ministers of the transactions which had already passed between himself and the Empress. Much as they all hated the idea of an alliance with the traditional enemy, the ministers agreed with Bernis and the King that this was the only course to follow if France were not to find herself completely isolated; they adopted unanimously the policy known as the *renversement des alliances*. On 1st May, 1756, the first Treaty of Versailles was signed, by France and Austria, not at Versailles at all, but at Jouy en Josas, at the house of M. Rouillé, the incompetent old Foreign Minister.

Voltaire says that this new policy, since it was inevitable, was perfectly natural; but his fellow countrymen could not think it natural at all. Were they now to find themselves shoulder to shoulder with the killers of their uncles, fathers and brothers? Was France no longer to defend the German states against persecution? Would there not result a new religious war? When the terms of the Treaty were published it was observed that France was obliged to go to the assistance of the Empire, whoever attacked it; while Austria was neutral in the Anglo-French quarrel. The King, isolated from the voice of public opinion, made, as he always did, the mistake of under-estimating its importance; nothing was done to prepare the French for the shock of suddenly finding themselves in the same camp as their erstwhile enemy. The people and the generals hated the alliance when it was made, and hated it even more violently when, after a few initial victories, French arms began to suffer a series of shocking reverses.

It was all blamed on to Madame de Pompadour. The Empress was supposed to have turned her little head with flattery; while Frederick had enraged her by giving one of his bitches the name Pompadour; the whole thing, from beginning to end, was due to feminine caprice. This is not quite fair. The responsibility for the Austrian alliance rested chiefly with the King, but also with the *Conseil d'Etat*, which, pro-Frederick as it was, thought the *renversement des alliances* preferable to isolation. Where the Marquise was greatly to blame was in having chosen the Abbé as secret negotiator. He had been quite at sea from the beginning, and was perfectly incapable of such a delicate task; by the time the professionals were called in, the Treaty of Westminster and the alleged English overtures to Vienna had deprived them of any bargaining powers. There was really nothing left for them to do but sign and look pleasant. The French had been thoroughly out-manœuvred by the Empress and her Foreign Minister.

The war against England started off, as such wars often do, very well indeed for her enemies. The Maréchal de Richelieu, by a brilliantly lucky coup, took the island of Minorca, of great importance as a vantage point for the English fleet. He had been besieging the supposedly impregnable Fort St. Philip, at Mahon, for a few weeks, and finding it a great bore in the absence of any women. His only pleasures were those of the table. But his cook was labouring under difficulties; there was no butter or cream on the island. He was driven to invent a new sauce, made only of eggs and oil, the Mahonaise.

At last the Duke became impatient and decided to finish the matter. Against all the rules of war and dictates of prudence, in spite of the fact that he had neither scaling ladders, engineers nor a map of the fortifications, he took his men up a cliff which no human being had ever climbed before, and captured the Fort with a loss of only six hundred killed and wounded. The whole island then fell into his hands (June, 1756). 'The Duke takes a town in the same light-hearted way as he seduces a woman,' said Madame de Pompadour, with grudging admiration. Indeed, scaling operations were all part of the night's work with Son Excellence, who was for ever in and out of bedroom windows.

The news of this victory, brought by Richelieu's son, M. de Fronsac, to the King at Compiègne at two in the morning, caused intense rejoicing. The exiled Archbishop of Paris ordered a Te Deum at Notre Dame; the old Maréchal de Belle Isle jumped out of bed and skipped for joy in his nightshirt; Madame de Pompadour gave a fireworks party at her Hermitage, distributing favours to her guests à la Mahon. She forgave Richelieu all his wickedness to her and wrote to congratulate him: Monsieur le Minorquin.

The English were as furious as the French were delighted. Bets of twenty to one had been taken in London that within four months Richelieu would arrive there as a prisoner-of-war; it had never occurred to anybody that Fort St. Philip could be captured. Popular rage was directed against Admiral Byng, who had failed to relieve the garrison; he was court-martialled and shot, in spite of, or perhaps because of, a letter written by Richelieu in his defence. Corsica was also occupied by French troops and everything looked very rosy for them in the Mediterranean.

Two months later Frederick, pretending to think that Maria Theresa was about to attack him, demanded a free passage for his troops through Saxony; when this was refused he occupied Dresden. The Dauphine received this news from her family early one morning. Clad only in a dressing-gown she rushed unannounced into her father-in-law's bedroom—such a thing had never been done before in the annals of Versailles. She besought him to send help to her father at once. The King was very nice to her and promised to do everything within his power. The Seven Years War had begun.

## Chapter Seventeen

# DAMIENS

IT will be remembered that on the thirteenth of December, 1756, the King went to Paris and made his *Parlement* register acceptance of the Pope's encyclical, and submission to himself. He was badly received by the population. He drove in state from la Muette to the *Palais de Justice*, through crowded streets, without hearing one cry of *Vive le Roi*, but did not appear to be at all put out by this. He was himself perfectly satisfied with the trend of events. The Pope's pronouncement solved an affair which had occupied too many people for too long. The alliance with the Empire—which also brought Russia and Sweden to the side of France—ensured the eastern frontier and the ports of the Low Countries. French troops were already being mobilized to go to the help of the Dauphine's family and implement the Austrian alliance, not perhaps a very popular move, but one which honour demanded. He had nothing with which to reproach himself, quite the contrary. He looked out of the window of his carriage, smiling a little at the sullen crowds, with the feeling of a father whose children do not understand that what he is doing is for their own good.

The winter was exceptionally cold, once again misery and unemployment were created by the absence of the *Enquêtes* and *Requêtes*, who had gone on strike as a protest against the King's action. Those of the courtiers who were in touch with Paris began to feel really worried about the situation. There was a vague fear abroad that some harm might come to the King.

Early in January, 1757, the Court went to Trianon. Versailles, with its enormous rooms and smoking chimneys, was desperately uncomfortable in cold weather. The *petits appartements* were fairly warm, but etiquette never could be relaxed; at certain times of day everybody had to be gathered in the state rooms, in full court dress: and every morning the King, in his nightshirt and bare feet, was obliged to run to the freezing, smoky state bedroom, and there hold his *lever*. Life was altogether more bearable at Trianon, though people shivered in front of the hottest fire. Madame Victoire, who had influenza, had been left behind in the big palace, and on 5th January the King went to spend the afternoon with her. At six o'clock his coaches were waiting outside the *Salle des Gardes* to take him and his gentlemen back to Trianon; the Swiss Guard was drawn up on each side of the door, a small crowd stood looking on, and the whole scene was lit with flaming torches.

The King was coming down the steps followed by the Dauphin, the Ducs de Richelieu and d'Ayen and two equerries. Suddenly a man pushed through the soldiers, gave the King what appeared to be a sharp blow, re-joined the crowd and stood there with his hat on. The King said: 'Duc d'Ayen, somebody hit me.' Neither the Dauphin nor d'Ayen had seen what had happened because they were looking for the bottom step in the uncertain light of the torches. Richelieu, who was behind them, said: 'It's that man, with his hat on.' The King put his hand to his ribs, found that it was covered with blood, realized that he had been stabbed with a knife, and said: 'I am wounded. Arrest the man, but don't hurt him.' He added that he was quite able to walk, and went up to his bedroom.

When he got upstairs he was bleeding very much, felt faint from the loss of blood, thought he was probably dying and asked for a confessor at once. Now the utmost confusion reigned. The

Court having been several days at Trianon, there were no sheets on the bed, no nightshirt could be found and, worst of all, no doctor. The King fainted, came to and insisted on a confessor. A priest was brought from the town of Versailles. The King confessed in a great hurry, and begged for absolution, saying he would confess again, and better, if he lived. 'I completely and entirely forgive my assassin,' he said.

Having received absolution he felt more at his ease. Then a surgeon arrived, also from the town, but having washed the wound he dared not do much more. At last la Martinière, the King's own surgeon, came from Trianon. He found that no vital organ had been touched and that the wound was not deep; all would be well, unless the knife was poisoned. This seemed rather likely, as the said knife, which lay on the chimney piece, the focus of all eyes, hardly constituted a lethal weapon. It was a penknife with two blades, the smaller of which had been used. Anxiety was redoubled at the idea of poison.

Various ministers were assembled in the ante-room, and the Dauphin asked them if a *Conseil d'Etat* ought to be called. Bernis said that, in his view, this was indispensable, and Richelieu was sent off to fetch the absent ministers. Mesdames now rushed in; seeing their father on a bare mattress, soaked with blood, they all fainted dead away. Then the Queen arrived and down she too went, on the floor. The Dauphin, though crying a good deal, kept his head and gave the orders. The King wanted to confess again, but his own confessor still could not be found, so they asked if he would see another priest from the town, who was held in very high esteem. The King spent a long time with him, and said he wished for extreme unction.

They sent for holy oil, which arrived, and the Cardinal de la Rochefoucauld, but he could not be found, so extreme unction was not administered. The King's own confessor appeared and the King had another half hour with him, after which he ordered everybody back into his room, and apologized publicly to his wife and daughters for the times when he had wronged her and scandalized them. Turning to the Dauphin he said he was happy to think that France would now have a good ruler. Everybody was in floods of tears. The courtiers, between their sobs, told each other that things looked very bad for the Marquise. The poor Marquise, who had also rushed back from Trianon, was in a state of mind that can be imagined. Of course she could not go and see the King, but had to wait in her own apartment, for news. Soon after midnight Quesnay came to her and said that he was out of danger; he could perfectly well go to a ball, if he wanted to. Great was her relief, but now she began to be tormented with fears for her own future. What had all these priests been saying to him? Would he send her away? She longed for a word from him, but no word came.

Meanwhile the man who had attacked the King, one Damiens, was being tortured by the Guards to find out if he had any accomplices. All he said was, take care of the Dauphin, and then, that people would soon be talking about him, Damiens, and that he would die in torments like Jesus Christ. Machault ordered wood to be brought and was about to burn him alive then and there. He was prevented from doing so by the Provost of Versailles, who had jurisdiction over criminals arrested outside the palace, and who carried him off to prison.

In Paris, where the news arrived very quickly, people flocked to the churches, and thousands stood all night outside the Hôtel de Ville, waiting to read the bulletins. The Duc de Gesvres lit two great bonfires to keep them from freezing to death. The Princes of the Blood, Ambassadors, and Presidents of the *Grand' Chambre* left immediately, in the full moon and terrible cold of that night, for Versailles; the road was covered with coaches. As for the members of the *Enquêtes* and *Requêtes*, who were still on strike, they went at once to church, and then dispatched a letter to Maupéou, the senior President, begging him to assure the King of their love. In spite of differences and irritations between the King and his people he was still the *Bien-Aimé* at this time.

Now, although the King was not much hurt in his body he had received a severe mental shock. He thought he saw in Damiens the instrument of the whole French people, and that this people whom he loved and to whom he felt himself joined, as in marriage, by the sacrament of the coronation, wanted him dead. In that case he had no wish, himself, to live. A short time ago, he had found a horrid little poem lying on his hearthrug, 'You go to Choisy and to Crécy; why don't you go to St. Denis?'[1] This, and many another lampoon, many another sign of his unpopularity, came back to him as he lay in bed. 'The body is all right,' he said, 'but this'—touching his forehead—'goes badly and does not mend.'

The wound healed, but day after day the King lay in his alcove, behind drawn curtains, speaking to nobody, and brooding. After eight days the curtains were drawn back and the courtiers saw that 'this superbly handsome man looked at us sadly, as who should say, "here is your King whom an unhappy creature wished to assassinate, and who is himself the unhappiest man in the land." ' He gave one or two orders; he would see the Ambassadors, he said, on Tuesday, instead of, as usual, on Wednesday; apart from that he hardly spoke.

The Marquise, for her part, was living through the worst time of her whole life. Day after day went by with no message from the King. Marigny went to see if he could have a word with him, but the Duc de Richelieu very rudely told him to be off. The Princesses and the Dauphin never left their father's room for a moment. Madame de Pompadour knew quite well that the faction which wanted to be rid of her, led by d'Argenson and supported, for religious reasons, by the King's children, would use

[1] Burial place of the Kings of France.

every means to further this end. It was now or never for them. Machault, whom she had hitherto regarded as her friend, and whom the public regarded as her creature, came to see her, and in a very different manner from his usual one with her, advised her to leave Versailles. He gave her to understand that this was the King's express wish. He had been talked into doing so by the Dauphin who had assumed a more authoritative manner since the attempt; the courtiers felt that he had suddenly been transformed from a fat, pious nobody into a man who might at any moment become their King. From now on he had a seat in the *Conseil d'Etat* and was altogether more important at Versailles. After the interview with Machault the Marquise, who was trembling, but otherwise calm and collected, gave orders for her carriages to be kept in readiness, and sent for her trunks. The Elysée was to be prepared to receive her and all her servants, and they were to start packing up at once. While they were doing so, in came Madame de Mirepoix. 'What is happening here? What are these trunks for?' 'Alas, dearest, M. de Machault says I must leave and that *he* wishes it.' 'I think your *Garde des Sceaux* is betraying you,' said the Maréchale, 'and I very much advise you to stay where you are until you get orders from the King himself. Who leaves the table loses the game.'

Soubise, Bernis, Gontaut and Marigny all gave the same advice, and between them they prevailed on her to stay until she heard directly from the King. They said he would be very angry with her if she went of her own accord, without waiting for his instructions. Her real friends had never been so good to her. The Duchesse de Brancas hardly left her, nor did Dr. Quesnay; Bernis and the other men came in twenty times a day to see how she was and to try to reassure her. She was extremely courageous, went quietly about her ordinary occupations and nobody could have guessed what she was suffering.

As for d'Argenson, the cards were on the table. Madame de

Pompadour sent for him; he kept her waiting for hours and when he came was perfectly insulting. She said that the King must be prevented from seeing seditious matter found in the mails; nothing could be worse for him, at present, than to read such stuff. D'Argenson replied that it was his plain duty to show the King everything. After a sharp interview: 'Monsieur, you are going too far. It would be pointless to prolong this conversation. I see quite plainly that you hope and think I shall have to leave the Court and therefore that you can say what you like to me. I have not seen the King for five days. It is possible that I shall never see him again, but if I do you can be quite sure that either you or I will have to go.'

'Madame, is this all?' said d'Argenson, and left the room. He was so sure which way the land lay that he wrote a letter to Madame d'Estrades telling her to cheer up, she would soon be back at Versailles, and then he and she would run the gambling den together. When he had gone, Bernis came to see Madame de Pompadour and found her in a characteristic attitude, standing by the fire, her hands in her muff; she was gazing absently out of the window. 'You look like a pensive sheep,' he said. 'It's the wolf who has made the sheep pensive,' she replied.

And still the days went by, and still no word from the King.

He was up now, in his bedroom, his hair curled and powdered, and walking about with a little stick. He hardly spoke—when the Ambassadors came to see him the interview took place in perfect silence—but he had more or less returned to normal life. It was noticed that the Dauphin never left his side and that they were friendly and affectionate together. But no chat, no gossip and no jokes with the men around him, who were beginning to feel the strain.

On the eleventh day the King was in his room with the Dauphin and the Dauphine, the tall Duchesse de Brancas, Messieurs de Croissy, Fontanieu, Champcenetz and Dufort de Cheverny.

Everybody else had gone off to dine, and the palace, as always at this hour, was utterly deserted. It was rather late and they were all hungry, waiting to be dismissed, but the King did not give the signal. He was wandering about in his dressing-gown and nightcap, leaning on his stick, in the sad silence to which they were becoming accustomed. At last he gave a sign to the Dauphine, who curtseyed and went out. Madame de Brancas was going to follow when the King told her to wait. The Dauphin looked up, very much surprised. 'Lend me your cloak, will you?' the King said to Madame de Brancas. She took it off and gave it to him; he put it round his shoulders, walked a few steps in it, said good-bye to her and left the room. The Dauphin made a move as though to follow him and the King said: 'No—don't come with me.' So the Dauphin went to join the Dauphine at dinner.

The gentlemen-in-waiting looked at each other with a wild surmise. Hungry as they were they agreed that it would be impossible to dine, it was all too interesting. They settled down to await developments. A good long time went by before the King returned, and when he did he was a different man; calm, agreeable, chatting away, laughing about his feminine cloak. He would dine now, he said, and advised the others to do the same. It was not difficult to guess that he had been to see the Marquise. In that one interview she had managed to put his mind completely at rest.

She told him, quite truly, that Damiens was mad, that he was not the instrument of any party or conspiracy, let alone of the French people as a whole, and that he had acted entirely on his own. The country was appalled by the attempt, she said, the Parisians would tear Damiens limb from limb if they could get hold of him, and nobody had been more sincerely shocked than the Magistrates. She spoke in her sensible downright way and the King believed her. Next day he got up, dressed, went out hunting and supped as usual with Madame de Pompadour. Marigny was there, treated more like a brother-in-law than ever. The good Barbier, in his diary, says: 'The King is beginning to amuse himself again, far the best for him and for us.'

D'Argenson and Machault were dismissed. 'Monsieur d'Argenson, your services are no longer necessary. I order you to resign your various charges and to go and live on your estate at Ormes.'[1] D'Argenson was in his bath when this intimation arrived. He quickly dressed and went to Paris, where a typically eighteenth-century scene took place. He found his wife, as usual, chatting to M. de Valfons. 'Don't go,' he said to Valfons, 'at such terrible moments it is better to be three.' He told them the news. Madame d'Argenson said that she would, of course, go with him to Ormes and M. de Valfons said he would, of course, come too, but d'Argenson would not hear of such sacrifices. Madame d'Argenson was a delicate woman, country air would be very bad for her, she must stay in Paris within reach of her doctor; and Valfons must stay within reach of her. That afternoon d'Argenson set forth, alone. At the city boundary he was met by Madame d'Estrades and they drove away to exile together. They both became very thin, with the boredom of country life. Not until after the death of the Marquise was d'Argenson allowed to go back to Paris; and then he only went there to die.

Machault's dismissal was couched in far more friendly terms. 'Monsieur de Machault, although certain of your probity and the honesty of your motives, circumstances oblige me to ask you for my seals and for your resignation as Minister of the Marine. You can rely upon my protection and friendship. You can ask favours for your children at any time at all. You had better stay at Arnouville[2] for the present. You will keep your salary and your honours.' Machault, in exile, became very fat.

[1] His beautiful château near Orléans.
[2] His estate in Seine-et-Oise.

He was nearly recalled to office by Louis XVI, but in the end was passed over, and he died in prison during the Revolution.

Were these two men sent away for crossing Madame de Pompadour or was it a matter of policy? During the days when the King lay behind his curtains he must have been pondering on public affairs, and on the war which was beginning. D'Argenson and Machault had always been publicly pro-Frederick, they disliked the *renversement des alliances* and were most half-hearted about the mobilization. It would have been very difficult to conduct the war efficiently with them at the head of affairs; they would have had to go sooner or later. Furthermore, Machault was at daggers drawn with the Magistrates and the King was anxious to come to a settlement with them. But the public thought they had been sacrificed to feminine spite.

The *Conseil d'Etat* was left a very much reduced and not very brilliant body. It consisted of the Dauphin; Paulmy, d'Argenson's nephew; Rouillé, who was in his dotage; the Maréchal de Belle-Isle, an excellent war minister but also rather old; Bernis, and St. Florentin, an authority on Court usage and procedure.

M. de Stainville, having done so well at Rome, was now promoted to the Vienna embassy; he came to Versailles to pay his court to the King and congratulate him on his escape. He had hardly been in the palace a week before giving further proof of his adroitness. He asked the Marquise if she really thought it wise to leave foreign affairs in such incompetent hands as Rouillé's. She said she and the King were both longing to get rid of him, but they were afraid of killing M. Rouillé who seemed very near to apoplexy as it was; he slept all through every council. The King thought that the shock of a dismissal might finish him.

Stainville said: 'Shall I get you his resignation?' The Marquise replied that nothing would be better received but that it was impossible. Madame Rouillé loved the Court as only a *bourgeoise* could love it, and she would never allow her husband to resign.

Stainville went straight off to see Madame Rouillé. He pointed
out to her that if her husband went on working it would probably
kill him and then she would have to leave Versailles. If he resigned,
on the other hand, they could keep their apartment and Rouillé
would be given the rich sinecure of the *Surintendance des Postes*. It
worked like a charm. He went with Madame Rouillé to her
husband's office and came away with the resignation.

Bernis, who succeeded Rouillé as Minister of Foreign Affairs,
saw eye to eye on every subject with Stainville. They both loved
Madame de Pompadour, both thought her influence on the King
entirely good and were both, whatever Bernis may say in his
memoirs, entirely in favour of the Austrian alliance, at this time.
When Stainville left for Vienna they promised to write to each
other constantly.

With the most important trial for years about to take place,
the members of the *Enquêtes* and *Requêtes* were of course most
anxious to go back to the *Palais de Justice* and participate in it;
while the King had no intention whatever of allowing them to
do so. A distinguished Magistrate, the Président de Meinières,
obtained, through Gontaut and Madame du Roure, an interview
with the Marquise which took place at the end of January. M. de
Meinières had two objects in view. His son, excluded from high
position in the army by his *bourgeois* birth, was excluded from any
legal employment by express order of the King. Many of the
*remontrances* with which the *Parlement* bored and annoyed the
King so continually, were known to have been composed by
Meinières with the help of his enormous library of legal documents. He was one of the cleverest and most intransigent of the
Parliamentarians and the King had decided to use such sanctions
as he could against him. The President was beginning to realize
that the precipitate action of the two Chambers, in leaving their
duties, had put them in a false position; his son's career too was

being adversely affected by their quarrel with the King. He came to treat on their and on his own behalf. In the end he saw the Marquise twice; he wrote an account of these interviews, which shows the impression she made on an elderly man, very important in his own sphere, who was, if anything, republican in feeling.

'Madame de Pompadour was alone, standing by the fire; she looked me up and down with a haughty air that will be graven on my memory as long as I live. No curtsey, no sort of greeting as she took stock of me; it was very imposing. When I came up to her she said, furiously, to her servant, to bring me a chair.[1] He put it so near hers that our knees were almost touching.

'When we were both seated, and the servant had gone, I said to Madame la Marquise, in very uncertain and trembling tones: "Madame, I have never wanted anything so much as the favour you are good enough to grant me to-day, I hope to have the honour to convince you of my deep respect, so that you can see for yourself that I am incapable of the cabals and intrigues of which I am accused. I hope, Madame, that when you have at last realized the injustice of such imputations, of which my poor son is the victim, your goodness, your humanity, and that natural inclination, which everybody knows you have, to protect the innocent and help the unlucky, will induce you to give me your powerful patronage, and to speak for me to the King in favour of giving a commission in a cavalry regiment to my son . . ."' And so on. The President says that during the whole of this speech, which was quite long for somebody dying of fright, as he was when he began it, the Marquise sat bolt upright in her chair with her eyes fixed on him most disconcertingly. When at last he finished, saying he had no idea what his crime was supposed to be, Madame de Pompadour spoke.

[1] In those days the difference between a chair and an armchair was a matter, not of comfort but of etiquette. Not to offer an armchair to the President was rude.

'*Comment, Monsieur*, you pretend not to know what you have done, what is your crime?'

'I have absolutely no idea, Madame.'

'Really! Have you then no friend?'

'You can see that I have, Madame, because it is entirely owing to my friends that I have the honour to pay my court to you to-day, but none of them has ever told me that he knew the reason for the way I am being treated.'

'Ah! You don't know in what consideration you are held?'

The President gave an uneasy laugh and said it was hardly a crime if he had acquired consideration while pursuing his trade. The consideration, observed the Marquise, came from the fact that he had been most useful to the other Magistrates, with his books and his manuscripts, finding precedents and quotations in them on which the various *remontrances* had been based. The result was that His Majesty had a prejudice against him which it would be very difficult to remove. The President admitted that he had an unusually profound knowledge of law, but said that, although he had put various facts at the disposal of his colleagues, the use they chose to make of them was nothing to do with him. In any case, he said, it was very unfair, and not like the King, to visit all this on his son.

'The King uses whatever weapon comes to hand,' she replied, 'and in your case it happens to be convenient to punish you through your son.' She then suggested that he should write to the King and offer his entire submission; several members of the *Enquêtes* and *Requêtes* had already done this privately, and the King was quite willing to make allowances for them. The President said at great length that he would not think it honourable to do so.

Madame de Pompadour laughed and said: 'I am always amazed when people begin putting forward their so-called honour as a reason for disobeying the King. They seem to forget that honour

consists in doing their duty and in trying to remedy the disorder
which reigns in every public department, now that justice itself
has gone bankrupt. Shall I tell you what honour dictates? You
should admit the silliness and the wickedness of a move which is
neither legal nor public-spirited, and try, by a different line of
conduct, to efface the bad impression you have made on the King
and his subjects. Everybody knows my deep respect for the
magistrature, and I only wish I had no reason to reproach this
august tribunal, this first *parlement* of the Kingdom, this French
court of justice, which always praises itself so pompously in its
writings and *remontrances*. In a quarter of an hour this wise body,
which is always trying to set the government to rights, falls into
a rage of blind, furious resentment, and abandons its duties. You
yourself left with these other irresponsible people and now you
refuse to cast them off? You would prefer to see the Kingdom,
the Treasury and the whole State collapse, that is what you call
honour? Ah! Monsieur de Meinières, that is not the honour of a
man who loves his King and country.'

The President was amazed, he says, by her eloquence; it was a
pleasure to listen to her. He defended himself as best he could,
and presently came back to the word honour, upon which she
said very sharply: 'Don't talk to me like that, M. de Meinières,
how can it be dishonourable to do something which is the plain
duty of a citizen?'

After this outburst they seem to have been on rather better
terms. They discussed the whole affair of the *Enquêtes* and *Requêtes*,
and the Marquise reminded the President of various political
events in the reign of Louis XIV. She knew her facts and talked,
he said, extraordinarily well. They went on for five quarters of an
hour; finally she went with him to the door while he protested
his great, tender and respectful attachment to the King. 'She made
an inclination of her head, and shot like an arrow towards her
bedroom which was full of people. As she went she never took

her eyes off me until I had shut the door, and I left her filled with amazement and admiration.'

The second interview was much shorter. They came to the point at once, and M. de Meinières told her that, like Louis XV, Henri IV had tried to reduce the *Parlement* to a single *chambre*, that Chancelier Séguier had explained that this was against the constitution and the King had given way. Now he, Meinières, had a solution in mind.

The Marquise: 'Have you got it in writing?'

The President: 'I have given it to M. de Bernis.'

The Marquise: 'It comes to the same. Let me have the opportunity to be useful to you. I wish it with all my heart.' She got up, curtseyed, and retired.

Madame de Pompadour and Bernis both worked during the next few months for a reconciliation between the King and the Parliament; the following September this took place and the *Enquêtes* and *Requêtes* resumed their functions.

Damiens was tried by sixty judges—five Princes of the Blood, twenty *Pairs de France* and members of the *Grand' Chambre* of the *Parlement*. He was a native of Artois, with a little property there, and had been a superior servant—between a butler and secretary— in *bourgeois* houses. His masters were for ever grumbling about the state of public affairs, he had taken their words seriously, supposed that the country was in danger, and thought he could draw attention to this danger by wounding the King. He said he never meant to kill him. He certainly wished to draw attention to himself; he was always saying that everybody would talk about him, and seemed quite to look forward to the terrible end which he knew was in store for him.

He was found guilty of an attempt to murder his sovereign and was tortured to death outside the Hôtel de Ville. As the Duc de Luynes says, his last hour does not make agreeable reading.

Thousands of Parisians and quite a few courtiers went to watch his agonies, and amateurs of torture came over from England for the show. But most educated people were rather shocked, not at the idea of the punishment, but at its being treated as an entertainment. Dufort de Cheverny says that he and his wife and a few friends, not caring for that sort of thing, made up a party and went to Sceaux for the day. Nobody could talk about anything else and it revolted them; they knew quite well that their servants had all been to see it and they gave out that they did not wish to hear any details. When the King was told that a certain woman of his acquaintance had been to the Hôtel de Ville, he put his hands over his eyes and said: '*Fi! La vilaine.*' He never spoke of Damiens by name, it was always '*ce monsieur* who wanted to kill me'. It seems rather curious that a humane man like the King, who had already said, 'arrest him but don't hurt him', and had forgiven him, on what he thought was his death-bed, should have allowed these fearful tortures. But justice was the prerogative of the *Parlement* and he may have felt obliged to abide by their decision; Damiens' punishment was the same as that suffered by Ravaillac, assassin of Henri IV. Paradoxical as it may sound, human life was valued high in those days; crimes of violence were rare and thought extremely shocking. There were astonishingly few murders, mass murder did not exist in Europe, and a sharp push administered to an Electress by Prussian soldiers constituted a German atrocity. No doubt people were more startled by the attempt than they would be to-day. Luynes got a letter from a friend saying: 'Is it possible that the age of assassinations is returning to this earth?'

The King was so accessible that it would be easy to kill him at any time, inside as well as outside his palace, and this made it necessary to deter would-be assassins; torture was supposed to be a deterrent. Pain was regarded with a different eye from ours. Everybody, sooner or later, was obliged to endure horrid pain.

There were no anæsthetics, the doctors applied their brutal reme-
dies and conducted their primitive operations on fully conscious
patients. Cardinal Dubois, for instance, must have suffered quite
as much during the operation of which he died the next day, as
Damiens on the scaffold; and they did not put him out of his
misery when it was over. Women suffered dreadfully in child-
birth; people with cancer had to bear it unalleviated until it killed
them. Of all the highly-civilized men who tell of this affair in their
memoirs only Dufort de Cheverny seems to have wondered
whether such an execution was necessary, and he only because the
King survived. Damiens is never spoken of in pity, no term of
opprobrium is too strong, *le monstre, le scélérat, le détestable assassin,
le parricide, ce misérable* and so on; even Voltaire, who hated torture, considered that his end was quite natural and inevitable.

The Dauphine's next baby was called le Comte d'Artois to
console that province for having spawned the reptile Damiens.

*Chapter Eighteen*

# THE SEVEN YEARS WAR

THE Seven Years War, which ravaged so much of Europe, never touched the sacred soil of France. But it cost her her colonial empire. Canada and large tracts of India were taken by the English while the French army was pinned down in Europe and the French navy neglected for lack of funds. As for the Prussians, when they came back to earth after seven years on their favourite planet, they noticed that their ally had been acquiring world-wide dominion at the cost of a few hundred English lives, while they had ruined themselves, lost the flower of their manhood, suffered from famine and Russian atrocities, made themselves loathed throughout the Empire, and all, it seemed, for the sake of a sandy plain.

In the nineteenth century the French could not forgive Louis XV for the loss of their colonies, but while it was happening they hardly noticed it. Public opinion was entirely against any form of colonization. The *philosophes*, two hundred years before their time, thought then as we think now on the subject and most of their fellow countrymen entirely agreed with them.

'What of the noble savage?' cried Jean-Jacques Rousseau, 'has he no rights?'

'An empire is like a tree,' said Montesquieu, 'if the branches spread too far they drain the sap from the trunk. Men should stay where they are; transplanted to another climate their health will suffer.'

Voltaire denounced the horrible crimes committed in America

by the Europeans and said: 'France can be happy without Quebec.'

The *Encyclopédie* devoted twelve lines to Canada, 'a country inhabited by bears, beavers and barbarians, and covered, eight months of the year, with snow.'

This line of thought was not unknown in England. Arthur Young speaks of 'richer fields to fatten Nabobs—what difference to me when I pay the malt and beer duty to be told . . . that it produced the acquisition of Canada?'

With so much propaganda pouring from such respectable pens, the literate classes in France rather naturally felt disinclined to expend large sums and the blood of their menfolk, in order to keep the territory which a few enterprising Frenchmen had conquered in these far-off countries, with their awfully hot, or awfully cold, climates. If the French provinces were dowdy and dull the colonies must be a hundred times more so. The unfortunate Montcalm and Dupleix, therefore, were, if not quite abandoned, quite insufficiently supported and though they accomplished miracles they could not but be defeated in the end.

Through all the diplomatic and political crises of recent years, life at Court had gone on exactly as usual. The only activity of the Austrian Ambassador to attract attention was the way he had his hair powdered, by two men with bellows. Members of the *Parlements*, grave and portentous, passed in and out of the King's council chamber as if their robes had the power of making them invisible; the courtiers never spoke of them, or seemed to notice them at all. The outbreak of war, however, made a certain impact at Versailles. As at the beginning of all wars, there was a great scramble to get into the army; Maréchal de Belle-Isle's antechamber was filled with young men clamouring for jobs. 'No hurry, my boy, it won't be over to-morrow.' As at the beginning of all wars, too, the women were for or against it, according to whether their husbands or their lovers were likely to be involved and whether they longed more for the safety or the glory of the loved one. No shame attached to the courtiers who preferred to stay at home and invent amusing songs about the French defeats. 'We can't help loving our defeats, they make such wonderful jokes.'

They could not help loving anything that made them laugh. The Lisbon earthquake was 'embarrassing to the physicists and humiliating to theologians'. It robbed Voltaire of his optimism. In the huge waves which engulfed the town, in the chasms which opened underneath it, in volcanic flames which raged for days in the outskirts, some 50,000 people perished. But to the courtiers of Louis XV it was an enormous joke. M. de Baschi, Madame de Pompadour's brother-in-law, was French Ambassador there at the time. He saw the Spanish Ambassador killed by the arms of Spain, which toppled onto his head from the portico of his embassy. Baschi then dashed into the house and rescued his colleague's little boy whom he took, with his own family, to the country. When he got back to Versailles he kept the whole Court in roars of laughter for a week with his account of it all. 'Have you heard Baschi on the earthquake?'

But the King and the Marquise were two changed people; gone was the charming carelessness of their early years together. Her red lacquer room became his office, here he received the Ministers and kept the state papers. Nothing was decided without her knowledge. If it be true that she marked the maps of Germany, which now replaced the Bouchers on her wall, with *mouches* (beauty spots) to show the course of the campaign, it was probably less out of a spirit of frivolity, than because they happened to be within reach, and were a convenient medium.

The voyages, such a pleasure to both of them, were cut down, and work in their various houses came to a standstill. Very sadly they gave up Crécy and sold it to the Duc de Penthièvre; the voyages there were supposed to be the most expensive of all. 'I regret nothing,' she wrote to Stainville, 'except my poor Crécy; I wouldn't even admit this if I were not sure of overcoming my weakness. I ought to be there at this very minute.' She went there for a last visit, without the King, to open the cottage hospital she had built in the village. It had forty-eight beds and a resident surgeon and she had sold her diamonds in order to endow it.

After the beginning of the war we know but little about Madame de Pompadour's private life. She was shut up in her apartment, working with the King and his ministers, and was seen much less at Court functions. In 1758 the invaluable diary of the Duc de Luynes comes to an end and we no longer have an almost daily account of the gossip and goings-on at Versailles. But everything we do know about her is rather sad. The Marquise had to a great extent lost her looks. She never ceased to mourn her little girl. Her heart troubled her, she was hardly ever well and often in pain. She worried very much over public events. The great compensation for all this was the companionship of the King. He went out hunting, he went off to his brothel, he saw a certain amount of his children, he performed his public duties; all the rest of the day he was with her. Their relationship was that of a couple happily married since many years.

By the spring of 1757, Frederick was in possession of Saxony, he also occupied Bohemia and laid siege to Prague. The Dauphine was so much upset by the news from her home that she had a miscarriage. Her mother was subjected to indignities which finally killed her; her father fled; and Frederick stole all their possessions, even the petty cash which he found in the palace. The only male member of that family who had ever been any good, Maurice de Saxe, now reposed beneath the most beautiful of all eighteenth-century tombs at Strasbourg. He had died in 1750, at Chambord, of making love too much. He was a Protestant or he would have been buried, like Turenne, with the royal family at St. Denis.

'How sad', remarked the Dauphine, 'that we can't sing a De Profundis for somebody who made us sing so many Te Deums.' Lowendal, too, was dead. The King remarked bitterly, and with truth, that he no longer had any generals, only a few captains. Out of these captains he and Madame de Pompadour did their best to choose wisely; those they appointed were all (except d'Estrées) members of their own circle and it must be said that none of them was worth anything. Madame de Pompadour set her heart from the first upon a high command for the Prince de Soubise, one of her greatest and oldest friends. He was given an army corps; the *Grande Armée* was commanded by Maréchal d'Estrées, who, with forty thousand men, instead of the twenty-four thousand promised in the Treaty of Versailles, set forth for Hanover.

D'Estrées crossed Westphalia, took Emden, subjugated Hesse and crossed the Weser, hardly meeting with any opposition at all. Cumberland, with an Anglo-German army, retreated before him to Hastenbeck. With lengthening lines of communication, it became more difficult to keep the army in provisions, and at this point d'Estrées fell out with Pâris-Duverney, who was as usual supplying it. Maurice de Saxe had always had such perfect confidence in Duverney that he used to consult him on his plans of campaign; d'Estrées took a different line, high-handed and rude. At the same time he left Soubise, of whom he was jealous, completely in the dark about his dispositions. In other words he alienated the friends of the Marquise, never a very wise thing to do. Duverney used his enormous influence with the King and with Madame de Pompadour to replace d'Estrées by Richelieu. It was a curious error for this usually good judge of human nature to have made; but he saw, rightly, that now was the moment to strike hard and win the war and he was, no doubt, dazzled by Richelieu's exploits at Geneva and Minorca.

The Maréchal de Belle-Isle, realizing that an intrigue to replace d'Estrées was afoot, sent him a secret message saying that he had better soon have a decisive victory to report if he did not want to be recalled. D'Estrées attacked the Duke of Cumberland and won the Battle of Hastenbeck (26th July, 1757). Too late, however. Duverney had by now persuaded the King, who in his turn had persuaded the Marquise, that Richelieu was their best hope, and they had decided upon his appointment. Madame de Pompadour wrote to Duverney: 'The King asks me to tell you, *mon nigaud*, that as your project has a political significance, you must confide it to the Abbé de Bernis. The Maréchal de Belle-Isle has been rather difficult; do stroke him when you see him. The King is speaking to M. de Richelieu to-night. I must warn you that he (Richelieu) tells everything to Madame de L. . . .'

So off went Son Excellence to replace d'Estrées. He would have been in time to claim the victory of Hastenbeck as his own if he had not stopped to spend a few days in Strasbourg with his mistress the Duchesse de Lauraguais who was on her way back from a watering place. The real victor of Hastenbeck was one Chevert, a regular soldier of great talent, debarred from higher command than that of Lt.-General because his family was not noble. The public, unaware of this, was outraged by the recall of d'Estrées immediately after such a success; a caricature circulated in Paris which represented him whipping Cumberland with a branch of laurel, while Richelieu picked up the leaves and crowned himself with them. Back at Versailles, d'Estrées compared his lot with that of Germanicus, also recalled a week after crossing the Weser, a piece of pretentiousness which lost him a good deal of sympathy.

Frederick's position now seemed to be desperate. He had been driven away from Prague by an Imperial army under General Daun, 'the most beautiful, the gayest army possible to be seen,' as Madame de Pompadour described it, and was also hard pressed on the Russian front. His thoughts turned to suicide, and then to making peace with France. He began by trying to bribe Madame de Pompadour, offering her huge sums of money and the principality of Neuchâtel. She thought this a great joke and forwarded his letters to the Empress. Then Voltaire seems to have suggested that Richelieu would be a more likely person to treat with.

The case of the Duc de Richelieu illustrates the fact that once a man has been convicted of treachery, he is better dead; the traitor will always betray. Frederick wrote to him in terms of fulsome flattery: 'The nephew of the great Cardinal is born to sign treaties as much as to win battles. . . . He who has merited statues in Geneva and conquered the Island of Minorca in the face of huge difficulties . . .' and so on. Richelieu sent this letter to Pâris-Duverney, as a sign of his good faith. But then, instead of pursuing Cumberland and his beaten army, he hung about in Hanover, wringing money from the civilian population. When the burgomaster of a town brought him the keys—always in solid gold—Richelieu would pocket them. The burgomasters sadly pointed out that Turenne used to take the towns, but give back the keys.

'Very likely,' said Richelieu, 'M. de Turenne was really inimitable.' He levied huge sums from householders who would rather pay than have soldiers billeted on them—in fact he was up to every known dodge by which a general in those days could enrich himself. His own soldiers called him *Papa la Maraude*, and they soon had no vestige of discipline left. Richelieu believed that an army should live off the country and gave his troops a free hand to rob and ravish the civilian population. At last he turned his attention once more to the campaign. He proceeded, as at Fort St. Philip, to ignore the rules of warfare and without any plan of battle, without any satisfactory arrangement for a supply line, he pursued the Duke of Cumberland to the banks of the Elbe. It was really asking for trouble. But his extraordinary luck persisted; he pinned Cumberland and his army between the Elbe and the sea, so that Cumberland had no choice but to open negotiations for a surrender. At this point the Seven Years War could have been won in a single campaign; Louis XV and the Empress would have had Europe at their feet and Madame de Pompadour, had she been given the credit for the Austrian alliance for which, subsequently, she had been so bitterly blamed, would have gone down to history as a political genius. If, when the Regent had enough proof to cut off four of M. de Richelieu's heads, he had cut off one, the history of France might have been different indeed.

Instead of taking Cumberland prisoner, and disarming his troops, Richelieu treated with him and let him go, on the promise that he and his allies would disband and never fight against France while the war lasted. This arrangement, known as the Convention of Closter Seven, was perfectly meaningless; neither Richelieu nor Cumberland was entitled to sign any form of treaty, and it was quite as badly received, at first, in London, and by Frederick, as at Fontainebleau. But the French suffered from it. Richelieu had signed, in his usual airy manner, without fixing any date for the execution of the articles, or remembering to prohibit Cumberland and his troops from fighting against the allies of France. Bernis was partly to blame for this fatal convention. Though in his memoirs he pretends that it came as a bombshell and that Richelieu presented him with an accomplished fact, his letters to Stainville show that he knew quite well that something of the sort was going on and did not entirely disapprove of it.

George II took no account of Cumberland's parole—'here is my son, who has ruined me and disgraced himself,' refused to ratify the Convention, and wrote to the Hanoverian council of regency at Stade: 'a victory gained by the King of Prussia would be a convenient occasion for falling unexpectedly upon the French, who are quartered in our states, in such a manner that they may be surprised separately in their quarters.' To do him justice, Cumberland keenly felt the dishonour and retired into private life.

Closter Seven was bad enough, but at least it had left the French army intact. Richelieu, now in full correspondence with Frederick, and probably receiving bribes from him, refused to send troops to Soubise in Saxony, who was clamouring for them. When finally, much too late, he did send them, no arrangements were made to feed them during their march and they arrived in a pitiful condition, quite unready for battle. The result was the crushing defeat of M. de Soubise and his army of French and Imperial troops at Rosbach, 1757. The blame for this must really be shared by Richelieu and the Duke of Saxe-Hildburghausen, in command of the Austrians. He had also been bought by Frederick; doubts as to his loyalty had already been expressed in France weeks before the engagement took place. Rosbach was one of the battles most enjoyed by the jokers at Versailles; songs and caricatures without end mocked the unfortunate Soubise. 'I've lost my army—wherever can it be—oh! thank goodness! I see it coming towards me—horrors! It's the enemy!' The Hôtel de Soubise was to let, they said, the Prince having gone to the Ecole Militaire. It would cost him nothing now to build a new house, he could do it with the stones that would be thrown at him. And so on.

Bernis wrote to Stainville that all this was very prejudicial to their friend (Madame de Pompadour); the public, which had disliked the appointment of Soubise, would only have forgiven it if he had won a victory—unfair perhaps, but the public is never fair on these occasions. M. de Soubise, who had behaved wisely before the battle, and like a hero during it, had better now retire and accept, with a good grace, a distinguished reserve in the allied army. He was in no way to blame, it had been a fatal mistake to have two generals.

As for Madame de Pompadour, she was in despair. She cried

all night after receiving a letter from the Prince in which he made no attempt to minimize the disaster which had befallen his army, a disaster the more heartrending, as so often happens, because of the hopeless gallantry of certain regiments and individuals. She wrote to Madame de Lutzelbourg: '. . . you know how fond I am of him, and can imagine how much I mind the things they are saying about him in Paris. His army loves and admires him, as he deserves. Madame la Dauphine is fearfully unhappy at the death of her mother the Queen—another victim of the King of Prussia. How can Providence allow him to go on making everybody so miserable? I feel desperate about it all. . . .' She fought like a tiger for her friend, refused to hear of his retirement and was furious at what she considered the unfair and revolting campaign launched against him by all the stay-at-homes. She was determined that he should have a second chance. That winter Madame de Pompadour made Soubise come back to Versailles on leave, and did her very best to console him; never has a beaten general been so well-received at home. She was in particularly good spirits again by then, fatter and looking perfectly beautiful; the King very gay and ready to be amused, and they were both talking a great deal about love. The little staircase was unblocked, and the King appeared and disappeared unexpectedly as he used to. Bébé, a water spaniel which Soubise had left with Madame de Pompadour, was enchanted to see his master. When the Prince mentioned his defeat one evening at supper, Madame de Pompadour told him not to talk shop.

At this time Madame de Pompadour and the King were seeing a great deal of that curious personage the Comte de St. Germain. He amused and distracted them, and they forced themselves to believe in him, rather as children force themselves to believe in conjurers, to heighten the entertainment value. St. Germain was a charlatan of whom not much has ever been known, except that he was very rich and spoke every European language. He has been accused, by French writers, of belonging to the English Intelligence Service and of being the father of Freemasonry. The English thought he was a Jacobite spy. But his own claim to fame was that he had lived for thousands of years and had known Jesus Christ.

He described to Madame de Pompadour the Courts of the various Kings of France where, he said, he had been *persona grata*. She decided that if she had not had the luck to live in the Court of her own King, she would have chosen that of François I, patron of the arts. One day St. Germain played a little tune on her clavichord and the King asked what it was. 'I don't know,' he replied carelessly, 'the first time I heard it was at the entry of Alexander into Babylon.' He astounded the King by removing a flaw from one of his diamonds. St. Germain said that his eternal life (not youth, for he was a well-set-up man of about fifty) was due to an elixir which preserved those who took it always at the same age. Madame de Pompadour eagerly swallowed both the story and the drug; she said that it had done her a great deal of good. But in 1760 St. Germain fell into bad odour with the police and Choiseul sent him packing. He wandered from one European court to another and died in 1780.

As soon as all the armies had gone into winter quarters, 1757–8, Richelieu, who was dying to see his mistresses again, asked for leave, not a very wise move if he had wanted to keep his command. Closter Seven had just been formally repudiated by Ferdinand of Brunswick, who had announced his intention of resuming hostilities at once. It hardly seemed the moment for the author of that unlucky armistice to go back to Paris and enjoy himself. The King granted him his leave but said that as it was impossible for the army to be without a commander-in-chief at such a critical moment he was sending the Comte de Clermont to replace him.

Richelieu once more demonstrated his capacity for getting away with everything. He came back to Versailles, where the King was delighted to see him, and happily resumed his lady-killing operations there and in Paris. Very soon he was observed sneaking into the bedroom of one of his mistresses, by means of a plank thrown over the street from an opposite house. He used the fruits of his treachery to buy the beautiful Hôtel d'Antin on the boulevards, and added a wing ending in a round room which looked out over fields. The Parisians called it the *Pavillon de Hanovre*. It was pulled down in 1930 and rebuilt in the park of Sceaux. 'I have seen it,' says Horace Walpole, 'there is a chamber surrounded with looking glasses and hung with white lute strings, painted with roses. I wish you could see the antiquated Rinaldo who has built himself this romantic bower. Looking glass never reflected so many wrinkles.'

The old mummy, as they called him at Versailles, was now sixty-two. His military career came to an end with the Convention of Closter Seven, his amorous career went on until he died, at the age of ninety-six. When he was eighty-four he pensioned off an old lady whose chief occupation in life had been finding girls for him and making all arrangements, and settled down with his fourth wife, a pretty young widow. She, worshipping him as much as all his other wives and mistresses, presented him with a son, who died at once, however—greatly to the relief of M. de Fronsac. Richelieu made up his quarrel with Maurepas when that minister was recalled, after twenty-seven years of exile, by Louis XVI; they used to sit together for hours on end at Versailles, which they alone, now, could remember under Louis XIV, regretting the glories of the past, perhaps, even—who knows?— regretting the Marquise herself.

'Poor posterity,' said Bernis, speaking of the Seven Years War, the personalities concerned and the dense atmosphere of intrigue in which it was conducted, 'what will you understand of all this? What a booby Truth will make of you!' After Rosbach he had but one idea, which was to make peace as quickly and as honourably as possible. The Prussian party in France, encouraged by two more allied defeats which followed almost at once, began to come out into the open. Pamphlets and memoranda poured from the pen of d'Argenson and found their way to the already discouraged officers at the front. Bernis told Stainville that 'Les Ormes' (d'Argenson and Madame d'Estrades) were quite as powerful with the army as the Ministry of War, but he took no steps to silence them. Cleverer in this than Hitler, Frederick had always courted the intellectuals, and from a very small outlay, consisting mostly of flattery, he now reaped rich dividends. The *philosophes* were on his side, to them he represented freedom of thought as opposed to the bigotry and obscurantism of their own King. He played upon the inborn distrust of all Frenchmen for Austria and the bogey of the Russian bear was invoked, not for the last time in history. Bernis was for ever saying that it would be *furieusement embarrassant* if the Russians began asking for more territory. The French home front was quite as demoralized as the army; people could take no interest in the war and only longed for it to stop. Worst of all, money was short.

Bernis became abjectly defeatist. Babet la Bouquetière was certainly no statesman. When the Austrian alliance was first proposed to him he was doubtful; then he supported it and actively helped to bring it into effect. At the beginning of the war he was enthusiastic about the alliance, and as soon as things began to go badly he came back to his orginal doubts, magnified a hundredfold. 'I told you so,' was the burden of his song to the Marquise. He told her other disagreeable things as well. Her enemies, he said, would accuse her of continuing the war in order to give Soubise his revenge. To Stainville he wrote: 'We have neither generals nor ministers, I find this phrase so true that I am quite willing to include myself in this category. ...' 'I pointed out [to the Marquise] that so far we have lost nothing at sea, that Minorca would more than make up for Louisburg ... but that in the long run the English, whose navy is so much stronger, could not fail to take away our colonies. Our allies can never make up to us for such a loss. ...' '... Our finances are no longer in a state to defray the enormous expenses.' 'I tell this to God and all his saints [Madame de Pompadour], we open big sad eyes, but nothing is done.' Page after page of this stuff went to Stainville in Vienna, copied, of course, by the Austrian secret police and duly read by Maria Theresa. 'What can be more blind than the courage which impels the Empress to try and defeat her enemy next year? What has she to hope for more than last year? The same men are in the same jobs, the King of Prussia is no different; our generals and ministers will always be inferior to him.'

He was not far wrong. The war now took a regular course. Every spring Frederick would be attacked on three sides by three armies converging on Berlin; every spring his position would look hopeless, and every summer and autumn, allied disunity, bad generalship, and lengthy supply lines fought his battles for him. Besides his own great courage and admirable troops he had two advantages, he was fighting on his home ground with unity of command. But the King and Madame de Pompadour, whose hatred of the Prussians, so understandable to us, bounded their horizon, refused to listen to the possibly reasonable advice of Bernis; and the Marquise began to see that if the war were to go on he would have to depart. He was obviously losing his nerve.

The Comte de Clermont, who replaced Richelieu in Hanover, was a Prince of the Blood, brother of M. le Duc and grandson of the great Condé. Though he had fought in many campaigns under Saxe, who had considered him a good officer, he was an Abbé and enjoyed the rich living of St. Germain des Prés. The chorus, led by Richelieu, of jokes, songs and epigrams about his appointment, may be imagined. 'His bottom is more suited to an arm-chair than a saddle,' etc. It would have been more sensible, they said, with some truth, to have appointed the pugnacious Arch-bishop, Christophe de Beaumont. However, as soon as Mon-seigneur arrived at the front and had taken a look at the troops he was to command, he got his own back on Richelieu with a crushing indictment. 'I found Your Majesty's army divided into three corps. The first is on the ground; it is composed of thieves and marauders . . . the second is under the ground and the third is in the hospitals.' The state of these was not very flourishing; those surgeons and nurses who had not deserted were as ill as the patients; filth and famine prevailed. Clermont was obliged to cashier eighty officers on the spot, for being absent without leave and for major offences against the civilian population. A whole regiment of hussars was broken up, and incorporated in other units, for pillage, theft and rape. To such a pass had hopeless generalship reduced the finest army in the world in eight years since the death of Maurice de Saxe. Apart from their demoraliza-tion the soldiers were physically in poor shape, worn out with marching on short rations.

Clermont was incapable of high command; almost immediately he began a series of retreats. Madame de Pompadour wrote to him continually to try and stiffen him up; he soon hated the post bag from Versailles more than any of his other troubles. He crossed the Weser. 'What can I say, Monseigneur? I am in despair that you should have been obliged to cross the Weser and even more so at the amount of casualties you have had to abandon. . . .' He crossed the Lippe and arrived at Wesel, having lost Hanover and Hesse as well. 'I hope your position on the Rhine is strong enough for you to be able to effect the necessary repairs . . . continue your good work, Monseigneur, and do not be discouraged.' News arrived at Versailles that he was preparing a further retreat behind the Moselle. The Marquise wrote a frantic letter—the Empress was now in danger of being dethroned, in which case France would be left alone, dishonoured and lost. 'This, Monseigneur, is an exact picture of our situation. I have no strength left to speak of anything else but my inviolable devotion to you.' At last the long agony ended in the crushing defeat of Clermont at Crefelt (23rd June, 1758).

This battle is chiefly remembered for the death of the Comte de Gisors, only child of the Maréchal de Belle-Isle. M. de Gisors, who was twenty-six, was one of those almost perfect young men who are so often killed in wars; he was truly mourned, by high and low, in Paris, at Versailles, in England and even in Germany; Frederick used to say he could forgive the French a great deal for having produced the Comte de Gisors. (It was he who once wrote from London: 'Whereas Madame de Pompadour shares the absolute power of Louis XV, Lady Yarmouth shares the absolute impotence of George II.') His short life was saddened by Richelieu's refusal to give him his daughter, the beautiful Septimanie. She married the Comte d'Egmont, an intensely dreary grandee of Spain. She and Gisors had been too virtuous to 'find each other in society', as her cynical old father had predicted; on the contrary they had been at great pains to avoid seeing each other. But their love had never altered. Gisors' little young wife, daughter of Nivernais, mourned him to the end of her days and refused to marry again. They had no children.

Everybody thought the blow would kill the Maréchal de Belle-Isle. Madame de Pompadour said that the King must go and see him at once, but he dreaded this visit and tried to put it off. '*Barbare*,' she declaimed, '*dont l'orgueil croit le sang d'un sujet trop payé d'un coup d'œil.*'[1] 'Who wrote that?' he asked. 'Voltaire.' 'Yes, I see. I suppose I'm the barbarian for having given Voltaire a post and a pension!' Finally he went in great state, accompanied by the Queen and all the Court, to offer his condolences. He

[1] Proud barbarian, you deem the blood of a subject amply repaid by a glance.

spoke nobly and with feeling to the Marshal, who found comfort in his words. So far from embarrassing the King with any display of grief he was perfectly stoical; he stayed at the Ministry of War, which the King had begged him to do, and buried himself more and more in his work.

After so much gloom and bad news the Duc d'Aiguillon's victory at St. Cast was very welcome at Versailles. M. d'Aiguillon, a great friend and protégé of Madame de Pompadour, was the governor of Brittany; he had very much wanted to resign this post and go to the war and she had dissuaded him from doing so. In September 1758 he and his Breton volunteers defeated a big English raid, a reconnaissance for invasion, at St. Cast; 3000 Englishmen were killed and 500 taken prisoner. D'Aiguillon's enemies said that he was hiding in a mill during the engagement: 'If our general did not cover himself with glory, at least he covered himself with flour.' But d'Aiguillon was not a coward, whatever his other faults, and certainly the Marquise had no such suspicions.

'We sang your Te Deum to-day,' she wrote, 'to my great satisfaction, always having predicted your success. Indeed how could it have been otherwise, with so much zeal, intelligence and so cool a head leading troops who only burned, like their commander, to avenge the King?' 'They say the mylords want to try again—I only hope it will be at the same cost to them.' 'I count on the good luck of Cavendish.'[1]

In 1758, too, Soubise took his revenge for Rosbach at the battles of Sandershausen and Lutzelberg, victories which, like that of Hastenbeck, are supposed to have been won by the unpromotable, because not noble, Chevert. In spite of these encouraging events Bernis went on bleating his despair. 'I am on the rack.' 'My brain is full of blood which keeps rushing to my head.' 'If I

---

[1] Lord Frederick Cavendish, Colonel of the 34th Foot, was taken prisoner at St. Cast. Madame de Pompadour always thereafter called d'Aiguillon 'Cavendish.'

were capable of dying, or going mad, I should have done both by now.' '*Nous avons été trahis de partout.*' The Marquise could hardly bear the sight of his depressing little face. She still believed in the Austrian alliance as much as ever and was determined to prosecute the war; in these circumstances it was no use keeping Bernis. Stainville, able, ambitious, young and energetic, a Lorrainer, heart and soul with the Empire by long family tradition, was the obvious man to step into his shoes. Stainville certainly thought so and did all he could to get into them; after a perusal of Bernis' long-winded whines to the Vienna embassy, it is difficult to blame him. They must have been unbearably irritating, especially as Stainville knew quite well that the Empress was reading them too, and that her suspicions of her ally were mounting daily. 'The French, it seems, are only invincible when they are fighting against me.'

It must be said that, if a politician who has once tasted power ever wishes to leave it, Bernis wished to. The whole thing had become too much for him. What he really wanted was to shelve the responsibility, which kept him awake at night, to surrender Foreign Affairs to somebody else, Stainville for choice, and to stay in the *Conseil*. At one moment it looked as if all this would be possible.

The King wrote: 'I am very sorry, Monsieur l'Abbé-Comte, that my affairs have affected your health so that you can no longer bear the weight of the work. Nobody wants peace more than I do, but it must be a solid peace, not a dishonourable one. I would sacrifice my own interests for it, but not those of my friends.' He went on to say that he would regretfully allow Bernis to hand over Foreign Affairs to Stainville and told him to advise Stainville and the Empress of this change. To sugar the pill of what was, in fact, his dismissal, a Cardinal's hat was procured for Bernis by Stainville, who, although Benedict XIV was dead, still had many friends left in Rome. In 1758 Stainville received a dukedom, and he was known henceforward as the Duc de Choiseul. An announcement appeared in the *Gazette de France*: 'The health of Cardinal de Bernis, which has, for a long time now, been far from good, has made it impossible for him to continue in the heavy task of Foreign Minister. The King has accepted his resignation and has named the Duc de Choiseul as his successor. The King has kept a place for Cardinal de Bernis in his *Conseil*. . . .' Bernis received his biretta with great pomp and ceremony at the hands of the King, who was very nice to him and said he had never made a finer Cardinal. But both he and the Marquise were determined to get him out of the palace.

The new Cardinal paid visits of state to the Queen, the Dauphin and Dauphine, the Duc de Bourgogne, the Duc de Berry, the Comte de Provence and the Comte d'Artois, aged one; to Madame Infante and her daughter the Infante Isabelle, to Mesdames Adélaïde, Sophie, Victoire and Louise. Then he left for his apartment in the Palais-Royal; it was six years before he saw Versailles again. The King wrote and told him to go and live in his château at Vic-sur-Aisne, near Soissons. No departing minister had ever been let down so lightly, but still there was no mistaking the fact that he had been dismissed and disgraced. Madame de Pompadour and Choiseul both felt rather guilty about him, and did what they could to lighten his exile, taking immediate steps to see that neither he nor his family should suffer financially. They wanted a bishopric for him, but this would have meant an interview with the King, who said it would embarrass him far too much and that he could not face it; but in 1764 they got his exile revoked, he came back to Versailles for a visit and was then made Archbishop of Albi. After the death of Madame de Pompadour Choiseul sent him as Ambassador to Rome, where he died in the middle of the French Revolution.

Madame de Pompadour had been truly fond of the little Abbé and was very sorry for what had happened. She told Madame du

Hausset that it was all the fault, in the first place, of the Bishop of Mirepoix who had stopped him from getting a pension. If he had had that, and the King had been quite prepared to give it to him, he would never have been made Ambassador but would have been master of the chapel at Versailles—far happier for him and she would not have had all these regrets. Now she was deprived of the pleasure, on which she had counted, of growing old in the company of this charming friend. She added that at the end of his first week in office, she had realized that he would not do.

The King was only too pleased to see the last of Bernis. He had never liked him and had been very much put off him by rumours, which had come to his ears, that the Abbé was having an affair with Madame Infante. Finally he had been unable to bear the sight of him since a certain incident at Versailles. Bernis, with an almost incredible lack of ordinary manners, took his gun, and went shooting in a little covert under the King's very windows. The Comte de Noailles and Madame de Pompadour told him that he must never do such a thing again; too late, the King knew about it. For years afterwards when he walked in that place he used to say: 'These are the pleasure grounds of Monsieur l'Abbé.'

*Chapter Nineteen*

# CHOISEUL

THE Duc de Choiseul was a very different sort of man from the false and smiling Maurepas, the haughty d'Argenson and the Abbé, his dear little face puckered with worry. To begin with he was an aristocrat, with all the airs and manners of one, and the King felt more at his ease with him than with any other minister he had ever had. He would never have gone shooting under the King's window. He was always in roistering spirits, had the capacity of explaining a complicated situation in a few pertinent words, did not go droning on about things, never hesitated nor havered and knew exactly what he thought should be done next. When the day's work was over, he cast aside the cares of state and was ready for a bit of fun.

In looks Choiseul was very much like Sir Winston Churchill, with bright red hair, bright blue eyes, a turned-up nose and an expression of humorous pugnacity. A *dogue* (mastiff), said his contemporaries. His friends loved him and were to prove unusually faithful when, having governed France for twelve years, he was disgraced and exiled to Chanteloup, his country home. Women found him irresistible and to his wife he was as God.

The Duchesse de Choiseul was an heiress, grand-daughter of the enormously rich Crozat, nicknamed *le pauvre* to distinguish him from his even more enormously rich brother, Crozat-*le-riche*. Her elder sister, the Marquise de Gontaut, wife of Madame de Pompadour's great friend, had been the mistress of Choiseul. She died giving birth to the future Duc de Lauzun who was very probably his son. When she knew that she was dying she made her twelve-year-old sister, Louise-Honorine, promise that she would marry Choiseul. Madame de Gontaut had seen that he was one of those people who need a great deal of money. Then she died, easy in her mind about her lover. By the time the marriage finally took place, however, the bride seemed to have become far less rich than she ought to have been, as the result of a law suit between the heirs of the brothers Crozat. Choiseul and Gontaut took the quarrel to the Court of Appeal. At this time Gontaut was in love with a certain Madame Rossignol, and he was for ever saying to Choiseul: 'Do you think Madame Rossignol loves me?' While the judge was reading the verdict, which would either make the brothers-in-law immensely rich, or leave them rather poor, Choiseul whispered to Gontaut: 'Do you think Madame Rossignol loves you?' and they then went off into such gales of giggles that they did not know which way the case had been decided. It was in their favour.

The Duchess, who is one of the amiable bores of history, fell madly in love with her husband and never looked at anybody else all her life. The only person who doubted the sincerity of her passion was Horace Walpole who said that she displayed it too much for him to believe in it. Choiseul himself was deeply devoted to her. 'Her virtue,' he wrote, 'her charm, her feeling for me and mine for her have brought more happiness to our married life than any amount of money would have done.' She had to put up with flagrant infidelity; at first it made her miserable, but in time she took the situation philosophically and made friends with her husband's mistresses. It was not only of them that she had cause for jealousy. M. de Choiseul had a sister whose lack of fortune had hitherto prevented her from marrying; at the ripe age of twenty-eight she was eating her heart out in the convent of Remiremont, a terrible fate for one who loved society above everything else. As soon as he was installed at Versailles he sent for this sister, and married her to the idiotic and vicious Duc de Gramont; they separated almost at once and the Duchess went to live with her brother. Though not so pretty, and not nearly so nice, as her sister-in-law she was more amusing and had more influence with Choiseul. The courtiers soon found this out, so that, while Madame de Choiseul was admired but neglected, Madame de Gramont was disliked but courted. Madame de Choiseul keenly resented the fact that even in her own house she was never now alone with her husband. Madame de Gramont made her feel a fool. One day the Duchesse de Choiseul was telling her guests at dinner that exile would hold no terrors for her, on the contrary, she would adore to live in some remote spot quite alone with Choiseul. 'Yes, but what about him?' said her horrid sister-in-law, from the other side of the table.

Madame de Pompadour loved the whole Choiseul family and could never have enough of them. She and the King supped with them three times a week; her own suppers altered very much in character, not more than eight guests of whom three were the Choiseuls. The Duchesse de Gramont amused the King and always sat next to him, Choiseul himself kept the whole table in a constant buzz of jollity and Madame de Choiseul was simply delicious.

The Marquise could feel at last that she and the King were being adequately supported in their work, and the comfort to her was all the greater because she was hardly ever well now; everything seemed to tire her. As the months went by she put more and more responsibility upon Choiseul. She kept the outward signs of power; the appointments, the rewards, the decorations and the commands were still distributed by her, the state papers still passed through her hands and the work was done in her room, but she ceased to be the moving spirit. Choiseul accumulated an unheard-of amount of ministries and honours; Foreign Affairs, War, the Navy, the Post Office, the governorship of

Touraine, the Golden Fleece (he already had the Cordon Bleu) and Colonel-General of the Swiss Guard, a post always hitherto occupied by a Prince of the Blood: in four years all were his. He used to say he was like the coachman in *L'Avare*, putting his hand to every job and doing whatever was wanted.

If the war, conducted by him, did not go much better than before, at any rate it went no worse and the prophesied disasters and ruin did not occur. It was hardly his fault that he took over a state near to bankruptcy, the shadow of a navy and a demoralized army commanded by the most incompetent generals France has ever known. He made the necessary financial reforms in an incredibly short time and with a minimum of fuss. In 1758 the budget for Foreign Affairs was fifty-seven millions; out of this came the maintenance of the Bavarian, Wurtemburg and Palatine armies, all paid by the King of France and very useless on the battlefield, and bribes, or what we should call *aid* to neutral countries. In 1759, the first year of Choiseul's administration, the budget was twenty-four millions, by 1763 it was down to eleven millions. This diminution never lost the King a single ally. The Duke also introduced reforms at Versailles. All the hundreds of people who held sinecures at Court were obliged to render an account of how much they got, and for what reason. The King himself had already cut down his expenses in many ways; he now kept only 1000 horses, had stopped all his private building, and had made economies even in his kitchen. The Marquise had sold most of her diamonds, which she always said was no sacrifice as she had never cared for jewels. They had both sent a huge quantity of silver to be melted down at the *Monnaie* and had induced the courtiers to do likewise. This served the double purpose of producing bullion and helping the factory at Sèvres; though it ruined the silversmiths. Every morning the King got a list of people who had done their duty by giving silver; they received one-quarter of the value in money and the rest in six per cent

Government bonds. Louis XIV had done the same in order to pay for his wars and the sad result is that old French silver is rarer than that of any other country. The Marquise had sold Bellevue to the King and had furthermore given almost her whole capital so that Ecole Militaire could be finished. The days of extravagance were over.

Maria Theresa was, of course, very much pleased by the appointment of Choiseul. She knew him well and had always known his family—his father had at one time been Austrian Minister to France—so she could be quite sure that he would never go back on the alliance. She now sent Madame de Pompadour the famous *escritoire*. When she first had the idea of giving the Marquise a present, she seems to have asked Starhemberg whether he thought a sum of money or a diamond aigrette would be the best. He replied that in his view the present that would give most pleasure would be one of the new writing tables now so fashionable, upright in design; these could be bought in Paris for about 4000 ducats. The Empress did not consider this valuable enough; she said it should cost at least 6000 ducats. She chose, out of her own enormous collection of lacquer boxes, two of the most perfect, and sent them to Paris to be made up and mounted in gold. This was done by the jeweller Ducrollay, Place Dauphine, and here is his bill.

|  | L. |
|---|---|
| Gold mounts for a lacquer desk, with flower vase, powder-box and sponge case, all in gold . . | 3,464 |
| Spent on lacquer . . . . . | 528 |
| Cabinet maker, joiner, and lock maker . . | 360 |
| Working the jewellery, engraving and chiselling . | 6,148 |
| For Lempereur (jeweller) . . . . | 66,000 |
| Miniature by Venevault . . . . | 600 |
| Box with copper mounts for packing the gift to go to Vienna and back to Paris . . . | 30 |

Packing up the gift and also those pieces of lacquer
   which were not used in its making    .     .     28

                                             77,158

The miniature of the Empress, surrounded by diamonds, was
evidently set in the lacquer. Nobody knows what finally became
of this remarkable piece mounted, it will be noticed, not in ormolu but in solid gold. Madame de Pompadour complained that
it was really too rich and that she had to hide it for fear of gossip;
she removed the miniature and had it framed in silver gilt, and
thus it appears in the inventory of her belongings made after her
death. But the *escritoire* itself seems to have vanished for ever.

Madame de Pompadour asked Starhemberg if she might take
the unusual liberty of writing direct to the Empress to thank her
for this present. '. . . If to be penetrated with enthusiastic admiration, Madame, for Your Imperial Majesty's charm and
legendary virtues is to be worthy of this precious gift then nobody
can be more worthy than I . . .' She signed Jeanne de Pompadour, 28 January, 1759, instead of her usual signature, Marquise
de Pompadour. (Letters to her relations and great friends had no
beginnings or endings, they were sealed with her three castles.)

Frederick, whose spies got hold of a copy of the letter for him,
circulated a parody which caused him the most exquisite delight:
'Beautiful Queen, the gracious words it pleases Your Majesty to
write to me are beyond all price. Incomparable Princess, who
honours me with the title of *bonne amie*, would that I could recon-
cile you to Venus the Goddess of Love as I have reconciled you to
my country . . .' and so on.

This did not do much harm to his victim; if anybody suffered
it was Maria Theresa who has been said by quite reputable historians to have written 'chère amie' and even 'chère cousine' to

Madame de Pompadour. Of course she never wrote directly to
her at all. The parody was rushed from the drum on which it was
written to the printing presses in Holland, and sent to all the
German states. Various copies went to Paris in the hope that one,
at least, would find its way to Versailles.

Voltaire was now back in Madame de Pompadour's life, a
reconciliation between them having been made by Choiseul,
who was a friend of his. In 1760 he dedicated *Tancrède* to her:
'Ever since your childhood I have seen distinction and talents
developing in you. At all times you have been unchangingly
good to me. It must be said, Madame, that I owe you a great
deal; furthermore I venture to thank you publicly for all you have
done to help a large number of writers, artists and other categories of deserving people. . . . You have shown discernment
in doing good because you have always used your own judgment.
I have never known a single writer or any unprejudiced person
who has not done justice to your character, and this not only in
public but also in private conversations when people are much
more inclined to blame than to praise. Believe me, Madame, it is
something to be proud of that those who know how to think
should speak thus of you.' No woman could ask for a greater
tribute from a man of genius.

Frederick soon discovered that Madame de Pompadour and
Voltaire were writing to each other again and began to use
Ferney as a post office for Versailles. Choiseul was anxious to
make peace, if it could be an honourable one, and he told Voltaire to see if Frederick could not be persuaded to reduce his demands and those of his English allies. 'Tell the King that, in spite
of our set-backs, Louis XV is still in a position to wipe out the
state of Prussia. If peace be not made this winter we shall be
obliged to take this decision, however dangerous.' He added
that France would be prepared to pay an indemnity.

Frederick pretended not to be interested in these overtures; Choiseul would soon be sent away, he said—he had already been minister for two years, a record at the French Court. Choiseul, thoroughly nettled, declared that he hated politics worse than death and lived only for pleasure; exile held no terrors for him. He had a beautiful house, a charming and faithful wife and delicious mistresses; there were only two ways in which anybody could harm him. The first would be to make him impotent and the second to oblige him to read the works of the philosopher of Sans-Souci. Frederick's reply was that peace would be signed— yes, by the King of England in Paris and by himself in Vienna. After this the letters became so acid that Voltaire stopped forwarding them; he saw that both sides would very soon round on him in their fury if he continued to be the go-between.

Choiseul's contribution to foreign policy was the *Pacte de Famille* among the Bourbons who reigned over France, Spain, Parma, Naples and the Two Sicilies; it was a Latin and Catholic block, fortified by an even closer alliance with the Empire, which was now drawn into the family. Louis XV married the two daughters of Madame Infante to the Emperor Joseph II and the Prince of the Asturias, while three little Archduchesses, in time, became Duchess of Parma, Queen of Naples and Dauphine of France.

The alliance between France and Spain, so ardently desired for so long, came too late to be of much use; Spain, exhausted by her efforts in the New World, had fallen a victim to the Roman Catholic religion in its most deadening and reactionary form, and had ceased to have much international importance. She was really more of a hindrance than a help to France in the war against England. As the war dragged on, it became obvious that the only course for Louis XV was to make the best peace he could, to build up a navy and perhaps resume the fight when England began to have difficulties with her American subjects. These difficulties were already foreseen by all the European statesmen of the day.

In 1762 the Empress Elizabeth of Russia died and her successor, Peter III, immediately made peace with Frederick, his hero from an early age. The withdrawal of Russia led to that of Sweden. All the European powers were sick of this apparently inconclusive war in which nearly a million people had perished. An armistice was agreed upon in 1762 and peace on a *status quo ante* basis was signed (February, 1763).

The fall of Pitt's government in 1762, and the fact that the new King, George III, seemed in favour of peace, decided the French to open negotiations with England. In September the Duc de Nivernais, 'crowned like Anacreon with roses and singing of pleasure,' set out for London as plenipotentiary. He very soon changed his tune. Most Englishmen were for continuing the war until they had taken the last inch of colonial territory from France. Nivernais' first night in England, at a delightful inn at Canterbury, cost him forty-six guineas; this extortion was the innkeeper's way of showing his patriotism. (When the gentlemen of Kent found it out they boycotted the inn and Nivernais eventually had to come to the rescue of his robber, now reduced to starvation, with a large gift of money.) The journey to London, however, charmed him, he said the country was all cultivated like the King's kitchen gardens. The Duke of Bedford's coachman took him, at an amazing speed, to the magnificent bridge of Westminster. Bedford himself had gone as envoy to France and made use of Nivernais' coaches while he was there—the usual arrangement between ambassadors in those days, who often used to live in each other's houses. Mirepoix and Albemarle had done so before the war began. Bedford left two houses ready for Nivernais, one in and one just outside London, 'very ugly but well situated.'

So far so good. But the smoke of London got on Nivernais' nerves, the fogs gave him a chronic sore throat and he could not bear the hours spent over the port after every meal. Very soon he took to leaving the table with the women; he would recite verses composed specially for them, or play the violin to them, in the drawing-room. They must have been surprised. Worst of all, Englishmen were extremely awkward to treat with, and things were not made easier by the fall of Havana. The news of this victory arrived when Nivernais was dining with Lord Bute; his fellow guests, unmindful of his feelings, burst into loud cheering.

Madame de Pompadour wrote: 'This cursed Havana, *petit époux*, I feel thoroughly frightened by it. What are the amiable Londoners going to say? The five fans you sent me are really not very pretty, though I admit that they are cheap. Send four more for two or three *louis* and let me know the total amount. . . . All my little friends send you their love, and so does your wife.'

The result of Havana was that, before the French could have peace, they had to blackmail the Spanish court into giving up Florida; the negotiations dragged on and Nivernais went to stay with various friends in their country houses. 'Wednesday to the Marlboroughs who have been begging me to go and will make a great fuss of me.' He very much enjoyed the fox-hunting, and his hosts enjoyed his company.

But the affair for which he had been sent was going too slowly for Madame de Pompadour, who wrote: 'There's never been such a gloomy *petit époux* in the world. You begin your letter: "My pen is falling from my hand"—no explanation, I thought all must be lost. But it seems, from what M. le Comte tells me, that you were talking of your tiredness. Really! You can rest afterwards but for God's sake finish now. The post we have just received has upset me very much, I tremble with fright and all our eloquence has not succeeded in reassuring M. de Bedford. *Petit époux*, how I would love you if you could tranquillize us quickly . . . As for your fans, they can go to the devil!'

He replied by sending a project for a treaty; 'not what I should have wished but the best I can do. . . . This is a cruel country to negotiate with, one needs a body and soul of iron. . . . I am quite done up, can't see straight, my stomach utterly destroyed, and every evening I have a horrid little cough brought on by the everlasting icy fogs . . .' At last, on 10th February, 1763, the treaty was signed. It was a personal success for Nivernais who had saved what he could, and more than another would have done, from the shipwreck. But it did not make cheerful reading for Frenchmen. Except for the territory which she still holds there to-day, France was evicted from India. In Canada she left 'a fragment of ancient France embedded in Northern ice' to be governed by Englishmen. Minorca returned to England; the French kept their West Indian islands, but lost Senegal.

The Duke went back to Versailles, taking with him his portrait by Allan Ramsay, spitting blood and in a sad state; '*une espèce de courbature générale.*' However, his wife, his mistress, and the good air of France soon got him quite right again, and in his letters he stopped talking of his own health. He could now only think of the Marquise, whose appearance had been a shock to him. She was evidently very far from well.

## Chapter Twenty

## THE END OF A DREAM

MADAME de Pompadour's health was failing and her spirits were very low. Two deaths in the royal family, which she now regarded as her own family, had recently saddened her and the King. In 1759 Madame Infante died, crying 'Au Paradis-vite-vite-au galop!' and in 1761 they lost the ten year old Duc de Bourgogne. He had endured the most cruel sufferings with extraordinary resolution. This child made a deep impression on all who knew him, and his mother, the Dauphine, was well aware that her other sons were of inferior stuff.

The Seven Years War, with its defeats and humiliations, had been a torment to the Marquise. She had put a brave face on it, the courtiers never saw her gloomy, nor did the King. She laughed and joked as she always had and they often thought she minded nothing. But her maid tells a different story. She could not sleep and she cried when she was alone. She worried far more than the King. His nerves were more solid than hers; the hunting took his mind off political matters for hours every day and made him sleep at night. Madame de Pompadour sat indoors, wrote letters and brooded; it was very bad for her. She had longed so much for France and her King to come out of the war covered with glory, and all had ended in ruin and shame. 'If I die,' she said, 'it will be of grief.'

To try and cheer her up, the King now put in hand a scheme, which they had long been considering, for a little country house in the gardens of Trianon. It was to be called the Petit Trianon and was intended to take the place of the Hermitage. They would be able to sleep there and occupy themselves with the farm which amused them more and more. The farm buildings, cow sheds, hen runs and so on were already there. The palace of Trianon was no good for their purpose as, by Court usage, too many people had the right to go there with the King and too much etiquette had to be observed there. Gabriel's plans for the small house were all ready; he started building in 1762 and it went up very quickly, but the Marquise only lived long enough to see the outside walls.

In 1763 Madame de Pompadour seems to have considered retiring from the Court to the Château of Ménars. She went there twice, without the King, an unprecedented absence and one that was much remarked on. She may have felt that she could not continue the struggle to keep his affections much longer. 'My life is like that of the early Christians—a perpetual combat.'

At this time the King had a new liaison, rather more disquieting than his usual commerce with little girls in the Parc aux Cerfs. His mistress was a lovely young woman, with long black hair, called Mlle Romains, the daughter of a lawyer from Grenoble. The King had first seen her walking in the gardens at Marly. She refused to be put in the Parc aux Cerfs and he bought her a little house at Passy, where she gave birth to a son. Madame de Pompadour went, disguised, to see her as she sat feeding her baby in the Bois de Boulogne; she and it were both smothered in beautiful lace, the black hair held by a diamond comb. The Marquise was greatly cast down after this outing.

'One must admit,' she said, sadly, 'that the mother and child are beautiful creatures.' But Madame de Mirepoix, as usual, consoled her in her sensible way: 'The King doesn't care a bit for his children, he has got too many and he won't want to be bothered with this mother and son. He never pays the slightest attention to the Comte du Luc, who is the dead spit of him—never speaks of him and I'm sure will do nothing for him. Once again, you must realize we are not under Louis XIV.' She was not quite right about this. He very soon got tired of Mlle Romains, as usual, but he did recognize her son, who grew up as l'Abbé de Bourbon, was adopted by Mesdames, but died of smallpox in his early twenties.

Peace was celebrated by the opening of the Place Louis XV (Place de la Concorde). As long ago as 1748, the King, after considering over sixty plans for this *Place*, and after much careful thought as to its position in Paris, had settled on a piece of waste land between the river, the Tuileries gardens and the Champs Elysées. He commissioned Gabriel to design the *Place*, and to build the two splendid blocks that contain to-day the Hôtel Crillon and the Ministère de la Marine. There was always a great deal of talk at Versailles about the plans, which were shown to all visitors. Old Stanislas never thought much of them. He had conceived the idea of the Place Stanislas, at Nancy, in bed one night and by the next afternoon he already had twenty workmen engaged on it; he was very scornful of the slow progress of his son-in-law's *Place*. Bouchardon had created an equestrian statue of the King for it which stood on a pedestal by Pigalle, with an allegorical figure at each corner—Force, Prudence, Justice and Peace. This was destroyed at the Revolution, but a small bronze of it exists at Versailles.

In June 1763 this statue was dragged from the sculptor's workshop and put up in the middle of the Place Louis XV—to a chorus of typically Parisian cheers and jeers; as usual they could not resist a joke and at the same time were pleased at the excuse for a party. The machine on which it was being transported stuck outside the Elysée: 'They'll never get him past the Hôtel Pompadour.' When the crowd saw the pedestal, with its four females, there were cries of: 'Vintimille, Mailly, Châteauroux, Pompadour,' '*Il est ici comme à Versailles, sans cœur et sans entrailles*,' and so on.

However, the processions, the fireworks, the sham battle on the Seine and the dancing in the streets, with free wine and meat, were enthusiastically attended. A great concert in the Tuileries gardens was ruined by a thunderstorm and tropical downpour, but the fireworks and illuminations in the *Place* the following night were a success. Nineteen boxes, for the King and his friends, had been built on the river in front of the Palais Bourbon, the Prince de Condé's house; they were tents of red linen lined with scarlet damask and each was lit by a beautiful chandelier. Madame de Pompadour and her brother were in one of these boxes. When the fireworks were over she gave another, even finer, display at the Elysée. An appalling traffic jam was the result. This really might have been foreseen, as there was then no bridge between the Pont Royal and the Pont de Sèvres; many carriages were unable to move again until the following morning.

This was Madame de Pompadour's last public appearance.

Bernis paid a short visit to Versailles in January, 1764. He was well received by the royal family, and the King overcame his embarrassment enough to bestow the Archbishopric of Albi upon him. The Marquise was loving and friendly; she seemed to have forgotten that he had once been so much on her nerves that she could hardly bear him in the room. Bernis never saw any of them again until Mesdames Adélaïde and Victoire arrived in Rome, refugees from their own country, during the Revolution.

Another friend of long ago called on the Marquise at this time, Madame de la Ferté d'Imbault. Madame de Pompadour had often begged her to come and live at Versailles, but she hated the Court, and never would do so. Her visit now was to thank her for the return of Cardinal de Bernis, a favour for which she had long been asking.

'I found the Marquise beautiful and serious, looking well, though she complained of insomnia, bad digestion and difficulty in breathing if she had to walk upstairs. She began by saying that I must be pleased with her for arranging such a brilliant return for my friend. She added that he had honestly done what he could, but that the country's misfortunes made him gloomy and depressing; she and the King had him too much on their nerves. She told me, in dramatic terms, how terribly she was affected by the deplorable state of the kingdom, the rebellious attitude of the *Parlement* and all that went on *up there* (pointing, with tears in her eyes, to the King's room).[1] She assured me that she only remained with the King because of her great devotion to him, that she would be a thousand times happier living quietly at Ménars but that he would be lost without her. Then she opened her heart to me, as she could do, she said, to nobody else, and told me all she had to put up with, speaking with more energy and eloquence than I had ever heard her. In short she seemed to me furious and demented; it was a real sermon on the miseries which ambition brings in its train. She seemed so wretched, so proud, so violently shaken and so suffocated by her own enormous power that I came away after an hour's talk feeling that death was the only refuge left to her.'

It was not far off. One evening, at Choisy, she was seized with such an appalling headache that she did not know where she was, and had to ask Champlost, the King's servant, to help her back to her own room. She had congestion of the lungs and lay between life and death for several days. The King put off his return to Versailles and stayed with her. After a while she seemed a little better and some people felt happier about her. Cochin made an engraving, to celebrate her convalescence, as a frame to a poem by Favart:

---

[1] The King was once more beset by difficulties which had broken out between Church and *Parlement*, and which resulted in the expulsion of the Jesuits from France at the end of 1764. This has been laid at the door of the Marquise, but there is nothing to show that she was implicated.

*Le soleil est malade*
*La Pompadour aussi*
*Ce n'est qu'une passade*
*L'un et l'autre est guéri, etc.*

(There had been an eclipse of the sun.) But the King was under no illusions. He wrote to his son-in-law, the Infant: 'I am as much worried as ever; I must tell you that I am not very hopeful of a real cure, and even feel that the end may be near. A debt of nearly twenty years, and an unshakeable friendship! However, God is the master and we must bow to His will. M. de Rochechouart has learnt of the death of his wife after much suffering; if he loved her I am sorry for him.'

In spite of the rule that none but royal persons might die at Versailles, the King brought her back there. The weather was terrible, there had not been such a cold, dark, wet, depressing spring for years; it was not a help to her and she got worse again. 'The winter is cruel to me,' she said. She sent for Collin and her will, and made various additions to it, leaving the King her house in Paris, respectfully suggesting that it would make a residence for the Comte de Provence, and her collection of engraved stones—they are now in the Bibliothèque Nationale.

Other bequests were: incomes on capital sums, varying according to length of service, to all her servants, as well as her clothes, linen, and lace to her three personal maids: her new diamond watch to the Maréchale de Mirepoix; portrait of Alexandrine framed in diamonds to Madame du Roure; a silver box set in diamonds to the Duchesse de Choiseul; a ring of pink and white diamonds set in a green bow, and 'a cornelian box he has often admired', to the Duc de Choiseul; an emerald necklace to Madame d'Amblimont; her dog, her parrot and her monkey to M. de Buffon. She left four thousand *livres* to Quesnay, and six thousand *livres* to Collin. The executor was the Prince de Soubise, to whom she left two rings and her tender love. Everything else went to her brother, the Marquis de Marigny, and after him, should he die without children (as he did), to a cousin, M. Poisson de Malvoisin. M. Poisson had two daughters, who lived at Ménars into the nineteenth century and died without children.

Collin cried so much while he wrote the codicil that the document is stained with his tears.

For the last few days the King hardly left her room. She could not breathe lying down, and sat in a chair, wearing a dressing-gown over a white taffeta petticoat; she had a little rouge and always smiled at everybody. Not one word of complaint passed her lips. When the doctors said that she was dying, she asked the King whether she ought to confess; she was not very anxious to do so, as it meant that she would not be able to see him again. However, he said that she must. He bade her a last farewell, and went upstairs to his own room.

A priest came. He told her she must send for d'Etioles; obediently she did so, but her husband begged to be excused, saying that he was not well. Then she confessed and communicated. The next day was Palm Sunday, the King was in church all day. Faithful Gontaut, Soubise and Choiseul stayed with her, until she said: 'It is coming now, my friends; I think you had better leave me to my soul, my women and the priest.' She told her women not to change her clothes, as it tired her and was no longer worth while. The priest made a movement as if to leave the room; she said: 'One moment, M. le Curé, we'll go together,' and died.

It was getting dark. The Duchesse de Praslin, who happened to be looking out of her window, saw two men carrying a stretcher, on which was the body of a woman lightly covered with a sheet. She clearly saw the shape of the head, the breasts, the stomach and the legs. Horrified, she sent her servant to find out what this could mean. When she heard that she had seen the last

of the Marquise she burst into tears. There was an iron rule that
no dead body could stay in the palace; the servants had not dared
to wait for her coach, and in any case it was only a step down the
hill to the Hôtel des Réservoirs. Here she lay, in a *Chapelle
Ardente*, until her funeral two days later.

Her old enemy the Dauphin wrote to the Bishop of Verdun:
'She is dying with a courage rare for either sex. Her lungs are full
of water, or pus, and the heart congested or dilated, it is an
unbelievably cruel and painful death. What can I tell you of her
soul? At Choisy she wanted to go and die in Paris and I hear that
she still asks to be taken there. The King has not seen her since
yesterday; she had communion last night; the Curé of the Mag-
dalen of Ville Evêque is with her all the time—here are reasons for
hoping that she will receive mercy.'

The Dauphine wrote by the same post: 'We have lost the poor
Marquise. Infinite is the mercy of God, and we must hope that
it will reach her, since He gave her time to communicate, receive
extreme unction and to profit by her last hours. They say that she
admitted all the evil she had done, and detested it. Now we can
only pray for her. . . . The King is in great affliction, though he
controls himself with us and with everybody. Our greatest wish
is that he could turn to his children, love them more than anybody, that God should touch his heart, draw him closer and
sanctify him. Farewell, my dear Bishop, be good, burn my letter
and don't answer it. Never write to me of the Marquise unless by
some perfectly safe emissary.'

Madame de la Tour Franqueville wrote to Jean-Jacques
Rousseau: 'The weather has been so frightful all the month that
Madame de Pompadour must have been less sad at leaving this
life. During her last moments she let it be seen that her soul was a
mixture of strength and weakness, never surprising in a woman.
Nor does it surprise me to see that she is now as much mourned

as she used to be despised or hated. The French, who win all the prizes, win that for inconsequence too.'

Voltaire wrote: 'I am very sad at the death of Madame de Pompadour. I was indebted to her and I mourn her out of gratitude. It seems absurd that while an ancient penpusher, hardly able to walk, should still be alive, a beautiful woman, in the midst of a splendid career, should die at the age of forty. Perhaps if she had been able to live quietly, as I do, she would be alive to-day.' 'Born sincere, she loved the King for himself; *elle avait de la justesse dans l'esprit et de la justice dans le cœur*; all this is not to be met with every day.' 'It is the end of a dream.'

The Queen wrote to President Hénault: 'Nobody talks here of *what is no more*, it is as if she had never existed. There's the world for you, worthy indeed of love!'

Diderot: 'Madame de Pompadour is dead. So what remains of this woman who cost us so much in men and in money, left us without honour and without energy, and who overthrew the whole political system of Europe? The Treaty of Versailles which will last as long as it lasts; Bouchardon's *Amour*, which will be admired for ever; a few stones engraved by Guay which will amaze the antiquaries of the future; a nice little picture by Van Loo which people will look at sometimes, and a handful of dust.'

Lord Hertford, the English Ambassador:

'Madame de Pompadour expired on Sunday evening about seven o'clock after a tedious illness. She saw the approaches of death with great courage; bid adieu to her friends with tenderness; and, I think, is generally regretted. She has died poor which wipes off the imputations of rapacity that popular clamour had thrown upon her.'

Like her houses, the very church where she was buried, with Alexandrine, has vanished. It was in the Place Vendôme, where the rue de la Paix now enters it.

The day after her funeral Marigny went to see the King, and

resigned all his charges and appointments; the King gave them back to him and furthermore said he would like him to have the Elysée; but later he exchanged it with him for another house in Paris.

And what of the King? So good at concealing all emotion, he was seen, by those who knew him well, to be very unhappy. Champlost, who had a bed in his room, said that for nights he hardly slept. He wrote to the Infant Philip: 'My anxiety is over, in the cruellest way. You can guess what I mean.' The day of the funeral arrived; a freezing storm howled round the palace. 'The Marquise has bad weather for her journey,' he remarked. At 6 p.m. the cortège was to leave for Paris; his servants shut the shutters, hoping to spare him the sight. But the King, by whose orders everything had been done, took Champlost by the arm and went out with him on to the balcony of his corner room. He watched the Marquise as she went back up the long Avenue de Paris; in the bitter wind he stood there without coat or hat until she was out of sight. Then he turned away, tears pouring down his cheeks. 'That is the only tribute I can pay her.'

After this a very great dullness fell upon the Château of Versailles.

# BIBLIOGRAPHY

## CHAPTER I

## VERSAILLES AND LOUIS XV

Gaxotte, Pierre, *Le Siècle de Louis XV*, 1933.

Saint Simon, Duc de, *Mémoires sur le Siècle de Louis XV et la Régence*, 1840.

Barbier, *Chronique de la Régence et du Règne de Louis XV*, 1885.

Young, Arthur, *Travels in the Kingdom of France*, 1793.

Marais, Mathieu, *Journal et Mémoires*, 1863.

Fleury, Comte de, *Louis XV Intime et Ses Petites Maîtresses*, 1899.

Luynes, Duc de, *Mémoires sur la Cour de Louis XV*, 1861.

Taine, *L'Ancien Régime et la Révolution Francaise*, 1875.

Ebeling, ed., *L'histoire racontée par ses temoins, Louis XV*.

Duclos, *Mémoires secrées sur les Règnes de Louis XIV et Louis XV*, Paris 1791.


## CHAPTER II

## PARIS AND MADAME D'ETIOLES

Barbier, op. cit.

Nolhac, Pierre de, *Louis XV et Madame de Pompadour* (1902?).

Luynes, op. cit.

Marquiset, *Le Marquis de Marigny*, 1918.

Dufort de Cheverny, *Mémoires sur les Règnes de Louis XV et Louis XVI*, 1908.

Croÿ, Prince de, *Journal Inédit*, 1906.

Ségur, Pierre de, *Le Royaume de la rue St. Honoré, Madame Geoffrin et sa Fille*, Paris, 1897.

Marmontel, *Mémoires*, Paris, 1891.

Goncourt, Edward et Jules de, *Madame de Pompadour*, 1888.
Valfons, Marquis de, *Souvenirs*, Paris N.D.
Aberconway, Lady, *Dictionary of Cat Lovers*, 1949.


CHAPTER III
## THE BALL OF THE CLIPPED YEW TREES

Goncourt, op. cit.
Barbier, op. cit.
Luynes, op. cit.
d'Angerville, *Private Life of Louis XV*, trans. Mingard, 1924.
Hénault, President, *Mémoires*, 1911.


CHAPTER IV
## FONTENOY

Fisher, H. A. L., *History of Europe*.
Luynes, op. cit.
Taine, op. cit.
Le Notre, *Versailles au Temps des Rois*.
Dufort de Cheverny, op. cit.
Bernis, Cardinal de, *Mémoires et Lettres*, Paris, 1878.
Voltaire, François-Marie Arouet de, *Oeuvres Complètes*, 1828–34.
Maurepas, Comte de, *Mémoires*, Paris, 1792.
Luynes, op. cit.
du Hausset, *Mémoires*, 1824.


CHAPTER V
## PRESENTATION AT COURT
du Hausset, op. cit.
Croÿ, op. cit.
Luynes, op. cit.
Williams, *The Fascinating Duc de Richelieu*, 1910.
Goncourt, op. cit.
Maurepas, op. cit.

CHAPTERS VI AND VII

## MOURNING AND THE STAIRCASE

du Hausset, op. cit.
Croÿ, op. cit.
Bernis, op. cit.
Luynes, op. cit.
Maurette, Madame, *La Vie Privée de Madame de Pompadour*, 1951.

CHAPTER VIII

## PLEASURE

Jullien, *Histoire du Théâtre de Madame de Pompadour*, 1874
Luynes, op. cit.
Taine, op. cit.
Dufort de Cheverny, op. cit.
Croÿ, op. cit.
Goncourt, op. cit.

CHAPTER IX

## ROYAL FAMILY AND POISSON FAMILY

Luynes, op. cit.
d'Angerville, op. cit.
le Chêne, Père, *Dauphin fils de Louis XV*, 1931.
du Hausset, op. cit.
Michelet, *Histoire de France*, Vol. 18.
Malassis, ed., *Correspondance de Madame de Pompadour avec son Père M.
Poisson et son frère M. de Vandières*, 1878.
L. Perey, *Un Petit Neveu de Mazarin*, Paris, 1893.
Marquiset, op. cit.

CHAPTER X

POWER

Barbier, op. cit.
Maurepas, op. cit.
Perey, op. cit.
Williams, op. cit.
Nolhac, op. cit.
Lt.-Col. Carré, *La Marquise de Pompadour*, 1937.


CHAPTER XI

FRIENDS AND TABLE TALK

Nolhac, Pierre de, Portraits du XVIII *ième* (*Voltaire et Madame de Pompadour*).
Maugras, Gaston, *La Cour de Lunéville aux 18ième Siècle*, 1925.
du Hausset, op. cit.
Lt.-Col. Carré, op. cit.
Croÿ, op. cit.


CHAPTER XII

TASTE AND INTERESTS

Dilke, Lady, *French Decoration and Furniture in the XVIII Century*, 1901.
Dilke, Lady, *French Architects and Sculptors in the XVIII Century*, 1900.
*Catalogue des Livres de Madame la Marquise de Pompadour Dame du Palais de la Reine*, 1765.
Marquiset, op. cit.
*Nouvelles Archives de l'art Français*, Vols. 19 and 20, 1094.
　　(*Correspondance de M. de Marigny avec Coypel, Lepicie et Cochin*).
Goncourt, op. cit.
Langlois, Mlle Rose Marie, *L'Ermitage de Madame de Pompadour*, 1947.
Luynes, op. cit.
*Correspondence of Mr. Joseph Jekyll with his sister-in-law, Lady Gertrude Sloane Stanley*, 1818–38.
*Revue de l'Histoire de Versailles*.

### CHAPTER XIII

## FROM LOVE TO FRIENDSHIP

Dufort de Cheverny, op. cit.
Fleury, Comte de, op. cit.
du Hausset, op. cit.
Nolhac, Pierre de, *Le Château de Versailles sous Louis XV*.
Marmontel, op. cit.
Maugras, *Le Duc et la Duchesse de Choiseul*, 1903.
Luynes, op. cit.
Bernis, op. cit.


### CHAPTER XIV

## THE *AFFAIRE* CHOISEUL-ROMANET

Marmontel, op. cit.
Croÿ, op. cit.
Maugras, op. cit.
Luynes, op. cit.


### CHAPTER XV

## POLITICS AT HOME

and

### CHAPTER XVI

## POLITICS ABROAD

Cambridge Modern History, Vol. VIII.
Michelet, op. cit.
Voltaire, op. cit.
Barbier, op. cit.
Luynes, op. cit.
Mgr. Knox, *Enthusiasm*, 1950.
Maugras, *Le Duc et la Duchesse de Choiseul*, 1903.
Hillairet, *Evocations du Vieux Paris*, 1952-3.
Nolhac, Pierre de, *Madame de Pompadour et la Politique*, 1928.

du Hausset, op. cit.

Gaxotte, op. cit.

Bernis, op. cit.

Croÿ, op. cit.

Carlyle, *History of Friedrich II called Frederick the Great*, Chapman and
    Hall, 1903.

Williams, op cit.

Duclos, op. cit.

### CHAPTER XVII

## DAMIENS

Barbier, op. cit.

Croÿ, op. cit.

du Hausset, op. cit.

Dufort de Cheverny, op. cit.

Bernis, op. cit.

Malassis, op. cit.    (in which is incorporated the interview with
    Meinières).

Valfons, op. cit.

Hénault, op. cit.

Luynes, op. cit.

### CHAPTER XVIII

## THE SEVEN YEARS WAR

Carlyle, op. cit.

Gaxotte, op. cit. and *Histoire des Français*.

Luynes, op. cit.

Croÿ, op. cit.

Nolhac, *Madame de Pompadour et la Politique*.

Williams, op. cit.

Bernis, op. cit.

Hillairet, op. cit.

Malassis, op. cit.

Rousset, *Le Comte de Gisors*, 1868.

## CHAPTER XIX

## CHOISEUL

Maugras, *Duc et Duchesse de Choiseul*.
Bernis, op. cit.
Croÿ, op. cit.
Dufort de Cheverny, op. cit.
Nolhac, *Madame de Pompadour et la Politique*.
Goncourt, op. cit.
Perey, op. cit.
Voltaire, op. cit.


## CHAPTER XX

## THE END OF A DREAM

Voltaire, op. cit.
Hillairet, op. cit.
du Hausset, op. cit.
Ségur, op. cit.
*Inventaire des biens de Madame de Pompadour, publié pour la société des bibliophiles français*, 1939
Dufort de Cheverny, op. cit.
*La Mort et les Obsèques de Madame de Pompadour, Revue de l'Histoire de Versailles*, 1901–02.
Nolhac, op. cit.
Le Chêne, op. cit.

# INDEX

# READ MORE IN PENGUIN

In every corner of the world, on every subject under the sun, Penguin represents quality and variety – the very best in publishing today.

For complete information about books available from Penguin – including Puffins, Penguin Classics and Arkana – and how to order them, write to us at the appropriate address below. Please note that for copyright reasons the selection of books varies from country to country.

**In the United Kingdom**: Please write to *Dept. EP, Penguin Books Ltd, Bath Road, Harmondsworth, West Drayton, Middlesex UB7 0DA*

**In the United States**: Please write to *Consumer Sales, Penguin Putnam Inc., P.O. Box 12289 Dept. B, Newark, New Jersey 07101-5289.* VISA and MasterCard holders call 1-800-788-6262 to order Penguin titles

**In Canada**: Please write to *Penguin Books Canada Ltd, 10 Alcorn Avenue, Suite 300, Toronto, Ontario M4V 3B2*

**In Australia**: Please write to *Penguin Books Australia Ltd, P.O. Box 257, Ringwood, Victoria 3134*

**In New Zealand**: Please write to *Penguin Books (NZ) Ltd, Private Bag 102902, North Shore Mail Centre, Auckland 10*

**In India**: Please write to *Penguin Books India Pvt Ltd, 11 Community Centre, Panchsheel Park, New Delhi 110017*

**In the Netherlands**: Please write to *Penguin Books Netherlands bv, Postbus 3507, NL-1001 AH Amsterdam*

**In Germany**: Please write to *Penguin Books Deutschland GmbH, Metzlerstrasse 26, 60594 Frankfurt am Main*

**In Spain**: Please write to *Penguin Books S. A., Bravo Murillo 19, 1° B, 28015 Madrid*

**In Italy**: Please write to *Penguin Italia s.r.l., Via Benedetto Croce 2, 20094 Corsico, Milano*

**In France**: Please write to *Penguin France, Le Carré Wilson, 62 rue Benjamin Baillaud, 31500 Toulouse*

**In Japan**: Please write to *Penguin Books Japan Ltd, Kaneko Building, 2-3-25 Koraku, Bunkyo-Ku, Tokyo 112*

**In South Africa**: Please write to *Penguin Books South Africa (Pty) Ltd, Private Bag X14, Parkview, 2122 Johannesburg*

# BY THE SAME AUTHOR

**The Sun King**

Nancy Mitford's magnificent biography of Louis XIV is also an illuminating examination of France in the late seventeenth and early eighteenth centuries. It focuses in particular on the Court of Versailles, which Louis transformed into Europe's greatest palace, and on the daily life of the king, government and courtiers as France reached the peak of its artistic and military achievement.

'A brilliant *son et lumière* performance' – *Guardian*

**Frederick the Great**

Among all the famous figures Nancy Mitford has portrayed, none, she owns, has made a greater appeal to her than Frederick; whether she is discussing his glee when he persuaded Voltaire to leave Versailles for Prussia, the rococo splendours of his palaces, or his cunning diplomacy, her enthusiasm shines out of every page of this lavishly illustrated biography.

**The Nancy Mitford Omnibus**

Nancy Mitford's immortal works – now in one volume.
*The Pursuit of Love · Love in a Cold Climate · The Blessing · Don't Tell Alfred*

Here is vivacious and passionate Linda, destined to fall in and out of love and marriage before finally finding happiness in a most unexpected form; and beautiful cold Polly Hampton, for whom life is to prove an altogether chillier business. So too the richly amusing tale of a charming French Marquis's courtship and marriage to his stubbornly English Marquise; and a witty exposé of life in the British Embassy in Paris under the administration of Sir Alfred Wincham.